ARNOLD

An Unauthorized Biography

ARNOLD

WENDY LEIGH

CONGDON & WEED, INC.

Chicago

Library of Congress Cataloging-in-Publication Data

Leigh, Wendy, 1950–
    Arnold : an unauthorized biography / Wendy Leigh.
      p.   cm.
    Includes bibliographical references.
    ISBN 0-86553-216-8 : $19.95
    1. Schwarzenegger, Arnold.   2. Bodybuilders—Austria—
Biography.   3. Actors—Austria—Biography.   I. Title.
GV545.52.S38L45   1990
646.7′5—dc20   89-78551
[B]   CIP

Published by Congdon & Weed, Inc.
180 North Michigan Avenue, Chicago, Illinois 60601
Distributed by Contemporary Books, Inc.
180 North Michigan Avenue, Chicago, Illinois 60601

022579

ST. JAMES-ASSINIBOIA

ACKNOWLEDGMENTS OF PERMISSIONS

Grateful acknowledgment is made for permission to use material from the following:

Bad News at Black Rock: The Sell-Out of CBS News by Peter McCabe, © 1987 by Peter McCabe. Reprinted by permission of William Morrow & Co.

"Bodybuilding: State of the Art, 1975" by Jim Stingley, © 1975 by the *Los Angeles Times*, November 16, 1975. Reprinted by permission.

Conan by Robert E. Howard. Reprinted by permission of Conan Properties, Inc.

"The High Price of Sudden Fame" by Jeanne Wolf, *Cosmopolitan*, November 1988.

"How Much Bigger Can Arnold Schwarzenegger Get?" by Lynn Darling, *Esquire*, March 1985.

"It's Not Easy, Being Arnold Schwarzenegger" by Christopher Ward, *London Daily Mirror*, March 8, 1968.

"The Money in Muscle" by Gene Stone, *California Business*, October 1988.

"Muscle Madness: The Incredible Boom in Male Body-Building" © 1977 by Leonard Todd, *Cosmopolitan*, August 1977.

Muscle Wars by Rick Wayne, © 1985 by Rick Wayne. Reprinted by permission of St. Martin's Press, Inc.

"*Playboy* Interview: Arnold Schwarzenegger," *Playboy*, January 1988; © 1987 by *Playboy*. Reprinted by permission. All rights reserved. Interview conducted by Joan Goodman.

"Pumping Arnold" by Nancy Collins, *Rolling Stone*, January 17, 1985; © 1985 by Straight Arrow Publishers, Inc. All rights reserved. Reprinted by permission.

"*Penthouse* Interview: Arnold Schwarzenegger" by James Delson, © 1981 by *Penthouse*; and "Schwarzenegger's Kurt Replies" by Sharon Churcher, © 1989 by *Penthouse*. Reprinted by permission of Penthouse Publications International, Ltd.

"The Self-Made Man" by Theresa Carpenter, *Premiere*, January 1989.

"Winning According to Schwarzenegger" by Marian Christy, *Boston Globe*, May 9, 1982. Reprinted courtesy of the *Boston Globe*.

Arnold isn't my book alone. It evolved thanks to the research, administrative skills, and interviewing talent of Stephen Karten, my husband. This is dedicated to Steve with my love and gratitude for making it *our* book.

Contents

ARNOLD

Prologue

ON APRIL 26, 1986, ARNOLD SCHWARZENEG-
ger married Maria Shriver at the Roman Catholic Church
of St. Francis Xavier, Hyannis. The international press
who had flocked to Massachusetts to cover the wedding
were convinced that they knew every single detail of the
groom's story: at twenty-one he had arrived in America a
penniless bodybuilder, born in an obscure Austrian village, armed only with the immigrant's time-honored weapons of hope, ambition, and an almost supernatural belief
in the great American dream.

Now, through the traditional virtues of hard work,
talent, charm, intelligence, positive mental attitude, and
persistence, Arnold Schwarzenegger had become a household name, a legendary hero whose life story thrilled millions of fans throughout the world. Seven times Mr. Olympia, he was the first athlete ever to make the transition from
sports figure to major box office draw. As Johnny Weismuller, Reg Park, Steve Reeves, Jim Brown, Fred William-
son, O. J. Simpson, and Merlin Olsen all fell by the cinematic wayside, only Arnold had successfully stormed the
silver screen, currently commanding a stupendous $10 mil-
lion per film.

Arnold Schwarzenegger epitomized the classic rags-to-
riches hero—a Horatio Alger figure who had conquered
America and made it his oyster. And today, eighteen years
after he had first set foot on American soil, he was about to
capture the richest pearl of all: marriage to one of America's great romantic prizes, John F. Kennedy's niece, Maria

Shriver. In the media's view Arnold Schwarzenegger's story was a great American saga of survival, triumph, and success, an inspiring tale of an immigrant who beat the odds. But that was only part of the truth.

Inside the church while the wedding guests waited with bated breath for the bride to appear, a canny observer could have divided them into groups. And within the fragments of each group each member represented a splinter of Arnold's past and held one of the many keys to its truth.

These groups were not only a testament to one of Arnold Schwarzenegger's most admirable qualities—loyalty—but also a demonstration of his continuing attachment to those who helped him attain his stupendous success. There was the German and Austrian faction, men well versed in the struggles of his early years, represented by Albert Busek, who was privy to intimate stories of his reckless Munich years. There was the British bodybuilding group, led by Wag Bennett, who guarded the truth about Arnold's youthful indiscretions with a fervent dedication. Then there were the American bodybuilders, the ones who knew him when he first came to the States and was defeated, the ones he then conquered and made his own. There were the celebrities, now his peers, like Andy Warhol and Grace Jones, who knew only Arnold the movie star. And there were the businessmen, like Jim Lorimer, men who had helped Arnold make millions through real estate and bodybuilding contests and who praised him for his financial acumen.

Finally, of course, there were the Kennedys and the Shrivers. Jacqueline Kennedy Onassis was there; so were Caroline, John Jr., Teddy, Joan, and Ethel, as well as Maria's father, Sargent Shriver, who gave the bride away, and her mother, Eunice, who used to be JFK's favorite sister. The Kennedys and the Shrivers, as the canny observer might have commented, appeared on the surface to be the most important group at the Schwarzenegger/ Shriver nuptials. But at the same time not only they, but also the bride herself, probably knew less about the groom than any other group present.

Only two wedding guests probably came close to knowing the entire truth about Arnold: best man Franco Columbu, his "blood brother," whose bodybuilding career mirrored his own, and his mother, Aurelia, resplendent in a violet dress, protected from the unseasonably cold New England weather by a full-length mink, most likely a gift from her son. As Aurelia watched Arnold and Maria walk down the aisle of the church where once both Bobby and Jack Kennedy had been altar boys, she must have marveled at how far destiny had brought her, had brought Arnold. Teddy Kennedy was her escort for the occasion, Gustav, her husband and Arnold's father, having died fourteen years before. But perhaps his spirit was watching. And perhaps only Gustav would have understood and appreciated the truth, applauding the incredible odyssey that had transported his son from a tiny Austrian village to America as Arnold embraced not only the radiance and the promise but also the ruthlessness and the dark side of the American dream—a dream that had finally swept him into the very heart of one of the most powerful families in America. Only Gustav would have truly appreciated the dazzling triumph of the will that is Arnold Schwarzenegger.

1
A Pride of Lions

THE CHARMING AUSTRIAN VILLAGE OF Thal, on the outskirts of Graz, in the province of Styria, would have made an ideal location for *The Sound of Music*. Surrounded by rolling hills, lakes, mountains, and forests of rich green trees, Thal is the epitome of serenity. Horses graze just a few yards from the heart of the village, where lilac bushes bloom in the temperate Styrian spring and sunlight-yellow buttercups grow under a sturdy oak tree that lends them shade as it has for decades past and will in decades to come.

If the beauty of the Thal scenery rivals anything shown in *The Sound of Music*, Gustav Schwarzenegger, Arnold's father, definitely was equal to Captain Von Trapp (as played by Christopher Plummer) in looks, charisma, and military bearing. Tall, handsome, and broad-shouldered, Gustav, an Austrian police chief, carried himself proudly, rather like a prince from one of Franz Lehár's operettas. Even as a child he had an air of nobility so striking that it attracted the attention of the Emperor Franz Josef, who had a summer palace close to Gustav's home. Franz Josef, said Gustav, had once invited him to ride with him in the royal coach. Gustav never forgot the experience of coming so close to the all-powerful emperor and would be obsessed by power in all its manifestations for the rest of his life.

He was a man of contrasts, both military martinet and debonair dandy, dressing beautifully enough to be described as an "Austrian Cary Grant." The cavalier of an otherwise down-to-earth family, Gustav was amusing, courteous, a musician who played six instruments, excelled at the flügelhorn, and was proficient at playing anything from military marches to Austrian folk music. Music, in fact, was his greatest joy, the fulcrum of his existence, so that in 1935 he joined the police band, the Graz Gendarmerie Musik, often led the band, and remained a member until he died. However, the Gendarmerie Musik wasn't the only organization of which Gustav Schwarzenegger was a member. For while 89 percent of Austrians did not join the Nazi party, Gustav Schwarzenegger, on July 4, 1938, applied for membership and was accepted.

Membership in the Nazi party was illegal in Austria from 1933 to 1938. But once Austria was annexed by Germany in March 1938, the law banning membership was repealed. This gave both pre-1933 Nazis and new enthusiasts the opportunity to join the now-legal party. Gustav was a member of the Austrian police force, but membership in the Nazi party was not mandatory for Austrian policemen, who, like other aspiring members of officialdom, were carefully vetted and subject to certain conditions. Indeed Gustav's application would have been rejected instantly had he not been of pure Aryan blood. Luckily his racial purity was unimpeachable. The Schwarzeneggers (a literal translation of their name is "black ploughmen") dated back over seven generations and were of entirely Styrian heritage (apart from one ancestor who moved to Austria via Czechoslovakia).

Styria, an Austrian federal county in the southeastern part of the country, is bordered by Hungary to the east, Yugoslavia in the south, and the rest of Austria to the west and north. Styrians are proud of their state and feel that, in comparison to the more lighthearted Viennese, they are tougher and more patriotic, priding themselves on possessing what they term *ein harter Kern*—a tough center. They have their own state costume, which all Styrians (including, at times, Arnold) don on state occasions. They speak in a broad dialect peculiar to Styria, which outsiders whose accent is "high German" find difficult to understand.

The Schwarzeneggers originated from Neuberg, near Mürzzuschlag, northeast of Graz, where they were locksmiths and steelworkers. Gustav's father, Karl, died young in an accident but was a big, strong man from whom, family lore has it, Arnold inherited his physique. Gustav's mother, Cecilia Hinterleitner, was also a well-built woman who lived until the ripe old age of eighty, her face unlined, dressed always in elegant blue silk. Karl and Cecilia had four children: Franz, Alois, Gustav, and, finally, a daughter, Cilly.

Before his death Karl Schwarzenegger spent some years in Vienna, working at the Schmidt Steel Works, leaving the children to be brought up by their grandmother. Gustav, for a time, followed in his father's footsteps and became a metalworker. Then he joined the Austrian Army, whose flamboyant uniform suited his regal carriage perfectly. He was witty and animated, a performer who loved attention. In later years, when his older brother, Franz, a dour man, fell into a depression, Gustav was always able to cheer him up by laughing and joking. An athlete and a champion in the sport of curling, Gustav was known as the "gentleman of the family" and was in no hurry to get married. Like his son Arnold after him, he waited until the age of thirty-eight before finally walking down the aisle.

Gustav met Aurelia Jadrny, who was born in Neunkirchen near Vienna, in Mürzsteg, Styria. A bright-eyed brunette with buckteeth, at the time she was working in a wartime office, dispensing food stamps, and was the widow of a certain Herr Barmuller. Although those who knew Gustav and Aurelia well say that Gustav spent his war years in the German military police, stationed in Belgium, Aurelia today says that, as she met Gustav after the end of the war, she has no idea exactly what he did during the war or even in which country he was stationed. Be that as it may, Aurelia and Gustav got married in Mürzsteg on October 20, 1945.

Gustav's wartime pursuits are not a matter of public record. His decision to join the Nazi party, however, gives some indication of his politics. Although many Austrians, unlike Gustav, did not go through the formal procedure necessary to join the Nazi party, many Styrians in particular welcomed Hitler into Graz—the capital—eagerly. In fact Hitler was so gratified by the Grazers' enthusiasm that he awarded the city an honorary title: *die Stadt der Erhebung*—the town of the elevation. Austrians, even now, remember Hitler's triumphant entry into Graz, how the crowds mobbed the street, climbing lampposts for a glimpse of *der Führer*, shouting *"Sieg Heil"* with strident fervor. Unemployment was high in Styria, and stories about prosperity under the Third Reich were prevalent, so, in the hope of a more prosperous future, Styrians flocked to support Hitler. Not only had he promised them employment, but by joining his Hitler Youth Movement their sons gained self-respect and hope, not to mention uniforms and knives—all serving to make them forget their oppressive poverty. Moreover, Hitler was also Austrian and cut a fine figure in his military uniform. So fine, in fact, that over thirty years later Arnold reportedly confided to his girlfriend Sue Moray that when his mother saw Adolf Hitler she almost swooned.

At the end of the war Aurelia and Gustav moved to Thal, which was situated approximately four miles outside Graz and, in 1947, had a population of around twelve hundred. There they lived on the top floor of a house that came with Gustav's new job as police commandant. The three-hundred-year-old house at 145 Thal-Linak, owned by a local dignitary, Baron Herberstein, was freezing, with wooden floorboards unprotected by carpeting. Central heating was nonexistent, as was indoor plumbing. Aurelia fetched water from a fountain 150 yards from the house and washed the family's clothes (which she sometimes made herself) in the local wash kitchen. Forced by circumstances to continually run up and down stairs carrying water or food, she eventually developed a weak heart.

Aurelia was a traditional wife who was content to obey her second husband and acquiesce to his rules, not suc-

cumbing to the new fashion of pants, because he forbade
her to wear them. Her role was to cook, clean, wash, knit,
sew, and mend. She was fanatical about cleanliness (a trait
her son Arnold acquired), her hair and nails were always
spotless, and she dedicated herself to polishing Gustav's
shoes and buckles until they shone, baked apple strudel,
and provided her husband with a clean shirt to wear to
work every day.

Money was always a problem in the Schwarzenegger
household, with Gustav earning the equivalent of only
$250 a month. His work, however, was not too taxing as
the Thal Gendarmerie existed mainly for the purpose of
controlling the day-trippers who walked from Graz to
Thal to swim in the Thalersee (lake) on Sundays. Gustav
was not an easy boss, and his men—Frederich Gsols, Franz
Stampler, and Anton Spuler—were often afraid of him. He
had a violent temper and, rumor had it, was once involved
in a serious altercation with the British high commissioner
of Graz, who had been stationed in Schloss Thal after the
war.

Temper may not have been the only cause of Gustav's
rumored conflict with the high commissioner. His drinking may well have been another. Gustav's day at the Thal
Gendarmerie habitually began with an eleven o'clock
snack of sausage with a roll. Then the drinking began.
During the forties and fifties it wasn't unusual for the
inhabitants of Thal, a village without a movie theater or
even a bus into Graz, to turn to drink for recreation, but
Gustav's drinking surpassed that of the average Thaler. An
eyewitness, who sometimes carried him home after a
drunken evening, remembers, "Gustav would drink two
liters of wine and then say, 'Now I will drink myself sober.'
But very often he drank so much that he didn't know where
he was and couldn't even walk. Aurelia was always terrified
that he would come home drunk, because then he got
violent."

Sometimes, though, life was pleasant for Aurelia, especially when she and Gustav spent an evening at Gasthaus

Schrott or Krainer, both in Thal. On warm summer days the Schwarzeneggers went to the Thalersee. Even today the *See* is surrounded by trees and is peaceful, with only the noise of quacking ducks breaking the silence. Couples stroll along the shore, stopping occasionally to kiss or to have a beer on the terrace of the Thalersee Restaurant and to watch the children boating on the lake. Aurelia sometimes helped out in the restaurant kitchen, perhaps taking refuge from her husband's drunken tirades in the serenity of the surroundings. As it turned out, the Thalersee itself was to play an important part in Arnold Schwarzenegger's strange and wondrous destiny.

Arnold Schwarzenegger was born at 4:10 A.M. on July 30, 1947. His older brother, Meinhard, was born on July 17th the year before. Psychologists claim that generally the youngest child is the favorite, loved and beloved by both parents. But although Arnold (like his mother and father) was born under the sign of Leo—the lion—he was never the king of the castle in which he grew up. From the start Meinhard was his father's favorite, the apple of his eye, while Arnold was often dispatched alone to stay with his uncle Alois in Mürzzuschlag. Gustav's favoritism was strong and blatant, stemming out of unfounded suspicion. On nights when he had been drinking heavily, Gustav would rant and rave, swearing to Aurelia that Arnold wasn't his child, that he was a bastard.

Judging by photographs of Aurelia during the forties, she was far removed from the classic scarlet woman, and reports of her indicate that she was faithful to her husband. Gustav, however, was violently possessive of his Reli, as he called her. Born in 1922, Aurelia was fifteen years younger than her autocratic husband, the age difference probably adding to his drink-induced delusions. His jealousy was irrational, causing him to forbid her to wear sleeveless dresses to church, even in summer.

By the time Arnold was three years old, Gustav's drinking and accusations had grown stronger, creating waves of unhappiness in the Schwarzenegger household that even the children could divine. On some nights little Arnold would wake up from a nightmare, crying bitterly, terrified and desolate. But no one, not his father, Gustav, or his mother, Aurelia, would come to comfort him. With a psyche marked forever by his childhood, even as an adult Arnold would continue to strive pitilessly and relentlessly for the attention he had once craved but had never received.

From the first, Meinhard was the charmer, Arnold the charmless. Even Aurelia seemed to favor her elder son, calling him by the affectionate nickname Meinhardl. On the surface, though, she wanted the boys to appear equal, treasuring locks of their hair and keeping their first baby teeth as mementos. In quest of equality she was obsessed by the notion that they should be the same height. If one boy grew taller than the other, she gave the other more food to eat.

Meinhard, however, was healthier than Arnold, who was often ill. In Thal, in those days, childhood illnesses could be fatal as the village didn't have a doctor; when Arnold was sick in the middle of the night, his life sometimes depended on his being hoisted onto a parent's shoulders for the walk into Graz, where the doctor would try to cure the little boy of whatever ailed him.

When Arnold was six, Gustav took him into town to see the former Olympic swimmer turned Hollywood actor, Johnny Weismuller, who was there to open a swimming pool. What Arnold thought of Weismuller is not on record.

By that time he had joined Meinhard at the Hans Gross School in Thal. From eight in the morning until one or two in the afternoon he went to school, taking ten minutes each day to walk there and back from his house.

Arnold and his brother shared a simple bedroom, overlooking the ruins of an ancient castle. He was a timid little boy who, for a time, wore thick glasses and had ears that stuck out. Next to his brother, blond and charismatic, in his lederhosen, a picture of the perfect Austrian child,

Arnold was a misfit, a child who was always treated as second best. One of his father's friends, aware of Gustav's attitude toward his younger son, felt sorry for Arnold and dubbed him "Cinderella."

He was petrified of his father, paralyzed with fear whenever Gustav reprimanded or questioned him. A source close to Arnold and his father remembers the following scene: "Arnold was such a poor child. One day, when Gustav was on the first floor of the police station, Arnold knocked on the door. He was ten years old and terrified of his father. 'Vati, Vati' ['Daddy, Daddy'], he said. Gustav barked, 'Arnold, what do you want?' Arnold trembled and then, because he was so afraid of his father, wet himself."

Gustav Schwarzenegger's love of discipline was legendary among his friends, neighbors, and colleagues. From the time the boys were able to understand him he drilled his sons in the credo of joy through strength and suffering. Hardship and pain were obstacles that had to be endured, worked through, and conquered. Power and victory mattered above all.

During the week Arnold and Meinhard were forced to get up each morning at six, fetch milk, and complete household chores before going to school. Sometimes Gustav inflicted military-style fetishes on the two boys, once demanding that they eat every meal with books pressed tightly under their elbows to teach them to keep their elbows by their sides while they ate.

There are indications, however, that sometimes Arnold managed to rebel. For example, when adults chanced to ask him the classic question "What do you want to be when you grow up?" Arnold would announce, "I don't want to learn anything, and I don't want to become anything. All I want is to go out in the world with a stick, a hat, and a monkey," probably knowing full well that this was the last answer Gustav, virulently ambitious for both of his sons, wanted to hear.

Weekends provided no relief from Gustav's strict upbringing; each Sunday Arnold and Meinhard were permitted to choose among hiking, visiting a farm, and going to Graz to see a play, an art show, or a museum. Or, if Gustav was performing with the police band, the boys would go to listen. Whatever the outing, it was underscored by a fear of the following day, when both boys would have to write the dreaded essay, describing in intricate detail every second of the excursion. However pleasurable the outing, neither Arnold nor Meinhard was ever able to relax and enjoy it, filled as they were with a fear of the essay. Years later Arnold would find it impossible to enjoy the moment; when he won a bodybuilding contest, his habitual reaction would be a joyless "Wait until next year!"

Gustav required the boys' essays to be ten pages long. On the Monday morning following the outing he examined every single page, correcting every mistake with a red pencil, while the boys watched, quivering, conscious that one spelling error would meet with a command that the culprit write the word fifty times. Mistakes, however insignificant, were definitely not tolerated. Meinhard inevitably made fewer errors than Arnold.

From the first Gustav encouraged an intense rivalry between his sons, taking great pride in pitting them against each other in boxing matches and skiing races. Capable of being charming and courtly to others, Gustav would watch gleefully as the two boys scrambled to outrun, outbox, outski, and outstudy each other, desperate for his approval. Each contest began with the portentous pronouncement from Gustav, "Let's see who's the best!" There was no doubt at all, as Arnold confirmed in later years, that both boys were competing to show their father who was the better son. Arnold, of course, had to fight more fiercely to be judged the best, knowing that Meinhard's grip on his father's heart was far firmer than his own. His battles were harder, his attempt to defeat his brother more desperate, and his need to win his father's love far stronger.

When approval finally came, Gustav awarded it only to the winner of each contest. To the loser went scornful derision. With an instinct for humiliation that came from some deep cavern in his soul, Gustav would force the vanquished brother to confront and acknowledge the winner. Their father would then ask, "Tell me, which one of you is the best?" Verbal salt would be rubbed into the wounds of the little boy who had lost, until finally the interrogation ceased with the loser, from the depths of his despair, acknowledging the winner.

Arnold didn't lose all the contests. But despite his occasional victories, he must have sensed that his father was still withholding the approval and love that he so deeply desired. Even if he heard the cherished words "You really beat your brother [this time]," the battle wasn't really over. There was still next time, another competition, another opportunity to beat his brother, win his father's love, and prove he was the best. Throughout his youth the competitions continued, fostering in Arnold a competitiveness that he would one day describe as being etched deep in his heart and mind.

At the age of ten Arnold's most notable talent was drawing, but apart from that, school didn't make him particularly happy or offer him solace from the hardship of living with an authoritarian, alcoholic father, a downtrodden mother, and a brother who was far more beloved than he was. He did have friends and often went skating with them on the Thalersee in winter and swam there or went boating in summer. He'd play table tennis, hike in the woods around Thal, or sometimes play cops and robbers with Freddy Kattner, who was around his age and was gratified that Arnold never minded which part he played—cop or robber. Other than playing a few children's games, his life was free from frills or self-indulgence. The Schwarzeneggers, both Catholic, always took the boys to church on Sunday and celebrated religious holidays but didn't make too much fuss over the two boys' birthdays, simply because they couldn't afford to buy them presents.

Poverty ensured that meat—usually Wiener schnitzel—was only a Sunday treat. Leaving food was considered a crime, for the Schwarzeneggers didn't own a refrigerator. In fact, as Arnold remembers it, one of the highlights of his youth was when the family bought a refrigerator. The entire family stuck their hands into the fridge, overcome with a sense of wonder. The advent of the refrigerator may have served as a reminder of all the material delights eluding the family and perhaps was the first step in the birth of Arnold's voracious drive toward financial gain. Naturally, the Schwarzeneggers didn't own a television either. Ironically, Arnold, who in later years would project himself to American audiences so successfully by way of television, grew up with only a radio as entertainment. Soon, however, he was able to devise a unique way of entertaining himself, one that would stay with him for much of his life.

Today Arnold's old schoolmates from the Hans Gross School are in their forties and in awe of their famous alumnus. Indeed, they are eager to talk about him but are careful with their words. Monika Zimmermann, a middle-aged Thal lady whose giggles still evoke the country schoolgirl she once was, mentions Arnold's celebrated sense of humor and all the pranks he played at school. At once she receives a warning look from the former headmaster's daughter, also present at the interview, and eager to protect Arnold. Frau Zimmermann clams up, but when coaxed volunteers that on one occasion he stood outside a nearby cake shop and begged passersby for a few schillings with which to buy pastries. Then, surprised by her own daring in revealing that small detail, Monika covers her mouth as if to silence herself. Helga Verschink, another schoolmate from Thal, says, "Arnold always protected me because I was small." And Franz Hormann, also a school friend, says, "Arnold was super, super, super." Perhaps. Then again, it also appears that during those early school days Gustav's upbringing had already taken its toll on Arnold's personality and that of his brother.

In her essays *Ego and the Mechanisms of Defense*, in particular the chapter "Identification with the Aggressor,"

Anna Freud writes of children who are afraid of their parents and cope with their fear by impersonating them. As a small child Arnold had tried to defuse his fear of his father by dressing up in his police uniform and pretending he *was* his father. And as he grew older his unrequited love for Gustav drove him not only to don his father's uniform but also to imitate his actions. Gustav had taught him to hate and humiliate rather than to love. Gustav had terrorized him; now Arnold, incited by his brother, began to terrorize other people.

Egged on by Meinhard, he began to taunt and torment others, just as Gustav had tormented him, was still tormenting him. On one occasion a source who knew Gustav well saw Meinhard and Arnold whipping a group of girls with stinging nettles. In disgust he complained to Gustav, who summoned Arnold for an explanation. Arnold denied everything, and Gustav, professing to believe him, let the whole matter drop. After that people thought twice before complaining to Gustav about his sons. And by the time Arnold left the Hans Gross School for the Fröbel School in Graz, Arnold's headmaster, Herr Stanzer, told a friend that he had prayed to be rid of the Schwarzenegger boys.

Meinhard was sent to the Marschall School but was eventually expelled on disciplinary grounds and sent to reform school. He had evolved into a bully, and Arnold, although not sent to reform school, was also involved in disturbing episodes. The man who had seen the boys tormenting neighborhood girls was once standing at the bus stop and witnessed Arnold, by then in his early teens, approach a twelve- or thirteen-year-old girl, pull her book-filled schoolbag out of her hand, and throw it into the river.

Sometimes it wasn't easy for Gustav to ignore his sons' transgressions. Although he was powerful, a demigod in the small world of Thal, where, as police chief, he reigned supreme, Arnold and Meinhard were fast becoming the terrors of the village. Finally Gustav was forced to confront the truth. A source who was there describes the incident: "Arnold and Meinhard were already in high school when it happened. The milkman drove along the street in Thal, and Meinhard and Arnold stood in the middle of the road and, for no reason, wouldn't let him pass. They hit him and he bled. He managed to rip one of the boys' schoolbags away from him and, with blood pouring down his face, drove to the police station. Gustav, reading the name on the schoolbag, couldn't deny that his sons were involved this time. He flattered the milkman into dropping the whole thing but didn't punish Arnold and Meinhard."

Arnold was learning about power—a lesson he was to put to good use in later life. Although he was afraid of his father, his father's power protected him. Meinhard too was adept at exploiting his father's position as police chief to the maximum. An eyewitness remembers, "When Meinhard was twelve or thirteen, an old couple named Schinerl, who were in their eighties, met him in the street in Thal. Meinhard was crying. He went up to them and begged, 'My grandmother has died, and my mother and father are already at the funeral. No one is here, and I want to buy a wreath for my grandmother, but I don't have the money. Frau Schinerl, can you lend me five hundred schillings?' The Schinerls were living on a pension, and five hundred schillings was a lot of money in those days. Meinhard's grandmother hadn't died at all, but he was a good actor. His father found out what he had done but didn't do anything to punish Meinhard."

It seemed that no matter what either of his sons did, Gustav never punished them. And, as an eyewitness says, "That is why the Schwarzeneggers were hated in Thal. Today everyone loves them, but forty years ago no one wanted to have anything to do with them."

Although Arnold often joined in his brother's questionable pranks, he was still only second best, unable to win his father's love and praise. To that end he joined the Graz Athletic Club, where he played a wing position on the local soccer team. By the time he reached the age of thirteen, however, as a result of the competitiveness Gustav had so forcefully nurtured, Arnold found that team sports no longer satisfied him. His father's legacy had already taken hold in his psyche; reacting against Gustav's love of the arts, he hated classical music, art, and antiques. And undoubtedly he hated Gustav as well.

At thirteen, he took things a stage further, compensating for his fear of Gustav by losing himself in grandiose fantasies. To protect himself from his father, his strength, and the power he wielded over his son, Arnold began to dream of becoming bigger and stronger than Gustav. He turned to surrogate supermen; first a comic book hero, Sieguard, a muscle man, and then other larger-than-life characters who lived in Germany's Black Forest.

Soon, however, he discovered that his comic book heroes had their counterparts in the flesh-and-blood stars of the silver screen. He began sneaking into the movie theaters—like the Gaidorf Kino in Graz, where a seat cost only six schillings—and devoured the films of John Wayne, Tarzan movies (starring Weismuller), and *Hercules*, featuring Steve Reeves and Reg Park. Already an iconoclast, Arnold favored Park over the more popular Reeves, believing that Park was tougher. He saw *Hercules* in the movie theater time after time, hour after hour, examining Park, judging him, admiring him, and, ultimately, promising himself that one day he, Arnold Schwarzenegger, then thirteen years old and poor as he was, would be like him, would even surpass Reg Park.

Somehow Arnold must have divined that he would feel safe only if he were on top. He was determined, he told himself, never to be like other people. There was more to life than his current existence. He told himself that he was born to be different, to be powerful, to be part of the small percentage of people who were leaders, not of the large mass of people who followed them.

Arnold has always claimed that the destiny he had chosen for himself all those years ago was born out of a combination of Sieguard, Hercules, and Reg Park. He also appears to believe that he conceived of that destiny out of his own free will. In reality, however, Arnold's escape route and ultimate rebellion against his father were derived from assuming his father's credo—the assertion that the pursuit of strength, competition, and victory should supersede all else, that some men are superior and others eminently inferior.

However much Arnold may have hated his father, it would seem that two dark forces would always duel within him: the desire to reject his father and the unconscious wish to be like him. If so, it seems equally clear which force won. His chosen path was to spend much of his life identifying with his father. He may have hated Gustav, but he never escaped him.

During those long nights in the gloomy Graz cinema, the thirteen-year-old Arnold may well have believed that he was eluding his father's stranglehold on his soul, that he was smashing the stifling power Gustav had over him, and that he had in his visions of becoming a superman found a refuge from him. So he sat in the dark Graz cinema night after night, conceiving for himself what he believed to be a new persona—that of a superman. And he would remain true to that adolescent vision of himself for the rest of his life.

2
Escape from Thal

BY THE TIME HE WAS THIRTEEN YEARS
old, Arnold had already made up his mind to leave Thal,
his father's drunken tyranny, and the family's poverty behind him. To do so in the future he knew he first had to
make the journey from Thal to Graz, which, although a
matter of only a few miles, was as long as any journey
between two opposing worlds. It was the first of three
journeys that the young Arnold was destined to negotiate
before he could begin to attain the success that he enjoys
today, and perhaps it was the most difficult. Thal, with its
winding roads and no sidewalks, is a rural community, so
peaceful that it is hard to believe that Graz, a major city, is
only a short drive away.

Yet after you travel by car for five minutes (a distance
Arnold, in his day, often had to walk), the countryside
begins to change; suddenly there are billboards, sidewalks,
traffic, and houses. Then, after a brief drive through a
commercial district, you enter the outskirts of Graz—dingy
back streets with salmon, gray, and yellow houses, lots of
people on bikes, a Central European city rather than a
Western European city, far closer to the Vienna of *The
Third Man* than to London or Paris.

Graz, however, is full of people who have never seen
London, Paris, or even Vienna, just 134 miles away, never
mind New York and Hollywood. Even today, thirty years
after Arnold made his first major journey from Thal to
Graz, middle-aged women—his contemporaries—still walk
around Graz in national costume with puffed sleeves and
ankle-length dresses, content never to leave Graz, let alone

Austria. The shop windows are full of *Mozart Kugeln*, the traditional Austrian sweets, flower girls sell their wares in the streets, and tourists while the hours away in sidewalk cafés, feasting on the Styrian specialties of piquant garlic soup, cheese soup, and thick white asparagus bursting with moisture. Graz, containing one of the most beautiful medieval sections in the world, belongs to another century, a place that even today seems relatively untouched by the twentieth century. And it is a miracle that Arnold, at thirteen, was able not only to venture outside Thal but also to conceive of leaving Graz at all.

Fantasies of Reg Park and of becoming a superman by now had formed the granite base of his hopes and dreams of escaping from Thal. He concluded that, as Reg Park was a bodybuilder, a bodybuilder was what he, Arnold, would become. Until now it seemed he had always been second best. He had always been powerless in the face of his father's tyranny, and his happiness had always been in the hands of other people, who invariably disappointed him. But now he had a goal, a chance to control his own life and work for his own happiness. Today bodybuilders who are jealous of Arnold's stupendous success, and there are many, often accuse him of leading a charmed life, of having been born under a spectacularly lucky star. That isn't entirely true. For by thirteen Arnold Schwarzenegger had already been inculcated with his father's competitive instincts. Already he was master of his own fate, director of his own scenario. For the first of many times in his life, Arnold selected and then contrived to meet a man who would play a vital part in the advancement of his goals.

In the early sixties Kurt Marnul, Mr. Austria, the most celebrated bodybuilder in the land, was Austria's answer to Arnold's beloved Reg Park. Marnul began bodybuilding in 1952 and in 1958 founded the Athletic Union Graz, the place where some of Austria's best bodybuilders now trained. Arnold, hearing that the swimming master at the Thalersee was one of Marnul's friends, was determined to meet him and begged for an introduction. Eventually fed

up with Arnold's persistence, the "Bademeister" finally told
Marnul about the aspiring young bodybuilder who was so
anxious to meet him and apparently wouldn't take no for
an answer. Consequently, one hot Sunday afternoon (which
Marnul remembers as having been in July 1961, although
there are others who say it was July 1962) Marnul, on a
whim—which would ultimately influence the course of
Arnold's life—decided to go swimming in the Thalersee
and make the acquaintance of his persistent young fan.

Arnold, Marnul recalls, was then nearly fourteen.
Marnul was immediately struck by Arnold's height (six foot
two) and his bulk. Marnul noted that Meinhard, who was
with his brother, was actually better built than Arnold and
was classic bodybuilding material—more muscular with
smaller hips. But it was obvious that it was Arnold who
had the bigger ambition. While Meinhard's attention wan-
dered to beautiful girls swimming in the lake, Arnold was
intent, passionate about becoming a bodybuilder. Marnul
invited both boys to train at the Union.

The sport that Arnold was about to make his own
dates back to Ancient Greece, where young men molded
their physiques into a more masculine form. It emerged
again in the late nineteenth century, when strongman
Eugene Sandow performed such great feats of strength that
he won the patronage of some of Europe's crowned heads.
Florenz Ziegfeld brought him to America, billing him as
"The Amazing Sandow," claiming that he was the strongest man in the world.

Ziegfeld put Sandow on display at the 1893 World's Fair
in Chicago, where he demonstrated his incredible power by
lifting weights, people, and even animals. After Sandow
came ex-wrestler Bernarr "Body Love" Macfadden, who
started America's first bodybuilding magazine, *Physical
Culture*. He also held America's first male physique contest
at Madison Square Garden in 1903, which drew large
crowds. The winner, Al Treloar, won $1,000 and the title of
"The Most Perfectly Developed Man in America." Over in

England, in 1905, the first British bodybuilding contest was held at the Albert Hall in London. The next notable bodybuilder was Angelo Siciliano, who came from Calabria, Italy. He renamed himself Charles Atlas and made a fortune selling courses in "dynamic tension," winning "The World's Most Perfectly Developed Man" title in 1922.

In 1939 the Amateur Athletic Union staged its first Mr. America contest; however, the sport was not taken seriously, nor did it have much of a following. It took the advent of World War II to jolt Americans into an awareness that both bodybuilding and exercise were beneficial. In California, Muscle Beach, south of the Santa Monica pier, was the center of the burgeoning bodybuilding universe. Those who took the red electric streetcar down to Muscle Beach could hear the clanking of weights in the distance long before they arrived. On a hot summer night hundreds of people would be on the beach, reading, eating, and, of course, exercising.

During the war the hotels near Muscle Beach were embarkation centers for servicemen about to be sent to fight overseas. They spent their spare time doing calisthenics by the north side of the pier, where sometimes thousands of servicemen were marching, exercising, and building their bodies. When they were exhausted, they relaxed at the Ocean Park Casino, a mile from Muscle Beach, where they listened to the big bands of Tommy Dorsey and Glenn Miller.

In 1945 Vic Tanny, one of the earliest bodybuilding entrepreneurs, had opened his first gym, in Rochester, New York. In the fifties, along with Bert Goodrich, Tanny also put on bodybuilding shows at the Los Angeles Shrine Auditorium. Amazingly, Tanny's shows attracted crowds of up to six thousand at a time. These early shows were produced with classic Hollywood pizzazz and featured not only bodybuilders but also live bands, strength acts, adagio dancers, and tumblers. Other bodybuilding pioneers included former weightlifting coach Bob Hoffman and Joe Gold, the founder of Gold's Gym—the Santa Monica–based bodybuilding mecca. With Jayne Mansfield's husband,

Mickey Hargitay, Gold had been one of Mae West's muscle men, touring cabarets throughout the United States. Last, but definitely not least, there were the Weider brothers, Joe and Ben, two Canadian powerhouses who founded the International Federation of Bodybuilders (also known as the IFBB) and published numerous bodybuilding magazines. It was Joe Weider who would eventually bring Arnold Schwarzenegger to America and promote bodybuilding to its present-day respectability.

That respectability, won only recently, wasn't easy to achieve. Bodybuilding, even today, is often termed a nonsport. After World War II Alistair Murray, national coach of the British weightlifting team, denounced bodybuilding as "muscular development without purpose." Bodybuilding was considered a bastard branch of weightlifting by both Olympic lifters and powerlifters. One disgruntled powerlifter exclaimed, "What the hell do they [bodybuilders] do with all those muscles? I'll tell you what they do. They get up on a little velvet platform and pose! That's right, *pose!* La-di-da." *Pose,* it was pointed out, suggests phoniness. Some label it an art, others a beauty contest. Bodybuilding has been stereotyped as an exercise in narcissism and exhibitionism performed by musclebound freaks who are all brawn and no brains. Rumors of homosexuality among both participants and fans have always pervaded the sport. But none of the slurs against bodybuilding deterred Arnold from making the profession his own.

On Monday, the day after he first met Kurt Marnul, Arnold was waiting on the doorstep of the Graz Athletic Union, situated in the Graz Liebenauer Football Stadium. In those days the Union was primitive; the equipment was minimal, the floors were uncarpeted, and the heating was nonexistent. The wall of the gym had a hole in it, usually stuffed full of newspaper, which would fly out on windy nights, letting the cold, the wind, and the rain whip through the room, chilling the twenty or so bodybuilders working out there.

Many years later, in his bestselling autobiographical *Arnold: The Education of a Bodybuilder,* Arnold suggested that he made many friends among the Graz bodybuilders, who accepted and encouraged him. That, however, wasn't the case. According to Helmut Cerncic, who worked as trainer at the Union from 1960 to 1967 and won the Mr. Austria title in 1963, Arnold did not make a good impression on the Union bodybuilders. On that first evening he introduced himself to all of them, one by one, solemnly announcing in tones that reminded Cerncic of a door-to-door salesman, "Good evening, my name is Arnold Schwarzenegger. I would like to do bodybuilding."

Cerncic noted that, although Arnold spoke in German, he isolated the word *bodybuilding* by pronouncing it in English. The effect was strange. Says Cerncic, "From the first night when he walked into the Union, we all thought Arnold had a big mouth. He had very bad posture, a slightly shrunken chest, fallen shoulders, very skinny legs, and used to train with his eyes half closed and his mouth half open, so that the whole effect was as if he wasn't all there. Soon after he started his first training session at the Union he turned around to another bodybuilder, Johnny Schnetz, who was around his age, and said, 'Well, I give myself about five years and I will be Mr. Universe.' We all looked at each other as if to say, 'This boy is crazy.'

"If you add to that the fact that every so often he would make a derogatory remark about one of the other bodybuilders, the result was that no one had much respect for him. In fact, he got on our nerves." In the context of the Union Arnold was a loner and a misfit, shunned by the other bodybuilders, whose overall attitude toward him, in Cerncic's words, was "You can train alone. Just keep your mouth shut."

Meinhard came to the Union a few times as well and made a halfhearted attempt to train. He proved to be much stronger than Arnold, with greater endurance, but became bored and gave up.

Early on, Kurt Marnul gave Arnold basic training

advice, telling him, "When you train, think of the muscle you are working on or developing and go to the farthest pain barrier. Go on until you cry out. That is the secret of the biggest bodybuilders. They train beyond the pain barrier." He had sensed Arnold's potential and advised him regarding diet, a topic about which the Austrian bodybuilding community, in that era, was ignorant. They didn't know about sticking to egg white and protein and, as they were unaware of the dangers of cholesterol, ate mountains of eggs. Marnul also told Arnold about steroids: how they increased growth and were necessary to win competitions. Arnold listened. Marnul offered him steroids. And Arnold took them.

Marnul had learned about steroids and their dosages from Steve Reeves, whom he had first met in France during a 1952 vacation, and was willing to give Arnold the necessary injections of the steroid Primobolin, the champagne of steroids, two or three times a week. The injections began almost immediately after Arnold started training as a bodybuilder. So did steroid tablets, namely Dianabol. An Austrian bodybuilder who trained with him remembers, "Arnold took steroids in doses that terrified the other bodybuilders. I saw him swallow eight or nine Dianabols at a time. Then he would take a gulp of milk, a handful of protein tablets, and while he was still swallowing and could hardly talk, say, 'Right, now I'm ready!' and start training." According to fellow bodybuilder Rick Wayne, steroids were still a part of Arnold's life in 1966, when he offered Wayne a month's supply of Dianabol. Wayne also says Arnold confided to him that he had been taking steroids since the age of thirteen.

Recently a great deal of publicity has surrounded the subject of steroids. From the bodybuilding point of view, steroids increase growth. They also have serious side effects, not only increasing aggression but also giving the user tremendous erections. At first, that is. Ultimately, however, steroids can cause the testicles to shrink, making erections virtually unattainable. According to current German bodybuilding star Ronald Matz, who has been Mr. Germany, Mr. Europe, and Mr. Universe, steroids have other consequences: "You get very horny. You think about sex all the time. Then your testosterone level goes below zero. The body stops providing it. You don't have any sexual feeling." Matz goes on to say that there are ways to counter some effects of steroid usage: "It takes a couple of months to recover, unless you take HCG, which comes from the urine of a pregnant woman. Today, though, there are other techniques apart from steroids; some bodybuilders have silicone put under their muscles by plastic surgeons. And bodybuilders still think that if one anabolic [steroid] is good, then two or three are better."

In the early sixties, however, the dangers of steroids were not fully understood. Marnul says he was in the habit of taking steroids three months before a contest. When the competition was over, he stopped for four months, resuming again for the next three.

Apart from giving Arnold steroids, Marnul also provided him with a new example to emulate. He was a big spender and a dandy, prone to wearing white denims and yellow-tinted glasses, driving around Graz in a Renault Floride, which excited the attention of all the ladies. Arnold was impressed, deciding that when he grew up he wanted to be like Marnul. One day he would far surpass him—in cars, in money, and in beautiful women.

Arnold was still a schoolboy living at home in Thal, but now his whole life was in Graz. If he missed the bus from Thal to Graz, he hitched a ride from a passing car. Each afternoon at five, when the Union opened, he would be there waiting, pounding on the door, insisting, "Let me in, let me in. I can't wait. I have to train." And in the evening, if he had a choice between finishing a set and catching his bus, Arnold always completed his set, then walked the four miles home. Karl Kainrath, a champion bodybuilder who trained with him, put it like this: "We all knew that the building could have fallen down, but Arnold would still have continued training." According to Cerncic, Arnold even confided, "If you told me that if I ate a kilo of shit I would put on muscles, I would eat it."

The Athletic Union was closed on Saturday and Sunday, but soon after Arnold began training there Marnul arrived at the Union to find that a window had been smashed. Finally Arnold confessed. He wanted to train seven days a week, he said, and in pursuit of his goal he had borrowed a ladder, climbed a wall, and smashed a window so that he could climb in and train. Marnul was angry but couldn't quite manage to lose his temper with this ardent young boy. Depriving him of training was akin to depriving him of air.

Gustav had taught Arnold to ignore pain and suffering and then move on. In that spirit he spent bitterly cold winter nights training without a break. One night, when he finally finished, exhausted, he looked down at his hands and realized that, in removing them from the frozen bars, he had ripped part of his skin away.

His dedication was total, unswerving, and heroic. He was almost a missionary in his attempt to convert his body into the perfect work of art he so passionately desired it to be. Nothing mattered anymore except training—not school, not friends, not girls, not his parents, nothing.

Anyone who talked to Arnold while he was training was ignored. Later, however, when his confidence had increased and the other bodybuilders had grown accustomed to his obnoxiousness and his habit of heckling them, he found he was able to disarm them by making them laugh. Sometimes they laughed so hard that they had to abandon their training while Arnold, to his satisfaction, continued. It would become a pattern of his career for him to play the gym jester, gaining attention yet in the same stroke sabotaging any rival who posed a threat.

Soon Marnul was no longer his only mentor. Sammi Adia Saad, a well-known bodybuilder studying in Graz, began to give him advice. So did Helmut Knaur, another bodybuilder who had been in the British Air Force and who taught him a few words of English. Then there was Alfred Gerstl, a local politician, whose son Karl was Arnold's age. Gerstl had a large apartment in Graz and soon offered Arnold the chance to train there on those days when the Union was closed. Alfred Gerstl was probably the first Jew whom Arnold had ever met, and despite his father's having joined the Nazi party, Arnold warmed to Gerstl instantly, treating him as an ersatz father. Although Arnold had, by then, built a makeshift gym in the basement of the house in Thal, training at Gerstl's often led to dinner, and he quickly found that it was more fun to spend the evening with Alfred and his family, listening to music and talking about bodybuilding, than to go home to Aurelia and Gustav.

Both of his parents still disapproved of Arnold, especially now that he had created a life for himself away from them. Gustav probably was not pleased that Arnold came in only sixth in the curling championships in February 1962. Aurelia, a deeply religious woman, was even more unhappy when he gave up going to church. Helmut Knaur had given him a book called *Pfaffenspiegel*, which Arnold was later to describe as being about how "horrible" priests were. Arnold announced to his parents that he no longer believed in church and didn't have time for it. There is little evidence to suggest that his attitude had altered radically by 1981 when, although seriously involved with Maria Shriver and the number-one candidate to marry into the very prominent and very Catholic Kennedy family, he remarked that he attended church on Sunday "when I think about it."

Gustav had striven always to diminish Arnold. Now Arnold retaliated by expanding himself. Literally. As his son grew larger and larger, Gustav himself seemed to shrink. In the spring of 1962 he was transferred from Thal to the police station in Raaba, on the outskirts of Graz. He had been moved on disciplinary grounds, after being drunk and making a nuisance of himself to a woman he met on a bus. To exacerbate matters, his favorite son, Meinhard, had defied him, leaving his latest school without permission and joining an electronics firm. And Arnold spent most of his time training, socializing with Alfred Gerstl, or seeing each of Reg Park's films at least three times.

Gustav was disturbed by Arnold's fanaticism and lust for victory—a lust that he himself had hammered into Arnold's soul. The truth was that he had, in a sense, created a Frankenstein's monster, who had now progressed beyond his control. To rectify the situation he told Arnold that he would never amount to anything, would never win the bodybuilding championships he so desperately craved. When that didn't deter Arnold from training, he threatened to send him to a psychiatrist.

Gustav never carried out his threat. Although there are those who claim bodybuilding is nothing but a narcissistic male beauty contest, Gustav, who worked out with weights himself, obviously wasn't one of them. He may have made the threat for Aurelia's benefit or out of jealousy and fear that his son might now be able to surpass him in machismo. Or he could have been motivated by altruistic parental concern over Arnold's megalomania.

Whatever the case, psychiatrists have developed theories regarding the allure of bodybuilding and the seductive siren song that the sport sings to its most fanatical acolytes. Dr. Maurice White, a British psychiatrist, analyzing some bodybuilders who demonstrate a compulsion to get bigger, says that although "a lot of people practice bodybuilding with acceptable motives, there are others who want to be admired, respected and feared." But, says White, "underneath the muscle is an empty shell, a hollow life, a sense of impotence."

British professor Laurie Taylor notes, "I always think that the bodybuilder has affinities with the obsessive masturbator who meticulously choreographs the steps of his own orgasm. There is the same assiduous concentration upon the body, the same precision, the same claustrophobic self-regard, the same fascination with chronicling performance. And there is the mirror: a crucial prop in all exercises in narcissism. . . . What's peculiar about the body-builder is that with weights, training methods, diets, and drugs, he can realize part of his fantasy. He can transform himself from a seven-stone [ninety-eight-pound] weakling into an Iron Man."

There is more. Dr. Stanley Riklin, a New York clinical psychologist, says, "The man who engages in bodybuilding to make himself feel stronger, healthier, and more confident so he'll be able to relate better to others is entirely different from the one who is preoccupied only with himself, with pumping his muscles up to an extraordinary size. But this second man, in my opinion, is usually quite insecure, and attempting to overcome deep anxieties—fears that he is small, damaged, inadequate. His energies are not going out toward other people, but *inward*; he involves others only to obtain admiration and allay anxieties about himself."

Frank Zane, three-time Mr. Olympia and one of Arnold's contemporaries, says, "Bodybuilding gave me the power to control and change my appearance. I thought that was tremendous." In the same vein Boyer Coe, four-time Mr. Universe and seven-time Mr. World, says that he believes people take up bodybuilding because they had inferiority complexes as children: "The way to overcome this is to build this big muscular body. Arthur Jones, who founded Nautilus, has labeled bodybuilders 'little boys hiding in gorilla suits.' "

In promoting bodybuilding as a sport, Arnold himself has repeatedly compared pumping up with sexuality, with having an orgasm. Ronald Matz adds, "Bodybuilding is sexual. When the muscle is blowing up, you look in the mirror and feel great. It is sexual. But you have to be a little bit of a masochist to go beyond the limit. You don't think of women; you just think of your own body."

Arnold, at fifteen, conformed to Ronald Matz's profile. Women were outside his realm of consciousness. His world

consisted only of bodybuilding and dreams of future success. To make money he had begun a three-year apprentice-
ship with a building materials firm in the Neubergasse in
Graz, doing carpentry for a salary of about two hundred
fifty schillings a month during the first year, seven hundred schillings a month the second year, and a princely one
thousand schillings a month the third year.

Arnold took part in his first bodybuilding contest in
Graz's most elegant hotel, the Steirer Hof. A proud Alfred
Gerstl invited his fellow politicians to the contest, hoping
to prove to them that bodybuilding was a worthy enterprise
that would keep growing boys off the streets. Pictures of
Arnold at that first contest reveal a handsome young boy
with a slightly petulant pout, his mouth not yet curled in
arrogance but exuding innocence and freshness. Arnold
didn't win that contest; he was only a runner-up. But he
was already at home onstage, the applause catering to his
love-starved nature, gilding him with a newfound self-
confidence.

The spring of 1964 found him once again literally
impersonating Gustav, when he became the city and national junior curling champion—in the same year that his
father became senior champion. Gustav began to sit up and
take notice, telling colleagues at work that Arnold resembled him and that they shouldn't forget Gustav's own athletic triumphs. At last Arnold was starting to win the
approval and attention from his father that he had once so
desperately craved. But it had come too late. The moment
had gone, and the die was cast. However much love and
attention Gustav was to give him in the future, it would not
compensate for the past. And nothing, not even the love
and admiration of the entire world, ever would.

Arnold had conquered Graz. But Graz was no longer
enough for him, and he began to make plans for the second
great journey of his life—the journey from Austria to Germany. In anticipation of broadening his horizons, Arnold,
demonstrating the planning and foresight that would be-

come one of his hallmarks, struck up a correspondence with Benno Dahmen and his partner, Peter Fasching, who published *Athletic Sportsman*, a German bodybuilding magazine. In 1963 Arnold had written to Benno, querying him on bodybuilding techniques. Gustav's essays had paid off in cultivating Arnold's literacy so that his letter was compelling. In consequence Benno replied and then began to follow Arnold's progress with interest.

Soon, however, Arnold's career would take a new and ultimately gratifying twist. On October 1, 1965, just a few months after his eighteenth birthday, Arnold began his compulsory one-year service in the Austrian Army. In many ways he was made for the military. After all, Gustav had run his family like a general, and Arnold had, until he discovered bodybuilding, invariably obeyed his commands. Accustomed to seeing his father's splendor when dressed in his police uniform, and perhaps again identifying with the aggressor, Arnold couldn't wait to wear one himself. The idea of medals, regimentation, and a firm, rigid structure, he later explained, appealed to him.

Besides, according to Arnold, Gustav had smoothed the path for his younger son by using his influence to have him stationed at a camp near Graz. He had also pulled strings so that Arnold, characteristically impressed by the size and power of tanks, could be a tank driver. Arnold claims that, thanks to Gustav's influence, the Austrian Army made an exception to the required tank driver's minimum age, lowering it from twenty-one to eighteen, thus enabling him to fulfill his ambition.

Driving a tank provided Arnold with a tremendous sense of power, and in *Arnold: The Education of a Body-builder* he describes how much he loved the recoil of the guns when they fired and how it fed something in his nature that was moved by demonstrations of strength. Sometimes, though, army life proved to be dangerous. Once he "parked" a tank but forgot to put the brake on. The tank rolled into the river. According to Arnold, there were no consequences.

For the first time in his life, thanks to the army, Arnold ate meat every single day. His body responded dramatically to the large amount of protein it was suddenly being fed. And Arnold blossomed. Which was just as well, because around the time that he joined the army Benno Dahmen wrote to him, inviting him to compete in the Junior Mr. Europe contest, to be held in Stuttgart on October 30th. Anyone who knew Arnold, his superhuman dedication, his unshakable belief in himself, and the impressive body he had now built was sure that the results were a foregone conclusion. For Arnold, at eighteen, was already a bodybuilding phenomenon.

Throughout his career, whether in bodybuilding or in films, Arnold has never sold himself cheaply. His first major contest was no exception. Throwing himself on the mercy of strangers, a tactic that was to serve him well in the future, Arnold wrote back to Benno confessing that he couldn't afford the fare to Stuttgart. Backed by his magazine, which hoped to witness and report the birth of a new bodybuilding star, Benno financed Arnold's trip to Stuttgart.

There is some confusion as to whether or not he used Benno's money to pay for the entire train fare from Graz to Stuttgart. Two of his fellow Austrian bodybuilders, Karl Kainrath and Hans Gobetz, remember making the journey by car. Benno, on the other hand, recalls picking Arnold up from the station.

Whatever route he took, Arnold's destination was never in doubt: Junior Mr. Europe. He knew exactly what he wanted. And he had taken great risks to obtain it. For despite being the product of Gustav's school of obedience and discipline, Arnold, as he would many times in his career, had gambled. To compete in Stuttgart he had gone AWOL.

The end, as was usually the case with Arnold, justified the means. Although observers at that early contest, like German bodybuilder Karl Blömer, who himself would become 1968 Mr. Europe and 1971 Mr. World, didn't think Arnold was very handsome, his size was indisputable.

Arnold won the contest to become Junior Mr. Europe 1965, in the process beating his future training partner, Franz Dischinger. But even if he had lost, he would still, in a sense, have won. Because on that October 30, 1965, at Stuttgart's Wulle Rooms, destiny set three vitally important players on the incredible stage of Arnold Schwarzenegger's now exciting life: Rolf Putziger, Wag Bennett, and Franco Columbu.

Franco Columbu, whom he met in Stuttgart that day, was, like Arnold, Aurelia, and Gustav, born under the sign of Leo. Six years older than Arnold, with his dark, pixieish good looks he often seemed younger. Only five foot five, born in Sardinia, he had ridden in Italian horse races and had been the lightweight boxing champion of Italy. He and Arnold had an instant rapport. Almost wordlessly they formed an indestructible bond.

Franco was to spend most of his career aping Arnold but never surpassing him. True, he was a great athlete in his own right, eventually winning most major bodybuilding titles at least once. He also had a fair share of charisma. But he was to remain forever in Arnold's shadow. Yet he was loyal to him, protected and loved him like a brother. Always Arnold's Sancho Panza, Franco could never beat him in anything. In a strange way he was Meinhard, vanquished. Which was just the way Arnold liked it.

Wag Bennett, British bodybuilding official, gym owner, and bodybuilder himself, over in Stuttgart to see the Junior Mr. Europe contest, had made bodybuilding the center of his existence. The sport was almost a religion to him. And as he watched Arnold Schwarzenegger on stage that October day in Stuttgart, he realized that he had found his messiah.

Putziger, the third man whom Arnold met as a result of his appearance at the Stuttgart contest, owned a gym in Munich and published bodybuilding magazines, beginning with *Hercules* and followed by *Sports Journal* and then *Sports Review*. He and his associate, Albert Busek, invited Arnold to Munich, offering him the job of trainer at the gym. Arnold said he would think about it. Putziger, a homosexual, said he hoped that Arnold would accept his invitation. He had great plans for him.

Victorious, Arnold went back to Graz and to certain punishment at the hands of the army. Arnold claims to have spent seven days locked in the army jail, with only a blanket, a cold stone bench, and practically no food. Word of Arnold's victory spread through the army camp, and he soon became a hero to the army, whose officers gave him all he wanted to eat and encouraged him to train even harder so that he could concentrate on bringing glory to Austria.

It would be easy to assume at this point that Arnold was a humorless fanatic who lived only for bodybuilding and had no other interests. However, at eighteen he had already developed a very important outlet that he would never relinquish—the practical joke, which appeared to be a more refined and socially acceptable form of the bullying that he had exhibited as a teenager. Today Arnold's sense of humor is legendary in bodybuilding circles. And although the stories illustrating it are legion, one story stands out among the rest: "the salt joke" that Arnold played on a naive bodybuilder around the time that he won his Stuttgart contest.

In Austria, while training at the Union, Arnold, Karl Kainrath, Kurt Marnul, and Hans Gobetz made the acquaintance of a certain Mr. C. Mr. C's father was a wealthy man who owned a guesthouse and meat store in Gleisdorf, just outside Graz. Mr. C adored Arnold, longed to have a body like his, and in his presence carried on like a lovesick girl.

Mr. C fawned over Arnold and adored him to distraction. There was a thin line between the attention Arnold had always longed for and mindless hero worship. He soon became repelled by both Mr. C's ardor and his slavishness. Once, Gobetz and Arnold, looking for a laugh, visited Mr.

C at his father's house. The father, eager to promote his calflike son's career, offered the "friendly" bodybuilders large portions of meat. Which they ate. The father immediately produced more. Which, again, they ate. Then they left. But Mr. C still didn't get the message.

Finally he gingerly approached Arnold and begged him for the secret of his success. What exactly were Arnold's training methods? What, for example, did he eat? Arnold's face lit up. As the spellbound young bodybuilder listened, he earnestly gave him this advice: "If you want to build a body like mine, you have to grind up nutshells and add them to a spoonful of salt. Eat one spoonful of this mixture on the first day. On the second day, increase it to two. On the third, three. And so on, until the thirtieth day, when you should be eating thirty teaspoons a day. Then you will put on a lot of muscle. And you will begin to build a body like mine."

Mr. C was delighted. He rushed out and began Arnold's salt diet, in his besotted state not realizing that a large amount of salt is lethal to the system of anyone, man or superman, and that even a small amount of salt is anathema to the bodybuilder, making his body retain the liquid that all bodybuilders are intent on eliminating.

All agree that Mr. C ended his diet on the seventeenth day, at the point when he was eating seventeen teaspoons of the salt/nutshell mixture per day. However, there is some disagreement as to the effect of Arnold's diet; some witnesses say Mr. C broke out in pimples all over his face and body; others that he ended up in the hospital. Two things, however, are indisputable. First, that today, over twenty years since Mr. C was the victim of Arnold's joke, he still turns deathly white at the very mention of Arnold's name. Second, that this was Arnold's first, and some say greatest, practical joke. It was certainly one that enhanced his mythology in the bodybuilding world, gained him a vast amount of attention, and caused him to explode in uproarious delight each and every time he told the story.

3
Munich

ARNOLD RETURNED HOME TO THAL A
hero. Aurelia was dazzled by his victory, polishing his
trophy until it glittered, then carrying it from house to
house, showing the neighbors what her younger son had
won. Gustav was not unimpressed, although he had other,
more serious concerns regarding Arnold on his mind.

Gustav, by all reports somewhat of a rake, was worried
about Arnold's sexuality. While Meinhard showed every
sign of becoming an accomplished womanizer, Arnold, at
eighteen, didn't yet have a girlfriend. The other bodybuilders used to dance the evening away at the Tenne Dancehall
in Graz, but in the four years that Arnold trained at the
Union, his trainer, Helmut Cerncic, never knew Arnold to
go to a disco or a dance hall.

Gustav, ever the general, marshaled his forces in aid of
his son's suspect sexuality. When Arnold finally brought
girls home when he was on leave, his delighted father
would be very encouraging and would provide them with a
bottle of wine and two glasses.

Arnold's sexual pattern was then set, as if in stone. He
viewed women only as tools for his sexual needs. With two
exceptions—his first serious girlfriend, Barbara Outland,
and his wife, Maria Shriver—he would never waste time
courting a woman. As his fame and prestige as a bodybuilder escalated, he discovered that the conventional small
talk and niceties normally inherent in the mating game
were completely unnecessary for him. Women became extremely available, and Arnold evolved a unique approach to

women, which in the future would either amuse or shock
anyone who encountered it.

In March 1966 Arnold won his second major bodybuilding title, that of Mr. Germany. However, his parents
were still not convinced that he should make bodybuilding
his career. After all, bodybuilders didn't make a living.
Arnold should settle down in Graz, get a "normal" job,
maybe as an officer in the army, and resign himself to
becoming a part-time bodybuilder.

The life that Aurelia and Gustav envisioned for Arnold
was probably close to the classic Thaler's lot. Many Thalers
were farmers or worked in the Graz pencil factory, but
Arnold, trained now as a carpenter, could probably make
more money working for a building company. He could
live in Thal (where, even in the mid-sixties, there was no
movie theater, no hairdresser, and little social life other
than evenings drinking at the local taverns), take the dawn
bus to Graz, do a day's work, and take the bus back to Thal
at twilight. But then Gustav and Aurelia didn't really understand the nature of the superman they had spawned.

Human beings essentially are divided between those
who remain with the tried and true, resisting change or
adventure, and those who have unlimited horizons, unafraid to risk the terror of the new. The first stay close to
home for their entire lives, sticking to what they know and,
better still, those who know them. Then there are those
who sever ties, leave home, take chances, and pitch their
tents far away from family, friends, and the familiar.

Another man in Arnold's position might have remained in Thal, winning minor bodybuilding titles year
after year and savoring his brief moment of glory. Perhaps
the attention garnered could have been sufficient, could
have satisfied another man's vanity, and might have won
him the requisite number of beautiful girls and a certain
amount of approval of parents and peers alike. But that
never would have been enough for Arnold.

He has never played it safe, has never picked the easy

route, the average, or the steady. Never afraid to take risks, he resisted succumbing to the lure of becoming an inflated fish in the exceedingly small pond that is Graz. Instead of opting for the safety of the anchored existence, mooring himself in Graz, founding a small empire right there among people he knew he could conquer and control, Arnold flung himself, as it were, into the open sea, confident that no shark was more lethal than the dangers of settling for stagnation and conventionality.

Arnold had listened well to his father's credo of joy through strength, had coupled it with the fanaticism of his fellow Austrian bodybuilders, laced it with the intoxicating euphoria of victory, and finally added to it the philosophy he had fashioned five years before as a thirteen-year-old boy sitting alone in the darkened Graz theater, watching Reg Park conquer the world. He would go to Munich, work at Putziger's gym, and leave the safety of his family and his country behind him. But rather than taking a hat, a stick, and a monkey with him, Arnold took with him his philosophy, the philosophy that his father had imprinted onto his soul.

At this point, then, it seems appropriate to study that philosophy—and the beliefs that Arnold took with him to Munich.

"I look down at people who are waiting, who are helpless. I like people who think there is more to life than eating or going to the toilet."

"Ever since I was a child, I would say to myself, 'There must be more to life than this,' and I found that I didn't want to be like everybody else. I wanted to be different. I wanted to be part of the small percentage of people who were leaders, not the large mass of followers. I think it was because I saw that leaders use 100 percent of their potential. . . . I was always fascinated by people in control of other people."

"Strength does not come from winning. Your struggles develop your strengths. When you go through hardships and decide not to surrender, that is strength. . . . You must want to be the greatest."

"As a kid I always idolized the winning athletes. It is one thing to idolize heroes. It is quite another to visualize yourself in their place. When I saw great people, I said to myself: 'I can be there.' "

"We all have great inner power. The power is self-faith. There's really an attitude to winning. You have to see yourself winning before you win. And you have to be hungry. You have to want to conquer."

"Good things don't happen by coincidence. . . . Every dream carries with it certain risks, especially the risk of failure. But I am not stopped by risks. Suppose a person takes the risk and fails. Then the person must try again. You cannot fail forever. If you try ten times, you have a better chance of making it on the eleventh try than if you didn't try at all."

"What I am most happy about is that I can zero in on a vision of where I want to be in the future. I can see it so clearly in front of me when I daydream that it's almost a reality. Then I get this easy feeling, and I don't have to be uptight to get there because I already feel like I'm there, that it's just a matter of time."

Arnold started working at Putziger's gym at 36 Schiller Strasse in Munich on August 1, 1966. That date was significant not just because it marked a new cycle for Arnold but also because it was his father's fifty-ninth birthday and the day on which his brother Meinhard first met the great and only love of his life.

Meinhard Schwarzenegger had always been a troubled boy. Despite having been Gustav's favorite son, he too had suffered from his father's harsh upbringing. A talented artist, he preferred to ignore his physical prowess and the sporting ability he had inherited from his father. Ironically it was Arnold, the rejected, unloved son, who had chosen to follow in his father's athletic footsteps while the favored son had repudiated Gustav totally.

On visits home Meinhard would argue bitterly with
Gustav about his politics. Politics, however, weren't the
only problem. Meinhard, who had once done his best to
con an old couple for five hundred schillings, now had
bigger financial fish to fry. Using his father's position and
sometimes his brother's growing fame, Meinhard managed
to borrow around thirty thousand schillings (which in
1965 amounted to $1,070) from a small number of people,
allegedly including Mr. C. Gustav's reputation began to
suffer until eventually, in an attempt to save a career that
had already been damaged by his drinking, Gustav was
compelled to protect himself from further problems by
making good every single one of Meinhard's debts.

Meinhard drifted from job to job, unwilling to support himself and jealous of his younger brother's success in
bodybuilding. While Arnold's star was ascending, Meinhard, who had always been the golden boy, found that his
own was setting. For Meinhard there was no glory, no
applause. His most valuable asset in life was his charm,
and, aware of his power, he set about using it to devastating
effect.

On August 1, 1966, while walking through the pretty
Austrian village of Kufstein, Meinhard noticed an adorable
twenty-year-old girl. The girl, with sky-blue eyes and blond
hair, could have represented Austria in the Miss World
contest. Just back from a holiday in Spain and on a trip
from Munich to her parents' house in Kufstein, Erika
Knapp was suntanned and buxom. Today, dressed in her
national costume as she was during her years with Meinhard, Erika is still a radiantly attractive woman.

Meinhard Schwarzenegger, with his sixth sense for
women, knew that Erika was for him. Erika had the same
feeling about Meinhard. He was tall, blond, and rivetingly
handsome. With uncharacteristic boldness, she asked him
for the time. He followed her home and invited her to
dinner. She refused.

With an instinct for strategy that his younger brother
also possessed in abundance and employed with startling

success, Meinhard, instead of risking a second rejection, asked Erika's neighbor for a date. Piqued, Erika naturally relented and went out with Meinhard herself.

After a few days in Kufstein she returned to Munich, where she worked as a dressmaker. Meinhard, dominated by passion, followed her. By November they were engaged. A month or two afterward, Erika and Meinhard were strolling along the bank of Munich's River Isar when she noticed five muscular men walking toward them. Snickering, she turned to Meinhard and whispered, "Look at them; look how inflated they all are." "Be quiet," said Meinhard. "That is my brother." It had been six months since they met, but until that moment, Erika hadn't known that Meinhard had a brother.

Arnold, too, was not eager to acknowledge his brother. When his new friends in Munich inquired about Meinhard, he would tell them not to ask him, but instead to ask his mother. The proud Aurelia always attended Arnold's contests, and Gustav corresponded with him on a regular basis. Unwilling to relinquish his habitual role, Gustav complained to Arnold that his handwriting was too big, asking if this, perhaps, was his son's ploy to avoid writing to his father at any length. Arnold denied the charge, but perhaps the ever-viligant Gustav was on to something. For at this stage, working for Putziger in Munich, Arnold had little to say to his father.

He was nineteen now, tall, enormous, with a gap-toothed smile that could, depending on his intentions, either enchant or mock. At first his strong Austrian accent was a liability at Putziger's, but no one dared make fun of him. Although he was, in essence, a country bumpkin, a farm boy who possessed only one suit, his self-confidence was remarkable, his presence formidable, and his ability to intimidate well honed. And, most amazingly of all, the charmless boy, gaining confidence from his bodybuilding triumphs, had grown into a charming man. He was, after all, the son of Gustav, whose charm was legendary, and the brother of Meinhard, whose charm he may well have imitated.

At first he slept in the gym. Officially he was a manager/trainer, but in reality he was a general factotum, sweeping the floor, cleaning bathrooms, and generally making himself useful. Universum Sport, Putziger's publishing house specializing in bodybuilding publications, was based in the same building as the gym. Run by Albert Busek, who had witnessed his Stuttgart triumph, Universum Sport's magazines would soon project Arnold as the new great hope of bodybuilding.

Albert Busek was to be, with Alfred Gerstl, the first of what could be termed the "Arnia"—men who believe in Arnold above all, worship the ground on which he walks, and do all they can to enhance his legend.

Even without them, however, Arnold would still have become the Arnold of bodybuilding fame. In Munich he trained for as long as seven hours a day, achieving stupendous results. Wrestlers trained at the gym, and their promoter offered Arnold a job, which he turned down. Bodybuilding remained his one and only Holy Grail.

Outside the gym Arnold began to couple his propensity for playing practical jokes with exhibitionism. On raucous nights, after swigging gigantic steins of beer in Munich's famous beer halls or in the Bavarian restaurant that was in the same building as the gym, Arnold would suddenly stand up, raise himself to his full height, and then, to the amazement of his fellow diners, rip off his shirt and flex his muscles.

For the first time in his life patently "one of the boys," he regaled his friends with the salt story, laughing so loudly that the spaghetti he was eating flew all over the restaurant.

Soon he became the scourge of Munich's restaurants; once he and a group of friends sat next to a lady with a tiny poodle on her knee. After Arnold wolfed down a mountain of food, he turned to the poodle and menacingly indicated that the dog was to be his next meal. The lady recoiled in fear.

In the same vein one bodybuilder in Munich was

treated to dinner along with five other friends, only to discover that when it came time to settle the bill Arnold's plan was to persuade them to leave the restaurant without paying.

He was wont to announce, "I am Styrian—I'll show you all!" And all who knew him during those adventurous Munich years agree that he certainly did just that.

Arnold and Franco Columbu, who was working as a trainer in Regensburg, became close friends, and they cut a swath through Munich's female population. By then, Arnold had become accustomed to the practice of sex without the preliminaries. According to an eyewitness, bodybuilder Helmut Riedmeier, when asked by a hapless waitress if he needed anything, Arnold, fueled by a large quantity of beer, replied, "Yes, to fuck you." He employed the same approach repeatedly, and although he never got seriously involved with a woman while in Munich, his bed was frequently occupied by one willing female or another.

His bulk, his status in the bodybuilding world, his charm, and his aggressiveness tended to win him whatever or whomever he chose to covet. It is important to note as well that Arnold's enhanced aggressiveness during the Munich years probably stemmed partly from steroids. According to Helmut Riedmeier, one of his training partners, Arnold "used to inject himself with steroids and took them for breakfast, lunch, and dinner quite openly."

Perhaps the steroids, apart from causing him to put on weight, also liberated the rashness he had been suppressing for so long under his father's regime. His dangerous driving was legendary among bodybuilders at the gym, most of whom refused to travel in any car driven by Arnold. He collected quantities of speeding tickets and traffic violations, some of which were never paid.

Arnold's aggression also found physical expression in barroom brawls. Fists flew when Arnold went to Munich's Oktoberfest, the traditional celebration that often degenerates into a notorious beer orgy and is renowned for its rowdiness. He did his best to contribute, heckling a group of Americans who were spending the evening at the fair. The Americans, deciding that they weren't going to stand for German presumptuousness, especially when it came from such a baby-faced lad, prepared to fight. Arnold, ever alert, aware that he and his friends, Busek's co-worker, Erich Janner, and his training partner, Franz Dischinger, were outnumbered, volunteered that fighting might not be a good idea.

The Americans reacted by pushing him. Arnold drew back. Then, turning to Janner, he said, "Hold my jacket." As he exposed his chest and flexed, the Americans capitulated, informing him that they too trained. There was a truce, and both sides went off together, laughing and joking, in search of more beer.

Although Arnold now dominated the Munich bodybuilding scene, he still kept in contact with the Union. His Austrian bodybuilding friends Gobetz, Kainrath, and Marnul came to visit him. Once they brought Gustav along with them, driving from Graz through villages populated by his relatives. Gustav, a gregarious man, insisted on paying his respects to family members in each and every village. Consequently, the journey took twice as long as normal. Once in Munich, he showed great pride in Arnold and boasted to anyone who cared to listen that the son had inherited his athletic abilities from his father.

By around 1967 Arnold was living in a small apartment where Helmut Riedmeier, who had won the Mr. Germany, Mr. Europe, and Mr. Universe titles, often stayed with him. And toward the end of his Munich time he was joined by Franco. All in all, life was congenial.

Then again, a few of Arnold's escapades during his Munich period had a slightly disturbing quality. As one of his training partners was to observe, "Arnold always made a fool of people he didn't respect. He'd make jokes of them." When reprimanded for his practical jokes, according to Marnul, Arnold dismissed his victims, contemptuously declaring, "They are so stupid. I would never do what they do."

He had been educated in the Gustav Schwarzenegger school of humiliation, and now he was on top. Now he could turn the tables and settle old scores, using strangers, acquaintances, and even friends as victims whose mortification served to dress his psychological wounds. He had been degraded and diminished. Now he would be the degrader. Now he would diminish.

The number of Arnold's victims during his Munich years may appear extraordinary unless one bears in mind his status during that time. He was a rising bodybuilding star, an example and an inspiration to those who aspired to succeed in the sport. His advice was sought and followed with a religious fervor by bodybuilders anxious to achieve his proportions. Mr. C, of the salt saga, was the first of many victims.

Arnold once told a fellow bodybuilder that if he ate two pounds of ice cream he would develop more muscle. Nowadays most bodybuilders are aware that water robs them of muscle definition; they take so many diuretics before major contests that sometimes, only seconds before a show begins, they can be seen backstage vomiting from the side effects. That information obviously hadn't filtered through to Arnold's victim, who proceeded to gulp down mountains of ice cream. Discovering that he was doing this on the suggestion of the divine Arnold, nine of his bodybuilding friends followed suit—and lived to regret it.

Then there was the sugar treatment. This was a variation on the salt theme, with Arnold counseling a bodybuilder to begin by eating one sugar cube on the first day, two on the second, three on the third, and so on, until the bodybuilder was eating thirty cubes of sugar a day.

Another bodybuilder nearly choked to death after Arnold persuaded him that instead of blending a favorite bodybuilder's concoction of egg whites and vitamins into a smooth paste, he should knead the mixture together and eat it as if it were an apple. When Kurt Marnul warned him that his advice could harm someone, Marnul remembers that Arnold laughed and merely reiterated that his victims were just stupid.

Arnold's role as gym manager/trainer was the ideal position from which to sally forth and play practical jokes on unsuspecting bodybuilders who had applied to join the gym. One novice bodybuilder who asked Arnold for an application was informed that acceptance was conditional on his passing a test related to his profession. What, asked Arnold, in fact, was the man's profession? "Mountaineer" was the answer. "Right," said Arnold. "Your membership test will be to climb out of the gym window and down to street level." The gym was on the second floor. Out the applicant went to complete Arnold's test.

It must be said that Arnold was completely democratic in the selection of his victims, not discriminating between old friends like Hans Gobetz, young bodybuilders who didn't stand a chance of winning any competition but unquestioningly drank in his words of wisdom, and total strangers, like the mountaineer applicant.

Arnold's practical jokes served to embellish his legend. Traditionally bodybuilders have been enthralled by power, their entire quest being to project an illusion of power by increasing their size. They are also accustomed to enduring pain in the process of training. And the flip side of enduring pain is, of course, inflicting it. Or watching another inflict it on one's behalf.

There was a further, even more seductive payoff to Arnold's practical jokes. Asserting his power not only made him feel strong and happy but also divided all with whom he came into contact into victims and predators. The victims had the jokes played on them. The predators watched, laughing with Arnold, triumphant that they had been chosen by him to take part in this delicious conspiracy of "them and us." Above all, they were acutely aware of his power. Each practical joke Arnold played served to cloak him in yet more impenetrably powerful armor, allowing him to win, bringing him friends, admiration, and supremacy.

Increasingly his jokes would have a more serious purpose: to undermine and destroy any competitors who might be a threat to him in future contests. In Munich he told one rival, "Power Mike," that the latest American bodybuilding competitive technique was to scream extremely loudly while posing onstage. "Power Mike" did so and, as Arnold gleefully recounted years later in *Pumping Iron*, made a total fool of himself.

Americans often trained at Putziger's—and provided the perfect target for Arnold's sense of humor. With an ingratiating smile he obligingly offered to teach them the few words of German necessary to facilitate their Munich stay. They gratefully accepted, telling themselves that this big young German was a regular guy. The lessons commenced, and they eagerly learned Arnold's phrases, then practiced so they could use them on the next German with whom they came into contact.

Arnold assured the Americans that, with the special phrases he had so thoughtfully taught them, they would definitely win friends and influence any German they might meet. So they used them—unaware that the true meaning of one of the nice young man's phrases was "Hello, you old pig. Do you still masturbate so much?"

Arnold himself, in his Munich days, however, had no need at all for masturbation. For he was surrounded by sexuality in all its variations.

During his stay in the city, Arnold—the very same young man who as a teenager in Thal hadn't been the least bit interested in women—went to Munich's most popular brothels. When Kurt Marnul arrived in Munich to visit him, an excited Arnold took him on a brothel tour, exclaiming, "All my life, all I have done is train. Graz is for old people. *This* is life."

And then there was the sexual life within the gym. Homosexuals have always been fervently attracted to bodybuilders. And many bodybuilders have taken financial advantage of that attraction. In some ways, as Peter McGough, a bodybuilding journalist who has been involved in the sport since the early sixties, points out, the logical conclusion to building your body so that others admire it is having them pay to admire it in a sexual sense.

In the mid-sixties many of Munich's homosexuals used to gather at Putziger's every evening and watch the bodybuilders train. Some of them readily offered money to any bodybuilder willing to pose for suggestive photographs. Arnold was their idol. But, as Arnold would repeatedly maintain over the years, there was nothing wrong with that.

In fact, in *Arnold: The Education of a Bodybuilder*, Arnold writes of one of the judges of the Junior Mr. Europe contest and, calling him by the pseudonym Schneck, says that the judge invited him to Munich where he owned a gym and a magazine. According to Arnold, he stayed with "Schneck" (who is actually Putziger), who made homosexual advances toward him. Arnold says he listened to Schneck's proposals but then rejected Schneck as well as other gay bodybuilders who hung around the gym.

He was young, charming, intelligent, witty, sought after, and talented in the extreme. He had paid his bodybuilding dues. He deserved every iota of success ahead of him.

4
London

LESS THAN TWO MONTHS AFTER STARTING
work in Munich, Arnold competed in the 1966 National
Amateur Body Builders Association (otherwise known as
NABBA) Mr. Universe contest in London. As Putziger was
paying him a pittance and he hadn't yet established himself
in Munich, Arnold's bodybuilding friends banded together
and paid his fare to London.

Helmut Riedmeier, a seasoned bodybuilder who knew
the British bodybuilding scene well and offered to show
Arnold the ropes, traveled with him as interpreter. They
stayed at the Royal Hotel, near London's British Museum,
training at the Westside Health Club in Kensington. The
NABBA Mr. Universe was a prestigious event; Mickey Hargitay was a past winner, and James Bond film star Sean
Connery was a past competitor.

Oscar Heidenstam, the chairman of NABBA, was
bowled over by the young Austrian who arrived in London
complete with crew cut, engaging personality, and a body
built for success. Today Heidenstam fondly remembers his
first insight into who and what Arnold really was. He was
sitting with Arnold when a friend (probably Riedmeier)
walked into the room and started talking to Arnold in
German. He was sharply reprimanded by Arnold, who said
reprovingly, "Don't you know it is very bad manners to talk
in German when we are with other people who don't understand?" Heidenstam was staggered by this example of
the nineteen-year-old youth's gentility and has never forgotten it. Many years later, although aware that Sue Moray

and then Maria Shriver didn't speak the language, Arnold would talk in German in their presence. But by then he was rich, famous, and established. Now, in London, about to compete in the Mr. Universe contest, his innate intelligence taught him to use the moment to the best effect: the powerful Heidenstam was impressed by his manners, and his German friend was humiliated and, at the same time, had been given a taste of Arnold's dominance.

From the moment he walked onstage at London's Victoria Palace that day at the end of September 1966, it was obvious to all who saw him that Arnold Schwarzenegger would soon reign unchallenged. Even before the start of the competition, the baby-faced giant strutted around backstage, draped in only a towel, while the contest favorite, the American Chet Yorton, pumped up next to him, convinced that victory would be his. Which it was.

Chet Yorton came in first in the 1966 Universe, but Arnold Schwarzenegger, the novice from Austria, came in second. Normally Arnold didn't like being in second place, but in this instance he probably didn't mind. In his heart he must have known that he had conquered. For, with his bulk, his innocence, and his nonchalant charm, he had taken the Mr. Universe contest by storm and bewitched the normally cynical British audience, receiving two curtain calls and a standing ovation.

American billionaire and bodybuilding aficionado J. Paul Getty sat in the front row and watched Arnold capture the Universe in all but name. So did British personality and NABBA president, celebrated disc jockey Jimmy Savile, a shrewd performer who was renowned for his long blond hair and trademark of greeting his TV audience with the words "Hello guys and gals," spoken in his broad Liverpool accent.

Savile was a showman, and he immediately recognized that in Arnold, only nineteen years old and inexperienced, he had met his match. He realized that Arnold's mesmerizing effect on the audience was due not merely to his immense size but also to his ability to play to the gallery, to project himself. In short, Arnold was overflowing with charisma.

In analyzing Arnold's appeal Savile later said, "Of course, he was young and had all the right measurements. But that wasn't it. It was his incredible personality. When he came onstage, it was like somebody had turned on all the spotlights. He just lit the stage up."

He would never again be a face in the crowd. For on that day at the Victoria Palace in September 1966, Arnold Schwarzenegger became an instant star.

Others associated with bodybuilding, however, were not so moved. John Citrone, who in 1968 competed with him in the Mr. Universe contest, commented on the fact that although Arnold had placed second and had aroused the enthusiasm of the crowd, his legs were lacking in development. Indeed, unlike their American counterparts, in those days German and Austrian bodybuilders tended to concentrate on developing their upper bodies and often disregarded their legs.

One of the most perceptive witnesses to Arnold's meteoric rise to fame and fortune who saw his 1966 Universe performance is Rick Wayne. Born in St. Lucia, where he currently publishes the *Star* newspaper, Rick, a former Mr. World, Mr. Universe, Mr. America, and Mr. Europe, spent ten years as a columnist for Joe Weider's *Muscle & Fitness* and was also associate publisher of *Flex*. Rick has followed Arnold's career since their first meeting in London.

Wayne describes his first meeting with Arnold, who had asked Helmut Riedmeier to introduce them: "Almost right away he was saying he was going to make a million bucks. . . . Here was this guy who could barely put two English words together, and he's telling me—talking in terms of movies and whatnot—that he's going to make a million bucks." Wayne goes on to say that part of Arnold's genius was the ability to show the right face at the right time. "There was Arnold . . . this baby-faced guy, but when you caught him in a more private atmosphere then you could see that what he was doing was arrogance; in other words, he could flash on the baby look—a conning baby look. He was anything *but* humble, but he had a way of making you think he was humble."

After the contest Arnold asked Rick if he thought he, Arnold, was capable of beating Weider's current number-one star, Dave Draper. Rick thought for a moment, then expressed his honest opinion. No, he didn't think Arnold could beat Dave. Arnold recoiled and announced, "I thought you were more with me."

Right at the beginning of his career he had formulated a strict code regarding the unwavering loyalty he expected from his friends. Implacably firm like his father, Arnold—who it must be said was always a good friend himself—demanded complete and utter loyalty from anyone with whom he came into contact. He came into contact with such a man at the 1966 NABBA Universe—Wag Bennett.

Wag, who had been bowled over by Arnold at his 1965 Junior Mr. Europe triumph in Stuttgart, was now a judge at the NABBA Universe. And, as he told Arnold a few hours later at the post-Universe dance, he thought Arnold should have won. Sitting by himself, dressed in a corduroy suit with badly fitting trousers, Arnold thanked Wag in broken English. Wag responded by inviting him to his home in Forest Gate, where he and his wife, Dianne, ran two gyms.

The Bennetts have always been an important presence on the British bodybuilding scene. Wag has been president of the European Federation of Bodybuilding, and Dianne, who publishes her own magazine, *Bodypower*, promoted female bodybuilding. In fact one of the star turns at the 1966 Universe was Dianne Bennett's Glamour Girls, who lifted weights to the tune of Roy Orbison's "Oh Pretty Woman."

Born Dianne Woolgar, to an ex–Tiller Girl (or British show girl), Dianne Bennett was a bit of a glamour girl herself. Her mother and father have always been fitness-conscious, running gyms in Portsmouth in the south of

England. At sixteen she met and married Wag, who was a few years her senior.

She and Wag made an interesting couple during the "swinging sixties" era in which they first met Arnold. Statuesque and prone to wearing big floppy hats, Dianne exuded sex appeal. Wag, on the other hand, was balding and overweight but, underneath his avuncular surface, capable of toughness. That toughness was enhanced by a combination of Wag's cockney accent and the fact that his gym was situated in London's rough East End. By the time Wag and Dianne met Arnold, they had constructed an intriguing mythology that held them in good stead among their peers in the bodybuilding community.

Today Wag and Dianne Bennett have erected a semishrine to Arnold Schwarzenegger in their home, not only filled with his photographs but also graced with a life-size statue of the superstar they befriended and still adore and admire. Arnold generously reciprocates, visiting Wag and Dianne whenever he is in England, inviting them to California and to his wedding. Wag, the keeper of Arnold's British flame, is naturally always delighted to recount the story of Arnold, his ambitions, and his early relationship with the Bennetts.

Arnold went home with them and, in no hurry to go back to Munich, stayed with them for a while, sleeping on a couch in the bedroom of one of their six children. Wag routinely asked all bodybuilders who crossed his path to define their life's ambition. He recalls, "Most bodybuilders would say, 'I want to be Mr. Britain, Mr. Universe, etc.' Then I would say, 'Yeah?' But that was it. That was the height of their ambition. But when I asked Arnold that question, his answer, in contrast, was 'I want to be the greatest bodybuilder in the world, the greatest bodybuilder of all time, and the richest bodybuilder in the world. I want to live in the United States and own an apartment block and be a film star. Ultimately I want to be a producer.' "

Wag, as he tells it, naturally was flabbergasted: "I thought to myself, 'Some hopes.' " Sensing Wag's reaction,

Arnold set out to convince him that he was serious. At first
he had probably underestimated Wag and had accepted his
invitation out of diplomacy. However, Wag surprised him
by disclosing that he was capable of bench-pressing five
hundred pounds. Then there was the matter of the orange
juice cans that Wag sold at his gym. A favorite gym pas-
time was to take an empty tin, crush it, then fold it. Arnold
tried and failed. Wag succeeded. Next there was the old
Sandow barbell that Wag kept in the gym. Wag was able to
press it, but Arnold wasn't. Wag believes these exploits won
him Arnold's respect. Arnold's respect won him Wag.

So Arnold spent time with the Bennetts, eating eight
eggs and a piece of steak for breakfast while simultaneously
convincing them that, in Wag's words, he was "a fantastic
boy." Obligingly he helped Wag keep the draft out of the
gym by pinning potato sacks up on the window. On
another occasion Arnold announced, "I am not going to
bed tonight until I weigh 255 pounds." His weight was
then 252 pounds, and, according to Wag, he then alternated
between voracious eating and getting on the scales to check
his weight. That process continued all evening until he
had achieved his goal.

In any interviews regarding Arnold, both Wag and
Dianne are quick to stress that Dianne played the part of
the motherly Wendy to Arnold's Peter Pan. Wag says, "Dianne idolizes him. Absolutely idolizes him," and says she
helped Arnold find girlfriends. Dianne adds, with a flash
of honesty, "We didn't need to look far. He had an animal
magnetism that attracts women to him." He certainly did.
Dianne Bennett herself was one of them.

Dianne has revealed her fling with Arnold to two
people, one a former bodybuilder and the other a bodybuilding journalist. According to the bodybuilder, Dianne's encounter with Arnold was a one-time event because
"She found him cold. Arnold didn't care. To him it was a
laugh." Far more important to Arnold than his brief moment of passion with the alluring Dianne was the fact that
Wag Bennett, a former competitor himself, not only taught
him to pose but also chose the ideal music for his posing

routine. The music he picked was "Exodus"—the theme that Arnold would use through most of his career—an ironic touch, given his father's membership in the Nazi party.

Wag had even more to offer him: he had once lived and trained with Arnold's idol, Reg Park. Dianne was soon forgotten and resumed her role of mother, confidante, and faithful friend. In later years, when Wag and Dianne were publishing a bodybuilding magazine called *Peak*, Dianne was featured heavily in the magazine and was often photographed with Arnold in its pages. The pictures sometimes verged on the suggestive—perhaps an in-joke among Arnold, Dianne, and Wag, who, like his protégé, was a masterful practical joker.

Wag Bennett, relishing his role of mentor, introduced Arnold to Reg Park soon after the Mr. Universe contest, inviting the two of them to guest pose at a show he was putting on at Stratford in East London. According to Wag, before the meeting Arnold was like an excited child. Reg, unaccustomed to seeing anyone as big as himself, couldn't believe his eyes when he saw the young Austrian and declared, "One day you are going to be the best bodybuilder in the world." Arnold was exhilarated and, ingratiating himself further with his idol, expressed a strong desire to visit him in South Africa, where the Yorkshire-born bodybuilder now lived. Gratified, Reg replied, "Win the Mr. Universe title, and I'll bring you out to South Africa." His promise was not made lightly, believing as he did that Arnold would, indeed, win the Mr. Universe title. For from the first he perceived Arnold as "a very sharp and ambitious kid. He had blinkers on. He knew just what he wanted and went after it." Time would prove Reg to be right about his new protégé. And when that moment came, he himself would become a victim of Arnold's sometimes ruthless and always relentless ambition.

Arnold's first trip to London for the 1966 Mr. Universe contest had earned him stardom and friends. He was now heir to the European bodybuilding throne, he was established in his chosen field, and he had fans and signed autographs. The Bennetts watched over him and promoted him, and his idol, Reg Park, actually believed in him. As Arnold left England for Munich, ready to resume his existence at Putziger's gym, he was aware of another new element in the increasingly stimulating roller coaster of his life. He was aware that his life was gathering momentum and that he was closer than ever to achieving his dream. However, not everything in his bodybuilding utopia was perfect.

Throughout his career Arnold has applied his genius for promotion and publicity to bodybuilding. One of his earliest goals was to eradicate the association between bodybuilders/bodybuilding and homosexuality.

To that end he has made the following statements. In 1975 he said, "I personally don't know of any competitive bodybuilders who are homosexuals. But, there is a lot of homosexual following around bodybuilding. Like when you go to a competition you will see them. And in gyms, like here, you will find homosexuals signing up to become members of the group so they can just watch you working out. Because we are to them what maybe some female sex symbol is to me. I mean I would love to watch Brigitte Bardot going to a gym and doing some bend-over lateral raises. A lot of people think we are homosexuals because we attract them. Because to them, you know, we are heaven."

And, in 1976, reacting to a scene in his film *Stay Hungry* during which a woman asks Joe Santo, Arnold's character, if he is a homosexual, he said, "It didn't belong in the movie. My character was obviously straight. Among bodybuilders there is almost no homosexuality. There are some [gays] among the followers. Sometimes they join the gyms so they can take showers with us."

He has also said, "The biggest cliché going around was that the sport attracted a lot of homosexuals. Now you hardly hear that from people, unless they are not up on the whole health movement. Yes, the sport attracts homosexu-

als, but it also attracts old ladies, young girls and all kinds
of men."

Although Arnold was relatively accurate in saying
that, yes, naturally gay men do admire bodybuilders, join
gyms to be close to them, and are obviously attracted to
them, there is still more. Before the advent of Arnold, who
raised the bodybuilding stakes to undreamed-of heights by
offering vast amounts of prize money, bodybuilders were
penniless, unwilling to work because they needed every
second of the day to train and eat, eat and train. Thus
Arnold, with his immense talent for public relations and
his slight propensity toward what is now commonly termed
disinformation, has omitted mentioning a vital factor present in the bodybuilding world through the years: the fact
that bodybuilders continually struggle to make ends meet
and often go to astonishing lengths to alleviate their financial problems.

Even today current bodybuilding champion Ronald
Matz says, "When a bodybuilder is very short of money, he
will do anything to survive. Some very rich gay men invest
in athletes and say, 'I'll give you a thousand dollars just to
pose.' Sometimes gay men first watch the bodybuilder pose,
then, after more money is exchanged, photograph them."

Then there is yesterday. British bodybuilder John Citrone, who, with his wife, Connie, used to tour Britain's
nightclubs, demonstrating his strength by blowing up hot
water bottles until they burst, describes the English bodybuilding scene of the mid-sixties: "We were all very enthusiastic about bodybuilding, but there was no money in it.
Some of the major bodybuilding photographers were gay.
And there were a lot of gay men hanging around."

In London in 1966, among the gay men "hanging
around" at bodybuilding contests were two patrons of the
sport. One was a Spanish millionaire Oscar Heidenstam
says is still an active supporter of the NABBA. For the past
twenty-five years this Spaniard was to be seen at the
NABBA contests. Years after the 1966 NABBA Mr. Universe
in which Arnold lit up the stage, the Spanish millionaire

met Rick Wayne in Geneva, talked to him for a few hours,
and then, to quote Rick directly, "he pulls out a stack of
pictures of Arnold at his house in a certain way, pictures of
him in his underwear." A second source goes even further,
claiming to have been shown the same pictures of Arnold
by the Spanish millionaire, who alleged that he paid Arnold $1,000 to spend the weekend with him at his house in
Spain and to pose for the photos.

Many bodybuilders have posed for seminude photographs, both gay and straight, some in magazines, others
for private collectors. The logic and the motivation are
inescapable: bodybuilders' stock-in-trade is displaying their
bodies for others to admire—so why not take that process to
a second stage and let the image of their admirable bodies
be preserved in time, by way of a photograph, in the bargain financing their existence?

Then there is the second gay man who was extremely
active on the British bodybuilding scene of the sixties. He
was a top British industrialist, then in his forties, not
overtly gay yet notorious for his generosity to bodybuilders.

Mr. R was a man who was used to getting what he
wanted. And hearing about the new Austrian bodybuilding
sensation, he decided that what he wanted was Arnold.

Arnold Schwarzenegger is not a homosexual. He is, in
fact, a red-blooded, heterosexually active male. Nonetheless,
at nineteen, determined to survive financially, conquer the
bodybuilding world, and become a superstar and a leader,
he was also somewhat of an opportunist. There were definitely plenty of opportunities for bodybuilders willing to
manifest a degree of compromise. That compromise was
lucrative, painless, and relatively easy to arrange.

Rick Wayne explains the general principle: "There
was a lot of temptation in those days." For example, a
bodybuilder came to Rick in New York once and said,
"Rick, this guy is a doctor, this guy is loaded, and he wants
to meet you. You don't have to do anything with him. He is
going to give me money just to meet you." According to
Rick, this was a standard line. Moreover, says Rick, some

of the guys would offer to share the money they earned as a result of having arranged the introduction.

As for Mr. R, Rick recalls, "He chased me for six months. He offered me an apartment, a regular allowance to spend time to do nothing but train and eat, if I would be his guy. Finally he said, 'Well, you can pass me on to a friend of yours.' Mr. R specialized in this. He would go to a bodybuilder, with whom he had either had an affair or hadn't, and then he would pay him to introduce him to another bodybuilder. He threw money around. Arnold was the top bodybuilder; he was hot stuff, could ask for anything he wanted, and would have been a big prize for Mr. R."

Mr. R set about meeting Arnold by approaching Helmut Riedmeier and asking for a favor. He had first met Riedmeier through a British publisher of gay magazines and openly stated his request. Would Helmut introduce him to that new sensation, Arnold Schwarzenegger? He planned to be in Munich in the near future, so could Riedmeier arrange a meeting? Riedmeier, Arnold's friend, interpreter, and guide through London, said he thought he could.

Whether or not money changed hands between Riedmeier and Mr. R at this point is not clear. According to Riedmeier—who tells the story quite freely, as if what transpired was, in those days, a matter of course—the man asked Riedmeier to introduce him to Arnold. "That's what I did then," says Riedmeier, who adds that Arnold didn't know how to handle the situation. Riedmeier told him, "Just relax. You know . . . just use your imagination."

"With Mr. R it was a money thing," says Riedmeier. "It was purely financial. I don't know what Mr. R paid Arnold. He got paid quite well. Afterward Arnold didn't go into details. He was pleased with the money. Mr. R thanked me for setting it up."

Whatever the nature of the relationship, it didn't end with a single meeting in Munich. Rick Wayne suggests that Arnold, much to Wag Bennett's chagrin, began to divide his London stays between Wag and Mr. R. As Rick tells it, at one point when Arnold was supposedly due to go back to Germany, Wag begged him to stay longer, but Arnold refused. Wag took him to the airport. Only to see him again, a few days later, on the steps of St. Paul's Cathedral, with Mr. R.

And according to Helmut Riedmeier, "Arnold stayed in touch with Mr. R for two years until he, Arnold, went to America in 1968."

Twenty-three years after his first meeting with him, Mr. R, who looks like an English version of Senator Daniel Patrick Moynihan, sat in an apartment in London's Chelsea district and, chain-smoking all the while, in well-modulated tones talked about his relationship with Arnold. "Yes, it is absolutely true that Helmut introduced me to him. In those days he knew I went to Munich frequently on business."

Although Mr. R didn't speak a word of German, he did, indeed, see Arnold in Munich on a number of occasions. "He was charming, always happy, and lived in the gym," says Mr. R. "He also ate an enormous amount. He ate as if he were at a trough. It was never one steak, always two. A good meal made him happy. Arnold would do anything for a good meal.

"I met his father in Munich, and I could see he was the harsh sergeant major type. He was very dominant, and Arnold was looking for someone to replace him. I also met his brother, Meinhard, who was very good-looking."

Arnold also saw Mr. R in London. Mr. R had a house in Kent, and Arnold visited him there. They also, says Mr. R, went sightseeing to the Tower of London and to St. Paul's Cathedral together. Sometimes Mr. R took Arnold to the theater, although, all these years later, he can't remember which plays they saw.

Mr. R, a charming and urbane man, a sophisticate who, by example, must have lent the young Arnold a certain amount of savoir faire, says that he advised him to invest in property once he was successful. "I always thought he was very smart," says Mr. R. "He was a country boy, but he was also street smart." Mr. R considered Arnold well mannered and always knew he was headed for the top. Arnold told Mr. R about his fling with Dianne Bennett, but, according to Mr. R, Arnold didn't have a serious relationship with a woman.

Mr. R admits that he has had affairs with bodybuilders. But was Arnold one of them? Did he, in fact, keep him? Here is Mr. R's reply: "This is a very lovely story. . . . I regret to say it is not true." Mr. R recalls being told that a German banker was keeping Arnold, but he discounted that rumor "because Arnold was always poor."

Mr. R says, "He did extremely well out of me," but denies having given him any cash. "I may have given him money for a taxi back to Wag's," says Mr. R, adding that Arnold ate extremely well with him and that Arnold was very charming. "He was a good tease."

5
Escape to America

By 1967 ARNOLD WAS BODYBUILDING'S MAN of the hour—in Britain at least. In London he gave a show in front of two thousand fans and signed autographs afterward. A few weeks before the 1967 Mr. Universe contest he traveled to Portsmouth to give some bodybuilding exhibitions and stayed with Dianne Bennett's father, Bob Woolgar. During that time he trained with Gordon Allen, now vice chairman of NABBA. Wag Bennett had primed Gordon to expect that Arnold would be a revelation; no one of his size had ever before been seen in Portsmouth. Allen remembers that, even at twenty, Arnold was very heavily into steroids.

Arnold posed at Portsmouth's Wedgwood Rooms, earning a few pounds and, according to Allen, changing before and after the contest in the men's toilets. He also toured Admiral Nelson's flagship, the *Victory*. As he walked up the gangway, off-duty Royal Navy sailors who were on board ship registered shock at his size. Seeing their reaction, Arnold bent down and picked up some ship's cannonballs as if they were tangerines. Interested in learning all he could about history, Arnold moved from room to room but encountered problems going through doorways that had been built to accommodate men half his size. Arnold made it clear to Allen during his short stay that he was very open to meeting any women to whom Allen cared to introduce him. A suitable candidate was found—small, sweet, and willing to succumb to the will of the charming Austrian. The lady, however, was in for a severe shock. Not that Arnold's sexual performance was lacking. Far from it. But two days after she tangled with him, spellbound by his personality and his prowess as were many women after her, believing that she had found the great love of her life, she traveled to London with Gordon Allen to see Arnold compete in the 1967 Universe. And although Arnold had arranged for her visit, he totally ignored her. She returned to Portsmouth in a flood of tears.

For Arnold wasn't, at that moment, interested in the woman, love, sex, or anything but the limelight—and the realization his grandiose dreams were now a reality. He had won the contest. In top form, at a weight of 235 pounds, Arnold, at six foot two, sported 22-inch arms, 28½-inch thighs, 20-inch calves, a 34-inch waist, and a 57-inch chest. The closest thing to a superman, he was powerful, strong, and far removed from the timid ten-year-old who had wet himself because he was so afraid of his father. Now, at twenty, he was the youngest Mr. Universe in history.

Mindful of Reg Park's promise to invite him to South Africa when he became Mr. Universe, Arnold dashed off a telegram to his idol: "I've just won the Universe. What's happening?" Reg, who was a force on the South African bodybuilding scene, was in the habit of inviting the reigning Mr. Universe to guest pose in South Africa and consequently offered Arnold a contract to guest pose in ten South African shows for a fee of fifty pounds per show. On a more personal level, Reg also invited Arnold to spend Christmas 1967 with him and his South African–born wife, Marianne. Ecstatic, Arnold accepted.

In *Arnold: The Education of a Bodybuilder*, he wrote that he was overwhelmed by Park's luxurious house, his pool, his antiques, and his servants and that he felt out of place. He did, however, apparently feel quite at home with the South African system of apartheid. According to Rick Wayne, who is black, when they discussed apartheid Arnold said he thought South Africa was right, saying things like "If you gave these blacks a country to run, they would

run it down the tubes." However, Rick was accustomed to
Arnold's reactionary views and quirky ways. He and Arnold had posed together in Munich. In his book, *Muscle
Wars*, a study of bodybuilding politics, Rick recalled that
after Arnold had "struck a pose reminiscent of the Nazi
salute," he received less applause from the German audience than he had expected. Arnold's response was to comment to Rick, "These people are nothing without an Austrian to lead them."

Back in Austria, Arnold wasn't yet regarded as the all-
conquering hero of his dreams. Especially not in Graz,
where he had never really won his training mates at the
Union over to his side. He had once come close to blows
with Karl Kainrath after telling him, "You know, for the
four years you've been training, you haven't got much to
show." Karl, a tough man with presence and the ability to
intimidate, looked Arnold up and down and said, "If you
ever tell me that again, I'll push your teeth out of your
neck." Arnold, stepping back, said, "Come on, Karl, you
understand a joke, don't you? I didn't mean it."

But now Arnold was the most famous bodybuilder in
Europe and the youngest Mr. Universe in history, and he
had every right to expect respect, awe, and deference from
his ex–Union colleagues. His former trainer, Helmut Cerncic, was involved in what Arnold must have believed would
be a triumphant return. In December 1967, just two
months after he had been voted Mr. Universe in London,
Arnold flew to Graz from Munich to compete in the Para-
dise Keller Lifting Championship. Cerncic remembers,
"Arnold arrived dressed in a beige-colored ski pullover that
added volume. His arm measured 50.5 centimeters [about
20 inches] in circumference. Everyone was impressed. Then
the trophies were brought in and placed in the middle of
the room. Arnold put his hands on his hips and said,
'What is this pile of shit? I've flown all the way from
Munich to win *that*!' Someone asked him if he was so sure
he would win. Arnold paused, then looked around, laughing. After a while he stopped laughing and started scrutin-

izing everyone. He started laughing again. 'Kurtl [Mar-
nul], you are good in bench-pressing, but put on five
hundred pounds for a squat and your legs will break off.
Addie [Ziegner], no, no, you've got good arms, but you are
not in my class.' Then he turned to Karl Kainrath and
said, 'Karl, I heard you have been pretty strong, but you are
not quite in my class.' Kainrath gave him a look. Then he
turned to me and asked what I bench-pressed. No one
would tell him. Arnold lost the contest. [Cerncic won.]
Suddenly he was like a little eighteen-year-old again."

The Graz bodybuilders may have had *Schadenfreude*
(joy in his misery) at Arnold's defeat, but on the other side
of the Atlantic the almighty Joe Weider, Mr. Bodybuilding
himself, knew only of his victories. An immediate consequence of Arnold's winning the Mr. Universe title was that
Weider instructed his European representative, Ludwig
Shusterich, to invite Arnold to America, where Weider
planned to pay him a small salary to train, write training
booklets for the Weider magazines, and in general allow
Weider to form him into an international (as opposed to
European) bodybuilding star.

Joe Weider is a unique, once-in-a-lifetime personality,
as iconoclastic, in his own way, as Arnold is in his. Born
in Montreal in 1922, Weider (in the words of his former
editor, Rick Wayne) "had a lifelong affair with bodybuilding." At thirteen a poor boy from an underprivileged family, he was enthralled by the richly masculine bodies he
saw depicted in borrowed copies of *Strength and Health*
magazine. His frailty, however, caused him to be barred
from gym membership. Undaunted, he discovered a fly-
wheel in a neighborhood junkyard and started using it as
a barbell. Within two years, with a total body weight of 155
pounds, he was able to press 222 pounds. At this juncture
he could have been classified as a weightlifter, but he soon
turned his creative powers to bodybuilding. Learning that
bodybuilders were despised and deducing that this was due
in part to the absence of a magazine exclusively featuring
them, Weider vowed to remedy the situation.

Using old editions of *Strength and Health* as a source, Weider compiled a list of eight hundred muscle men and did a test mailing announcing his intention to publish a bodybuilding magazine. Subscriptions amounting to $500 rolled in, and in no time at all Weider had mimeographed the first few issues of his new publication, *Your Physique.*

Weider and his brother Ben went on to found the International Federation of Bodybuilders, eclipse bodybuilding publishing rivals Bob Hoffman and Dan Lurie, and ultimately reign supreme over the bodybuilding world. In American bodybuilding their word was law, their reputation larger than life, and the stranglehold they had established on bodybuilding unbreakable. They were promoters and businessmen, kingmakers and legend makers. Some said that if the Weiders decided to promote a bodybuilder in their magazine he could win great popularity among the public without having once competed in a single contest. In short, the Weiders were omnipotent. And it was only a matter of time before they turned their overwhelming attention to Arnold.

Arnold, however, wasn't prepared to rush into anything. Now that he was Mr. Universe, NABBA officials like Oscar Heidenstam, who felt a strong sense of rivalry with the Weider organization, warned him against becoming involved with Joe Weider. Moreover, he was enjoying his life in Munich. With his never-failing sense of timing, he decided to delay making any decisions about moving to America and putting himself into the notoriously devious yet brilliantly capable hands of Joe Weider. As yet, he did not know just how much he and Joe had in common.

He did, however, agree to see Weider's emissary, Ludwig Shusterich, who met with him at the Royal Hotel in London a few days after the contest. He listened to Shusterich, stalled, then went back to Munich. He was now champion; the world was at his feet.

On October 6, 1967, the new Mr. Universe gave one of his first press interviews ever—to the *Münchner Merkur.* In the interview Arnold said that he trained for four hours a day and claimed to be an idealist who wanted to be an example to youth, teaching them that there was more to life than sitting on a bar stool and drinking whiskey. After that the interview went downhill. Arnold confessed that he had no time to read but that he often went to the opera with his father. Which opera? asked the interviewer. Arnold was lost for words and couldn't name a single opera. And when he did manage to speak, judging by the writer's report, he spoke in an almost unintelligible Austrian accent, punctuated by "Naa!"

Arnold would soon rival Muhammad Ali in self-promotion, but at that time he had not yet learned how to handle press interviews engendered by his newfound fame. In 1968 he was interviewed by journalist Christopher Ward of the London *Daily Mirror*. To comprehend how far Arnold, his fame, and the image of bodybuilding itself have come, it is telling to study the tone of one of Arnold's first English-speaking interviews and to observe the contempt in which he and the sport were held.

The dateline is London, March 8, 1968. The headline reads "Christopher Ward, weight 10 st 2 lbs, chest expanded 36½ inches, meets Mr. Universe, weight 18 st 2 lbs, chest expanded 58 inches—It's not easy, being Arnold Schwarzenegger." Next to the text is a picture of a bare-chested Arnold above the caption, "Arnold Schwarzenegger: misunderstood muscle man."

Ward then proceeds to slice up his hapless victim.

Arnold Schwarzenegger can, when the mood takes him, punch a hole in a wall. If you ask him nicely, he will blow up your hot water bottle until it bursts, and overturn your car with one hand.

When he's really trying, he can hold above his head a weight equivalent to eight Twiggies. This is only half a Twiggy less than the world record of eight-and-a-half Twiggies, or 710 pounds. I hope you're impressed.

Unhappily Arnold, who at twenty is the youngest-ever Mr. Universe, is a very misunderstood man.

Do you know what people are saying about him? They're saying he's all muscle.

Well, people will jump to conclusions just like that, but it's very upsetting for poor 18 stone Arnold with his 58-inch chest. All muscle indeed!

So the other day when Arnold arrived in Britain for a few shows of strength up and down the country, I dropped in to offer my condolences and to view the body beautiful itself.

"Please understand that I am like ordinary man only bigger and stronger," said Arnold, who comes from Austria, where he is weightlifting champion, underwater swimming champion, high-diving champion, and curling champion.

"I have normal feelings like other men. Why do people treat me with fun just because I am biggest, strongest man in world?"

"And most beautiful," I ventured.

"And most beautiful," agreed Arnold.

(If you would like to dispute any of these points, Arnold will be happy to settle the matter at the time and place of your choosing.)

Arnold's muscle-rippling life is taken up traveling round the globe making Miss World–type guest appearances and being offered film roles as Hercules, Tarzan, Jason, or Samson. There are, however, rather a lot of disadvantages.

For a start, when people meet him, they do not launch into a discussion about the amplitude and frequency of neural response. Indeed, they treat him more like an object than a person. They give him a push here and a prod there. Some even greet him with a jovial thump in the guts. They seem quite surprised when they discover it hurts him.

Another snag is that a lot of girls don't fancy big strong he-men these days. They prefer something feebler. It's a bit of bad luck for Arnold, that. When he started out on the long, painful road to the body beautiful, Charles Atlas figures were the trendy thing.

Worst of all for Arnold is that weedy-looking people—like you and me—are forever picking fights with him.

I would have thought that no taxi driver would have told Arnold what to do with his sixpenny tip. No cinema commissionaire in his right mind would have ordered Arnold to the end of the queue when he arrived to see *Mary Poppins*. But they do, brave fellows. They do.

Arnold didn't get to be like this on a spoonful of malt before breakfast every day. He survives on eggs, milk, steaks, concentrated foods, and drinks nothing but beer. He eats about three times more than most men.

"I hope you're not going to go away and write that I am, how do you say, all brain and no brawns?" said Arnold.

"All brawn and no brains is what you mean," I said.

"Ah," said Arnold. "You're very kind."

Arnold was livid when he read Christopher Ward's article. He had been alternately patronized and laughed at. His English had been mocked, his profession slighted, and he, Arnold Schwarzenegger, had been made a figure of ridicule. Inexperienced with the British press and hamstrung by his feeble grasp of the English language, he had failed to project an iota of his true personality. In a fury he vowed to Rick Wayne that he would never again allow a journalist to make a fool of him. Nevertheless, the article betrayed Arnold's attitude toward the press and foreshadowed his subsequent approach to his own image and publicity. Even at this stage, despite his limited English and the newness of his status, he attempted to dictate to the journalist and control the article he was writing.

Although Arnold failed to impose his will on this, one

of the first journalists he had ever encountered, he could console himself that at least Christopher Ward had spelled his name correctly. That would suffice until the not too distant future when Arnold, by then in total command of the English language and the intricacies of self-promotion, would use the press more effectively than almost any other public figure of our era.

Arnold seemed to be enjoying his newfound status immensely. About the time that Christopher Ward's article was published, he went to Newcastle, in the north of England, to star in a show run by John Citrone, who was soon to be his rival in the 1968 Mr. Universe. He stayed with Citrone at his house on Chesterly Street, just eight miles outside of Newcastle. Citrone draws a telling picture of Arnold's brief visit: "He could hardly speak English, but he was bigheaded and told everyone, 'These are the biggest arms in the world.' Then he said, 'I am going to America to become one of the most famous men in the world.' We weren't wealthy people, but he ate us out of house and home."

In 1968, too, there was news from Arnold's home back in Austria: on February 2nd, Erika, Meinhard's fiancée, had given birth to a son, Patrick. The couple hadn't yet married though, because, according to Erika, Meinhard refused to settle down. Also, as Arnold was to learn three years later, Meinhard had secretly chosen him as Patrick's godfather. And on that distant day when Arnold discovered the truth, Meinhard's choice would assume great significance and reveal a new facet to the enigma that Arnold had by then become.

His bodybuilding success, however, was plain and simple. In September Arnold traveled to London to compete in the 1968 Mr. Universe contest. Asked about his performance in the NABBA contests, NABBA president Jimmy Savile said, "What got him his wins was his incredible personality. He could walk onstage in such a manner that he got people to applaud. He had an easy personality. In the pop business we would call him 'a moody merchant.' Which means that he knew how to kid very nicely the people. Arnold, who was deadly serious, always gave the impression that he was happy-go-lucky. One of his most loved remarks to me was to say 'Hello, Jimmy, how are you? How is everything? Come and meet some of my skinny friends.' Then he would introduce me to the other bodybuilders competing against him. He was using me to psych them out. He had supreme confidence."

It was certainly warranted. On Saturday, September 21, 1968, at London's Victoria Palace, Arnold was voted Mr. Universe for the second time. Arnold's victory in the 1968 NABBA Universe was predictable. His next move, however, definitely was not.

Joe Weider, American bodybuilding promoter par excellence, had been wooing Arnold for the past year, via his European representative, Ludwig Shusterich. "Lud" and his wife, Pat, first met Arnold in Munich in early 1967, where they had lunch with Arnold and another young bodybuilder and his new bride.

Looking back, Pat Shusterich remembers that Arnold's much vaunted charm repelled her. Pat repeated her impressions to Lud. But Lud, an uncritical man who tries firmly to focus on the positive in everyone, preferred not to get involved in criticism of Weider's new protégé. He was, however, shocked by Arnold's actions during that first Munich lunch. While X, the muscular and attractive newlywed bodybuilder, went to the men's room, Arnold turned to his young wife and said, "Listen, I only live down the block. Why don't you come up to my apartment with me?" Lud Shusterich, who was old enough to be Arnold's father, stepped in and delivered a stiff lecture, telling Arnold in no uncertain terms that he was no gentleman.

The fact that Arnold took Lud's lecture without protesting indicates that his mind was not set against moving to America. To that end, in August 1968, during one of his many visits to England, he accepted Lud and Pat's invitation to a California-style barbecue at their home in Purley, Surrey. During the afternoon, conversation turned to Arnold's possible American trip. Lud Shusterich remembers telling Arnold not to forget that he would need a visa if he wanted to travel to America.

Although he had conquered Europe, it was patently obvious that Arnold was not yet in sufficient shape to storm America. As a result Lud was extremely surprised when, just before the NABBA Mr. Universe contest, Arnold came to him at the Royal Hotel in London and suddenly informed him that he wanted to leave for America immediately. True, Joe Weider had indeed invited Arnold to compete in the IFBB Mr. Universe contest in Miami, due to be held in a matter of days. But Arnold, according to Shusterich, was not in shape—not for America and a crack at the IFBB championship. He hadn't trained for America. He hadn't even *packed* for America and had only one gym bag with him. Be that as it may, Arnold arranged to meet Lud at the Air India counter at London's Heathrow Airport.

In *Arnold: The Education of a Bodybuilder*, Arnold explains his lack of form and the fact that he had only a gym bag with him when he first went to America by saying that he had originally planned to stay only for the contest, then return to Germany. According to Lud, that isn't strictly true. For Weider's contract, which Lud took to Heathrow for Arnold to sign, committed him to spending time in America at Weider's expense. And there are those who claim that Arnold's impulsive decision to leave for America at a moment's notice was not governed by rashness but by calculation.

In his book, Arnold refers to having had "scrapes" with the Munich police. There are rumors that Arnold's "scrapes" may well have been more serious than they sound, although there is no indication that they led to a criminal record.

Mr. R remembers that Arnold telephoned him the night before he left England, telling him that he was going to America because he had problems in Germany. Whatever those problems may have been, at Heathrow Airport, just before he was about to leave for America, he encountered an obstacle to his plans. For as he handed his papers to the Air India ticket clerk, there was consternation. He didn't have a visa.

Weider was waiting for him in America. The contest was imminent. Now he was stranded in London. Lud too was horrified, knowing that visa applications took a few days to process.

He had been in the midst of congratulating himself for having succeeded in claiming Arnold for Weider. A former world champion bodybuilder himself, Lud was also delighted to play a part in the career of someone he believed was destined to become a legend in the international bodybuilding field. Yet now, through Arnold's surprising stupidity, Weider would be disappointed, Arnold would miss the Miami contest, and Lud himself would have fallen short in his assigned task. He thought for a few moments, then hit on a solution.

Lud, an officer in the U.S. Air Force Reserve, belonged to the Columbia Club, a London club for U.S. Air Force Reserve officers. And, as it turned out, all eighteen of his fellow club members happened to work in high places. And naturally, given Arnold Schwarzenegger and his sometimes charmed life, one of them happened to work for the visa section at the American Embassy. So Lud picked up the phone, called his fellow officer, and asked for a favor, telling him that he had with him one of the world's top athletes, who needed an instant visa for America. Lud's fellow officer hesitated, then spoke the following words: "Lud, I wouldn't do this for anybody in the world. I will only do this for you because you are a fellow officer and your word is your bond. I will get you an instant visa if you will personally vouch for Arnold Schwarzenegger. If you vouch as to his lack of a criminal record, I will accept your word as a fellow officer, knowing that our word is our bond." Lud looked at Weider's great hope, the young and seemingly innocent Arnold, overflowing with promise, ambition, and charisma, and agreed.

Lud and Arnold raced to the embassy in a taxi. Once there, Lud read the visa application, which included the clause attesting that the applicant did not have a criminal record. He knew that by signing it he would be sticking his neck out, as was his fellow officer, the American Embassy employee. For a moment Lud thought back to Arnold's astonishing behavior toward the young bodybuilder's wife when they had first met in Munich, but he brushed those thoughts away. After all, Arnold was young. He would change and flourish in America. Lud signed the form vouching for him, and Arnold, then and there, got a visa to enter America.

If Arnold hadn't gotten his visa that day at Heathrow Airport, he would have antagonized the powerful Joe Weider by letting him down. And his American bodybuilding career would have been doomed before it began. But Arnold had had an almost supernatural stroke of good luck. Lud Shusterich took a risk by vouching for a young bodybuilder he didn't really know. But, as it turned out, even if Lud had been unwilling to take a risk for his boss, Joe Weider, another emotion did prompt him to take that risk for Arnold himself. For Arnold's ace, as far as Lud was concerned, was this: Ludwig Shusterich, who today seems as American as Henry Fonda, was, in fact, born in Predat, Yugoslavia, which at one time had been Austrian and is not far from Arnold's hometown of Thal. He would not have abandoned a fellow countryman. Fate had chosen Ludwig Shusterich to be the one man who could facilitate Arnold's escape to America and to a new life.

6
Florida and California: 1968

MAKING THE THIRD AND MOST SIGNIFI-
cant journey of his life, Arnold arrived in America at the
end of September 1968. Although he was overweight and
out of shape, his last words to Lud Shusterich were "I'll eat
them up in America. I'll eat them up, baby." Shusterich
was a trifle disturbed by Arnold's overweening self-confidence.

The Arnold who first set foot on American soil at
Miami International Airport wasn't prepared for either
America or the IFBB Mr. Universe contest. Years later he
recalled, "I could not speak the language well at all. I
couldn't listen to the news. I couldn't read the papers. . . . It
was the most difficult time in my life." Later he added, "I
had no money. I had only one gym bag with me, because I
did not plan to move here at that point. I was kind of like
a helpless kid in a way."

Just one day after he arrived in America, Arnold was
defeated by Frank Zane in the IFBB Mr. Universe contest.
The audience at the Miami Beach Auditorium didn't dis-
agree with the judges' verdict, either. Zane, seventy pounds
lighter than Arnold, had just won the Mr. America title,
looked "finished," posed gracefully, and was bronzed to
perfection. Arnold, on the other hand, at 250 pounds, was
out of condition, chalk-white, and personified quantity as
opposed to quality.

That night Arnold, alone in a strange country, thousands of miles from the continent where he had always
conquered, lay in his bed and cried himself to sleep. As in

years gone by, he had only his own words and his own unshakable will with which to comfort himself.

In *Arnold: The Education of a Bodybuilder*, he described his reaction, saying that it took him only one day to recover from his defeat and that ultimately it had only served to increase his determination. He would learn from Americans, use their techniques, eat their food, and then, finally, he would vanquish them in their own sport. He vowed that he would show them who was really best. And that vow, as always, became his driving force, the impetus for his future.

The resolution he made during those first few days in America set in motion a new journey that would bring Arnold fame and fortune. "That which does not kill you will make you strong," wrote Friedrich Nietzsche—words used at the beginning of *Conan the Barbarian*. He had been humiliated and defeated, but he would emerge stronger. And although he had been "killed" in the bodybuilding arena, he would turn defeat into victory and emerge triumphant.

It is fairly likely that one member of the audience at the Miami Beach Auditorium grappled with a strange mixture of emotions as he watched Frank Zane beat Arnold Schwarzenegger. That man was Joe Weider, Arnold's patron, the man who had signed him to a year's contract and had paid for his flight to America. Says Weider today, "There was absolutely no question that Arnold was a sleeping giant just waiting to be roused to reach the greatness he was slated for. My work with him the week during the Universe revealed quickly just how talented he really was. . . . I knew, with a capital K, that Arnold was going to be the greatest bodybuilder of his time." Some bodybuilders, however, claim that the outcome of the 1968 IFBB Mr. Universe provided Joe with a badly needed advantage over Arnold.

Joe, an extremely astute man, probably noted Arnold's arrogance, filed away that perception, perhaps concluding that young Mr. Schwarzenegger needed taking down a peg or two. And although Joe Weider obviously played no part in engineering Arnold's Miami defeat, it was, of course, useful. His new protégé had exhibited remarkable self-confidence. Perhaps now, in the wake of his defeat, he would be more malleable and easier for Joe to handle.

Joe Weider has never been the kind of man to experience problems in handling bodybuilders or, for that matter, any other species of human being. With his unique Canadian twang making him sound like a cross between a gangster and a stand-up comic, he is a man to be reckoned with, a man with absolute power who expects everyone connected with bodybuilding to acknowledge his supremacy. If Machiavelli were ever to return to earth, he might well meet his match in Joe Weider. Indeed, it is debatable whether even he would be able to build a powerbase as impenetrable as that of the Weider empire.

In October 1988 *California Business* summed up the magnitude of Weider's current operation: "Weider and his brother Ben, president of the International Federation of Body Builders, the worldwide professionl bodybuilding organization, almost completely control the bodybuilding game. It's as if Walter O'Malley owned not only the Dodgers, but also Chavez Ravine, NBC Sports, *Sports Illustrated*—and most of the players."

In 1968 the number one "player" Weider naturally expected to own was Arnold Schwarzenegger. For although his business wasn't yet fully established, Weider was still the only game in town. And the contract Arnold had just signed stipulated that Weider would pay Arnold a relatively small weekly salary in exchange for Arnold's training hard, then lending his name, face, and physique to any advertisements and public appearances Weider desired. He would associate himself with a number of articles, written by a ghost and published under his name, explaining his training techniques. Weider would then promote him as bodybuilding's newest idol.

As far as bodybuilding insiders were concerned, the

stage seemed set for Weider to become Arnold's Pygmalion, transforming a gauche European into a slick American superstar. Those close to Joe assumed that Arnold would now, after his Miami defeat, be putty in Weider's hands. But they had gravely miscalculated. For although Arnold needed Weider to launch his American career, he still intended to do things his way.

At first, though, their relationship was one of student/ teacher, with Weider coaching Arnold in many areas, including the financial benefits of both buying real estate and collecting art. They were also mentor/protégé, with Weider teaching Arnold about publicity, business, and how to trim one's sails to fit the wind. Weider, a perceptive man and a brilliant promoter and manipulator, also taught Arnold how to separate business relationships from friendships. In *Arnold: The Education of a Bodybuilder*, Arnold writes of Weider's pragmatism, his ability to suspend even the deepest friendship once business dealings began. Arnold was able to learn that lesson well, and later, despite their subsequent friendship, became as tough as possible when negotiating with Joe.

On the surface it appeared that Joe had complete control over Arnold. The truth, however, was this: In the depth of his soul, Weider was conquered from the very first moment he set eyes on Arnold. And although he did nurture and promote him, laying the American foundations of his fame and fortune, Weider would never exercise complete control over his disciple.

Soon Arnold had the whip hand over Joe, with the pupil outstripping the teacher and the protégé eclipsing the mentor. In the words of Armand Tanny, "Arnold was bright, confident, and assertive. He literally overpowered Joe." Weider had met his match in Arnold. According to bodybuilder Dan Howard, who encountered Arnold when he first came to America, Arnold was "the only bodybuilder ever to come out on top when dealing with Weider." This still holds true. A leading bodybuilding journalist comments, "Joe visibly shrinks in Arnold's presence. Arnold is like a child who went beyond the father." In a way perhaps Arnold is the son Joe never had. Joe, on the other hand, appears to have represented the father that Arnold, in fact, *did* have.

The major factor that tilted the balance of power between Joe and Arnold lay in the coincidence that, like Gustav, Joe Weider is a powerful and dominant personality. And if Gustav hadn't succeeded in crushing Arnold, there was little chance the mighty Joe Weider would do any better. Many a time Joe sighed to Rick Wayne that Arnold looked on him as a father. But as Arnold must have hated his father, it seemed natural that he eventualy took that hatred out on Joe.

Arnold has always regarded Weider with ambivalence, reportedly saying at one point that "the man he most admires is the man he also hates most: Joe Weider!"

In any case, Arnold continued to be a credit to Joe Weider throughout his career, making money for Weider's magazines and the IFBB, run by Weider's brother, Ben, but he often fell foul of Joe by failing to acknowledge his debt to Weider when being interviewed by the media. And nineteen years after Joe first brought Arnold to America, even though he tried to paint a favorable picture of Arnold in an interview for this book, he exposed the depth of his wound by claiming how, in the past, Arnold had not mentioned him enough.

Omission, however, was not Arnold's only sin. Rather like a rebellious son who is set on separating from his father once and for all, Arnold sometimes used the media as a vehicle to proclaim his distance from Joe.

He launched an overt attack on Weider relatively early in his career. In 1974, in a comprehensive *Sports Illustrated* interview, one of the first to handle bodybuilding with a degree of seriousness, Arnold made a full frontal attack on his former mentor:

All of these magazines—Weider's, Hoffman's, Lurie's—I call them comic books, circus books! Those headlines! HOW ARNOLD TERRORIZED HIS THIGHS! Hah! THIS IS JOE'S BICEPS SPEAKING! Why are Joe's biceps talking to anybody? It is not that much of a biceps. Joe exposes Lurie and Lurie exposes Joe and Hoffman is against everybody and can't tell Ben from Joe, or says he can't. Why won't these guys get together? I will tell you why. It is because none of these silly people are really interested in bodybuilding anymore. They are only interested in the money that can be made from it. Each of them says that he is for bodybuilding, but these men are not. They are knocking the sport down. I ask Joe why he prints such junk—why is everybody bombing and blasting and terrorizing, all these silly words?

There was more—with Arnold saying he wanted to publish his own magazine: "I would like to get hold of Joe's magazine. But he will not give up such a sales manual. I will have to start my own magazine, a *real* magazine, a bodybuilding magazine, not just something to sell products to fourteen-year-old boys."

In the first few years of Arnold's time in America, Weider continued to play a dual role in his life. On a friendship level Weider took Arnold around to art galleries and antique shops and socialized with him. On a work level Joe paid him a weekly salary and paid for his apartment and car while Arnold became the world's number one Weider star, helping Joe sell his magazines, his products, and the image of bodybuilding in general.

It is a measure of the interdependence of Joe and Arnold that, despite the vitriolic tone of Arnold's remarks over the years, their business relationship and friendship have survived, and Weider, who considers Arnold a close friend, has never publicly retaliated. Nor would Arnold ever really disown Weider, still appearing at IFBB shows, giving inter-

views to Joe's magazines, and including him in his life
even after he had far surpassed the man who had brought
him to the United States.

Before moving to California, Arnold spent some time
in New York, then went to visit one of bodybuilding's top
photographers, Jim Caruso, in Montreal. Caruso had
taken pictures of Arnold during the Florida contest and
had invited him to his home in Montreal. There Jim took
yet more pictures of him; then, when Arnold expressed an
interest, Jim led him on a tour of the city and its beautiful
cathedrals. In Montreal Arnold tried to buy a pair of jeans
but was unable to find any that could accommodate his
gigantic calves.

Next it was on to California, where he was met at Los
Angeles Airport by Weider's photographer, Art Zeller. Like
Joe Gold, now of World Gym, Zeller is a founding member
of the California Arnia—men whose love for Arnold pul-
sates with devotion, emotion, and loyalty. According to
Zeller, the new arrival spoke English tolerably well but was
angry that Frank Zane, whom he termed "a chicken with
seventeen-inch arms," had beaten him.

On Weider's instructions Zeller photographed Arnold
constantly. Zeller remembers that from the start Arnold
was ready to sacrifice everything to achieve his goals, getting enough sleep and training hard. Always prepared to
admit to his deficiencies and to devote himself to eliminating them, Arnold immediately took posing lessons from
Dick Tyler. Tyler, deciding that Arnold merited "heroic"
music, picked for his posing routine *Thus Spake Zarathus-
tra*. Years later Tyler commented that if Hitler had wanted
to advertise the Aryan ideal, Arnold would have been its
perfect representative.

Tyler's remarks may sound a trifle barbed; however,
since 1977 rumors have circulated in the bodybuilding
world that during the filming of *Pumping Iron*, the
pseudo-documentary film that transformed him into a
legend, Arnold said he admired Hitler. When contacted for

a newspaper article in 1988, George Butler, the producer and director of the film and still a close friend of Arnold's today, admitted that during the filming of *Pumping Iron* Arnold definitely did say that he admired Hitler. Butler then conceded that the remark was cut from the final version of the film, adding that Arnold expressed his admiration of "Hitler and Kennedy in almost the same breath as people who were leaders." When asked why Arnold admired Hitler, Butler replied that the context in the film was that Arnold was saying he had "always wanted to be remembered like the most famous people in history, like Jesus and so on. And I think his admiration is for people who were so striking that they would be remembered always."

According to Charles Gaines, who wrote the book *Pumping Iron* on which the film of the same name was based, *Pumping Iron* was not scripted. Says Gaines, "If what you mean by scripted is that there was a written script that the actors read from in which every camera angle and scene was carefully plotted and written—no, it was not scripted in that sense. It was laid out strictly—it was story-boarded. Big segments of the movie were very carefully conceived and to some degree scripted in the conventional use of the term. But so far as the entire movie being scripted, no, it was not."

Gaines, unlike his partner, George Butler, says that he can't remember Arnold saying in *Pumping Iron* that he admired Hitler and adds, "My own feeling is that Arnold doesn't admire Hitler. If he did, in fact, say that, it was in a teasing and ribbing sense."

Manfred Thellig, who worked with Arnold in Munich, offers a similar interpretation. According to Thellig, Arnold "definitely admires the Teutonic period of the Third Reich. He just loved those leftover relics of the Third Reich in Munich—those Teutonic statues." He added that Arnold would say, "If I had lived at that time, I would have been one of those Teutonic breeders" but explains, "Whenever he opened his mouth and it sounded like 'Oh, there is a neo-Nazi,' this was just playing Tarzan. It wasn't serious."

It must also be pointed out that the second of the four most important women whom Arnold has loved is half Jewish and that he has sustained deep and sincere friendships with many Jews, some of whom are his closest business aides. He is also on record as a friend of the Wiesenthal Center in Los Angeles and of fellow Austrian Simon Wiesenthal himself. Arnold attended his birthday celebration as well as other Wiesenthal Center events.

There are, nevertheless, witnesses over the years who have seen Arnold break into the *"Sieg Heil"* salute and play his records of Hitler's speeches.

Arnold responded to this issue during a 1989 *Penthouse* interview with journalist Sharon Churcher. According to Churcher, a former associate of Arnold's during the seventies had heard from a mutual acquaintance that Arnold had Nazi paraphernalia in his apartment. According to the associate, Arnold's reaction at that time was to claim, through *Pumping Iron* producer George Butler, that his interest "was only that of a student." Butler, professing to have forgotten the above exchange, says that he had never seen any Nazi paraphernalia at Arnold's house.

The article goes on to quote Arnold as saying, "I totally hate the Nazi period." He adds, "When you come from a background like Germany or Austria, then you sometimes are joked about and people give you sometimes gifts that maybe had something to do with that [Nazi] time." When asked if he kept any such presents, Arnold replied, "No. I am so much against that time period. I despise it."

There is yet another possibility. As one bodybuilder, who observed Arnold in America doing the *"Sieg Heil"* salute, commented, "It was expected of him." Arnold personified Aryan supremacy and Germanic strength of will. To top that, his father had been a member of the Nazi party. Both his heritage and his image were inescapable. Inescapable, but not ineradicable. Yet Arnold, far from underplaying his roots, embraced and advertised them.

Essentially always an entertainer, a performer who gloried in satisfying his audience, Arnold must have known that the Nazi aura surrounding him did not displease his admirers. After all, the goal of many bodybuilders is to carve for themselves bodies befitting a master race, and to that end power and dominance are valued above all. Bodybuilding journalist Dick Tyler, who was Joe Weider's West Coast editor and who met Arnold during his first months in America, sums up the allure of the jackboot in bodybuilding terms: "I used to tell bodybuilders, 'When you go out there, think of yourself as the very best. There is no other. It will come across to the audience and they love it. That's why they are there. They are sitting there with their skinny bodies and they are looking up at that stage—looking up at their heroes.' They want that arrogance, and Arnold knew this. You didn't need to give any advice to him about being arrogant." All in all, allegations of Arnold's veneer of Nazism probably didn't hurt him in the unique arena that is bodybuilding.

Weider had found a small apartment for Arnold on Strand Street in Santa Monica and sent him to train with bodybuilding veteran Vince Gironda, whose gym was on Ventura Boulevard between Studio City and Universal City. However, according to one bodybuilding insider, Gironda's first impression of Weider's latest protégé was far from favorable. Arnold introduced himself to Vince with the words "I am Arnold Schwarzenegger, Mr. Universe." Vince, a crusty eccentric and respecter of no man, not even one being groomed for superstardom by the great Joe Weider, eyed the flabby Arnold and retorted, "You look like a fat fuck to me."

Presumably Arnold took Vince's remarks quite well, for he continued to train with him for nine months before moving to Gold's Gym on Pacific Avenue in Santa Monica. Though still a small club at that time, Gold's was the hub of the bodybuilding universe. Arnold, with his unusual sense of humor and seductive charm, naturally became the center of attraction there, but his time at Gold's was devoted primarily to training and to becoming number one.

Former Mr. America Bill Grant, who now runs Bill Grant's Olympia Fitness Center in Verona, New Jersey, met and trained with Arnold during his first few months in America. "Bodybuilding back then was closely knit, and we were like a family. We all knew what we had to do, but Arnold had more of a goal in mind than any of us. It was a stepping-stone for him, a tool.

"He was more imaginative and creative than the rest of us. He had a vision. Arnold had a lot of intensity when he trained. You could look into his eyes when he came into the gym, and it was all business. I think we all had it, but Arnold had it more. He had the eye of the tiger.

"He was incredibly competitive and determined to win. Once we were doing squats with 365 pounds on our back. Arnold did twelve reps, and I did thirteen. Arnold looked at me and said, 'You will never beat me again.' I trained hard, but I never beat him in squats again. No matter how hard I tried, he never let me beat him again.

"Arnold would never tell you when he really had an injury. You never knew when he was hurt. I think that he was injured a lot, but never wanted us to know because he wanted to continue to train. He had this fierce determination. Arnold trained six days a week. Three days a week he did chest and back in the morning and came back at night and did legs.

"For example, on chest and back, he did five sets of bench presses [each set is doing twelve repetitions]. We started out at 135 pounds on the bar and worked up to 345 pounds bench press. Arnold got the most out of his workouts by his constant concentration. There is a lot of pain. You go to the burn, as if your body is on fire. We would do a set until we dropped. We would do a bench press and have somebody standing next to the bar, and when we couldn't do any more at 335 pounds they would pull the weight off and we would keep going. That way you keep going until that 135 pounds feels like a ton.

"In one exercise—say squats—with ten reps lifting 315

pounds at a time, Arnold would lift a total of fifteen thousand pounds of weight in one exercise. You could say that he lifted tons a week. Arnold sometimes fainted—passed out unconscious—from the strain of a workout. He even threw up. But he just got up again. He had guts and determination. He could motivate anyone with his dedication."

Arnold trained until he dropped, showing grace under pressure and determination through suffering. One of his other training partners comments, "Arnold was dedicated beyond belief. Once I was doing twenty sets of biceps work with him and said, 'Boy, Arnold, we have fourteen sets to go.' His reply was, 'No, we only have one. The one we are working on.' "

From the first, Arnold loved America. He loved the politics; Nixon was in power, and that, to Arnold, was heaven. He loved the fast cars, gathering an impressive number of speeding tickets while striking terror into the heart of any passenger riding with him. Once he challenged Art Zeller to a car race, roaring through red lights, careening over sidewalks, doing anything to win, until Dick Tyler, aware that Arnold's car had been given to him by Weider, commented that Joe would have done better to have given Arnold a tank!

He loved the climate, telling his former mentor Benno Dahmen, "It is so warm. In Graz I am always cold. Here is where I will stay. The sun shines."

Above all, America was fun. Arnold was a star with an admiring following of bodybuilders who clustered eagerly around him at the gym, hoping to learn his training secrets. No salt jokes for them. At least not at first—not while Arnold concentrated on employing his skill at making friends and influencing people. There was Don Peters, a bodybuilder and actor with whom he trained and who invited him for home-cooked meals. There was Dan Howard, who roomed with him for a while and took him skeet shooting and bowling. Also Joe Gold, who adored him on sight. And, of course, Weider himself, who continually advanced Arnold's education in art and self-promotion while furthering his rise to stardom in the bodybuilding world.

During those first few months he quickly made friends with his old adversary Frank Zane, trained with him, and, always eager to improve himself, took math lessons from Frank, who was a math teacher. Arnold impressed Frank as being a brilliant student, best at gathering information by ear: "Arnold uses the principles of bodybuilding and applies them to the rest of his life. In bodybuilding you have to do repeated behavior. Arnold took that analogy into his real life. He applied bodybuilding to math. In the Weider principle of forced repetitions, when you are doing reps with weights, you get to a point when you feel as if you can no longer go on because your muscles are exhausted. If somebody helps, you can force yourself to do more. There is another way. You can force out reps by taking weight off without resting or go to lighter weights to go beyond failure. Arnold would study up to the point that he didn't want to do it anymore. Then he would make himself study for another hour. It is all weight training." He reciprocated by giving Frank a deep massage before they worked out together. Once they drove to Tijuana in Arnold's white Volkswagen, running out of gas on the way back because it was Arnold's policy never to check the gauge. He and Frank went bowling, did archery together, and talked ceaselessly about bodybuilding, with Arnold picking the brain and learning the professional secrets of the man who had once managed to beat him.

Bill Grant describes Arnold's average day: "We would begin at ten with a two-hour workout at the gym. On Monday, Wednesday, and Friday, Arnold would work on his chest and back in the morning; then he would come back in the evening and do his legs. On Tuesday, Thursday, and Sunday, he did chest and arms. In between we would all leave and go to the beach. We would go to a hamburger joint on Santa Monica Beach that we called

'The Germans.' At night we were like a family and gave parties."

Sometimes the bodybuilders would take a break at places like the Bicycle Shop on Wilshire, the Green Door on Muscle Beach, the WindJammer at Marina Del Rey, and the Little Swede on 4th and Santa Monica. Close to Vic Tanny's gym, the "Swede" was a favorite for exhausted bodybuilders who used to pay $2.25 for the buffet, then arouse the management's resentment by eating three times as much as the regular customers.

Although he was the new boy in town, Arnold soon reverted to his aggressive Munich tactics, telling an old lady who ran an antique shop to "fuck off" after she warned him to be careful not to knock over some of the expensive items on her shelves. In a less malicious vein he took great delight in mooning Gold's Gym manager Ron D'Ippolito, who, when he washed the gym's windows, found himself confronted by Arnold's extremely impressive and undeniably naked derriere.

And although he later claimed to be shocked by the lassitude of the other bodybuilders who were spending most of their time on the beach getting a tan, in reality he did the same thing and managed to get in his fair share of beach fun. Armand Tanny remembers the story of a bronzed Arnold sitting on the beach during those early 1968 days and catching sight of a beautiful bikini-clad girl. Sidling over to her, Arnold announced, "I want to fuck you." One of his friends, hastily intervening, explained to the girl, "My friend doesn't understand our ways. He is foreign." The girl, brushing away the excuses, insisted, "No, no, let him talk." And Arnold, as was his pattern, got exactly what he wanted.

Soon his pickup "techniques" entered the annals of bodybuilding folklore. Even during his first few weeks in America, photographer Jim Caruso, in Florida with Arnold for the Mr. Universe contest, witnessed him approach a girl in a restaurant with the words "I want to sleep with you tonight." The girl left with him. So great was his confidence that, according to fellow bodybuilder Wil McArdle, who first met him in 1968, Arnold walked down the street, saw a girl, asked if she would "like to fuck"—and got results.

He was irresistible, exuding bonhomie. During his first few months in America, Arnold enchanted everyone he met with his *Sound of Music* accent, Teutonic self-confidence, sense of fun, and childlike infectiousness. The combination of overwhelming charm, winning personality, and impressive physique was Arnold's passport to prosperity, success, stardom, and, for the first time in his life, true love.

7
Love and Victory: 1969–1970

BY 1969 ARNOLD'S BREATHTAKING ODYSSEY had come to a halt; after leaving Austria and the overpowering grip of his authoritarian father, finding his vocation, conquering his rivals, spending days of high drama in Munich, rollicking from bed to bed in London, attracting mentors along the way, while at the same time perfecting and polishing his alluring charm, educating his extremely sharp and receptive mind, and building his stupendous body, he had finally settled in California. He was only twenty-two years old.

Already he had lived through more adventure than most people manage to encounter in a lifetime. Yet one experience remained foreign to him: passion and love. However, in July 1969, in a Santa Monica restaurant named Zucky's, Arnold met the girl who would become his first serious involvement.

At that point he had already begun to educate himself to be an American, mastering all things American and savoring the free spirit of the country, its size, and its promise of power and success. He was in love with America's sweeping potential. And Barbara Outland was the logical conclusion of his newfound passion.

At twenty she was a pretty all-American girl, a blue-eyed blond, not far removed in looks from Meinhard's fiancée, Erika. But although she was California born and bred, Barbara definitely didn't conform to the stereotype of brainless suntanned surfer. Throughout his life Arnold has always deviated from the norm and opted for the unusual.

And Barbara was no exception. Despite the fact that she was working as a waitress at Zucky's when Arnold met her, that wasn't her vocation but a summer job she took to support herself during her last year in San Diego, where she was studying to be a teacher.

Barbara was gentle and home-loving, a woman who, like Arnold's mother, possessed a strong will under her compliant surface. She was literate and poised, born to an affluent California family, and was instantly smitten with Arnold. He was tanned and muscular, spoke broken English, and was, in Barbara's eyes, utterly adorable.

Barbara was innocent and idealistic. She had never heard of Arnold and knew nothing about his titles. She was suggestible and sensitive. Fortuitously for Arnold, Barbara also specialized in teaching English.

Prone to one-night stands, Arnold applied a new and more formal approach to Barbara, asking her to go out with him on proper dates. She was a Madonna figure to him, a woman he respected. Those who saw them together say that the pretty young woman was obviously spellbound by the bodybuilder, on whose every word she hung. The situation didn't displease Arnold.

By now Arnold was one of the boys, the life and soul of the party. According to fellow bodybuilder Dan Howard, "There wasn't anybody you could have had more fun with on a night out on the town than Arnold. He could get as wild as you wanted to get. He was fun."

Bodybuilding great Boyer Coe, four-time Mr. Universe, met Arnold in Chicago in 1969, just after Boyer won the Mr. America contest. Arnold was there both to see the contest and to meet his archrival, the magnificent Cuban-born "king" of bodybuilding, Sergio Oliva. A few weeks later, at Weider's invitation, Boyer flew to California. Arnold met him at the airport, and the two men spent the week hanging out together. "Arnold always wanted to be the center of attention," remembers Boyer. "He did whatever necessary, be it pushing something off the table or talking very loud. He definitely loved attention."

By that time he had been joined by his old friend, Franco Columbu, having induced Weider to import Columbu to California. According to Rick Wayne, who began working for Weider in 1969, "Arnold insisted that Franco come to America. He didn't want American friends. They were his competitors, they were people he planned to beat. He wanted someone he knew well." Wayne believes that Arnold does not really like Americans, "because he sees them as pampered, soft in every way. He has never respected Americans and thinks they should be more nationalistic."

Franco started out by sharing Arnold's small apartment on Strand, then they both moved to a two-bedroom apartment on 14th Street in Santa Monica. Barbara, not yet living with Arnold on a permanent basis, stayed with him on weekends. Naturally, while she was away, Arnold and Franco devoted themselves rigorously to playing the field. Dick Tyler remembers, "Franco and Arnold told me that they had so many women that they couldn't keep track of who was who. They would just wake up in the middle of the night, and they would each have a girl with them. Women were there for their pleasure."

Back on a business level, it was on to New York and the twin events of the IFBB Mr. Universe at the Brooklyn Academy of Music followed by the Mr. Olympia. And yet again, Arnold met with an American defeat, this time by Sergio Oliva. Later he told Rick Wayne, "I was with him in his dressing room . . . shortly before we were called out to pose. Sergio was covered, as usual, in his butcher's overalls. It was obvious that he was nobody's turkey, of course.

"But after he'd pumped up and undressed, I just couldn't believe what I saw. Then Sergio walked past me and spread out his lats, ever so casually, you understand, but that was enough to freeze my blood. Right there and then I knew it was all over for me. I was completely psyched out. . . . He took away my determination to beat him. When I went out to pose it was just a matter of going through the motions. I'd lost the contest before I stepped onstage."

There was, however, some consolation. Arnold went

back to London for the 1969 NABBA Universe, which he won easily, telling another rival, handsome black bodybuilder Serge Nubret, that he intended to beat every bodybuilder alive.

After the Brooklyn contest Arnold returned to New York to appear in his first film, *Hercules Goes to New York*—sometimes also known as *Hercules Goes Bananas* or just *Hercules*. Weider had won the part for Arnold by convincing the producer that he was a well-known European stage actor. The ninety-one-minute film, made for Italian television on a $300,000 budget, was a spoof of the Steve Reeves and Reg Park films that the young Arnold had devoured in Graz. And although, owing to his heavy accent, he had to suffer the indignity of having his voice dubbed by another actor, Arnold must have relished the experience. The late Laurence Olivier once said, "To oneself, inside, one is always sixteen, with red lips." And to Arnold, who, at twenty-two, to himself, inside, was probably still thirteen, unhappy, and unloved, being equal to Reg must have been more gratifying than anything that had ever happened to him or ever would.

Hercules Goes to New York is sometimes shown on television, even today, and every time it airs Arnold gets twenty or more calls from friends laughing hysterically after seeing his abortive film debut.

He spends most of the film dressed in only a brief toga, playing the part of Zeus's illegitimate son, who has been thrown out of Olympus and catapulted down to earth, landing in New York City. The sound track is saturated with Greek music of the local taverna variety.

Hercules arrives in New York with no money, the classic big lug, a poor man's Crocodile Dundee who is completely bemused by the metropolis. In the words of the film distributor's press release, "The action never stops. He is chased by beautiful girls, fight promoters, grizzly bears, gangsters and an angry Zeus hurling thunderbolts, all culminating in an uproarious chariot race through Times Square."

Later, when he was a success and was promoting his talent at career management, Arnold often professed to have picked his film parts with extreme care. *Hercules*, patently, is one exception. Arnold appeared in the film under the pseudonym Arnold Strong. And after his charmless performance it is a miracle that his film career didn't end the moment that it so shakily began. However disastrous his debut, one thing was radiantly clear to Arnold: acting was the answer, satisfying his ego and feeding his hunger for attention. Later he was to say of acting, "Myself, I like the money. And the ego satisfaction. People recognize you and say, 'This is the guy who just did the film.' That makes me feel wonderful."

By Christmas 1969 Arnold and Barbara were dating on a regular basis. Arnold had also stepped up his training, determined that 1970 would be his year. With that end in mind he abandoned his European training technique of working for five or six hours at a time. Instead he switched to the Joe Weider method of split and double split sessions, training four or five times a week, in two or three daily sessions, each lasting just under an hour.

He began to study his rivals, one night amazing Dan Howard by doing all the other bodybuilders' routines, which he had memorized. He also pushed himself to the extreme.

All through his grueling training, Arnold kept the image of Sergio Oliva in front of him. Black bodybuilder Dave DuPre, who would appear with Arnold years later in *Pumping Iron*, says Arnold declared one time while working out at Gold's, "Serge is your only black hope to beat me. Black people are inferior. You are not capable of achieving the success of white people. Black people are stupid." Black people weren't the only target of his venom, for as usual he was completely democratic in his heckling. According to DuPre, "He would make fun of Jews. If anybody looked Jewish, he would point it out and tell them that they were inferior. I would remind him that it was a Jew who had brought him to America. Then he would shut up."

In DuPre's view, "He was always upset that all the black guys were able to go out with all the white girls. He couldn't stand that." And he did his best to reverse the situation. Once, having dinner at a New York restaurant with Rick Wayne and Joe Weider, Arnold noticed a beautiful black hatcheck girl. He began talking to her, then asked Joe to lend him his car. Joe complied, and Arnold left with the girl. Rick recalls that the next day Arnold made a point of telling him, "You know, the girl said I was better than any black guy she had ever had."

Rick asked Arnold how he had managed to persuade the girl to leave with him. His answer crystallizes his notorious approach to women: "He told me that he said to her, 'Why you American girls work so hard?' The girl said, 'I just started.' Arnold countered, 'Aw, come on, let's go fuck.' "

As Arnold had planned, 1970 was his year. With Weider's encouragement he had set up a mail order business offering bodybuilding aids and booklets published under the name of Arnold Strong (but featuring his photo) and written mostly by Weider's editor, Gene Mozee, sold through ads in the pages of Joe's magazines, and business was booming. Barbara too was proving useful, eagerly helping with the massive amount of paperwork necessary to run the business. Arnold, however, did all he could to streamline things. When letters arrived, he held each envelope up to the light. Those that contained checks were opened. The others, presumably from fans seeking autographs and advice, were tossed unopened into the wastepaper basket.

According to Arnold and Franco's subsequent publicity, they also set up an enterprise called Pumping Bricks, a bricklaying business. Although they were to make much of the business in years to come, there are those who claim that Pumping Bricks was merely a promotional gambit, not a reality, but a concept that provided anecdotes through which Arnold and Franco could explain just how they had supported themselves during their early years in America. In any event, they both eagerly revealed their bricklaying anecdotes to talk show hosts, who laughed indulgently at the stories of two European adventurers taking advantage of American naïveté. On the ABC news magazine show "20/20" Franco told the following story: "One of our workers nearly ruined a patio job by laying the bricks crookedly. Arnold said, 'Don't worry, we will talk to the lady.' I said, 'Talking to the lady won't move these bricks.' Arnold said, 'No matter what happens in a construction site, you have to be able to sell what you have created.' Arnold convinced the lady that the bricks, by being off, were a new European style. She was fascinated. She said, 'I like it that way. I want it that way.' "

Another Franco anecdote, in the same vein, tells of the duo's exploits when they visited damaged houses after an earthquake. According to Franco, one woman asked them to demolish a chimney. Franco says, "Arnold looked at it and said, 'What if we got a big rope and swung like Tarzan onto the roof and laid on our backs and pushed the chimney over with our feet?' So it took us about ten minutes to knock down the chimney once we got the rope on it, and we made a thousand dollars. The lady was so happy she gave us the bricks. Arnold promptly sold those bricks to another client, calling them 'antique bricks.' "

Franco's willingness to project Arnold as the éminence grise of their tiny enterprise is telling. He was always happy to play the part of sidekick, following admiringly wherever Arnold led. Sometimes, however, even Franco had to concede that Arnold was not infallible. After reading about a new supersonic airport that was due to be built in Palmdale, northeast of Los Angeles, Arnold and Franco invested $15,000 (made from mail order sales) in fifteen acres of the land. As Franco tells it, he and Arnold were lured to Palmdale by a fast-talking salesman: "He spoke to us for two hours on the bus about how they are making this freeway into Palmdale. The Intercontinental Airport. They were going to other planets. And to us, it was like,

'Wow!'" Six months later they discovered that the super-sonic airport had been canceled and the land was next to a dump. A rueful Columbu, perhaps mindful of the fact that it is sometimes good publicity for winners to appear vulnerable in the media, confided, "We still have the land sitting there. I don't know if we can ever sell it. We learned once and for all what to do and what not to do."

Over in London, Wag Bennett, sometime before the 1970 NABBA Mr. Universe, had sent his old friend Reg Park a letter proposing that he attempt a comeback. Wag obligingly also enclosed pictures of Arnold, the reigning champion for the past three years, suggesting that the king could easily be deposed. Reg, probably very grateful to Wag for his advice and the photographs, and no doubt tempted by the prospect of teaching his young admirer a lesson, took Wag's advice and entered the 1970 Universe, completely unaware that the pictures Wag had sent him were old photographs of Arnold taken in the days when he was out of condition.

Gordon Allen, who was at the Universe competition, watched as Reg "strutted around backstage while some colored guy from South Africa toweled him down. Then Arnold came onstage. And there was a gasp from the audience. He was so muscular. Reg was shocked." Shocked and vanquished. For Arnold had, once again, been true to his pattern: to find a mentor and then eclipse him entirely.

Looking back on the contest, Arnold told Rick Wayne that he was sorry to have burst Reg's bubble because Reg had been his boyhood idol, and Arnold hoped he would recover. And in *Arnold: The Education of a Bodybuilder* he tried to make it clear that Reg's participation in the contest had been a surprise to him.

According to Rick Wayne, "Witnesses had it that while Park was furiously pumping up backstage, a fully attired and clearly unconcerned Arnold had babbled on and on about every irrelevant subject under the sun . . . until finally the older man lost his cool. 'Damn it, Arnold,' he exploded, 'will you can the bullshit till after the contest!' To which Arnold was reported to have replied, 'Contest, Reg? What contest?' "

There is, however, another side to Arnold's treatment of Reg, one that highlights his ability to separate business from friendship as well as his strong paternal drive and capacity for love. A few years after Arnold defeated him, Reg's son, John-John, moved to California to study in Newport Beach. According to Reg, "Arnold drove down to Newport Beach every single Friday to visit John-John. The round-trip journey to and from Los Angeles was an hour and a half, but Arnold still went to see John-John each and every Friday. He'd take him out for a meal, make sure he was eating properly and that he had enough money. He really looked after the kid." And Reg, the mentor whom he outstripped, is still friends with Arnold, has had him to stay at his home in Johannesburg's Morningside Heights as many as five times, visits him twice a year in California, and was invited to his wedding.

On September 19th, the day after Arnold's victory in London, another contest took place, in Columbus, Ohio. Titled the Pro Mr. World contest, it was run by a man who was to play an important part in Arnold's financial future and also was destined to become one of his closest friends.

Jim Lorimer, the Pro Mr. World promoter, had phoned Arnold at Gold's Gym a few weeks earlier and told him that the contest was due to be televised nationally on ABC's "Wide World of Sports." Lorimer suggested that, the moment the curtain fell on the NABBA Universe, Arnold take the first flight out of Heathrow. Lorimer would have a private jet waiting in New York, ready to whisk him to Columbus and the contest at the Veterans Memorial Auditorium. Mindful of the television exposure, Arnold agreed.

The flight from London to New York, depending on the winds, can take up to eight hours and is exhausting. Jet lag too, precipitated by the five-hour time difference between London and New York, also takes its toll. Yet Arnold not only weathered the long flight, negotiated the long customs lines at JFK International Airport in New York, and managed to switch to his Columbus-bound jet; he also arrived fresh, rested, and determined to win. And despite having traveled nonstop for over twelve hours, he was victorious, defeating Sergio Oliva to win the Pro Mr. World title along with $500 and an electric watch. To top that he was also interviewed by ABC-TV. More important, though, was the fact that he also met Jim Lorimer.

Twenty years Arnold's senior, Lorimer is an impressive man. Arnold spotted him immediately as a man who could be useful as mentor, friend, and business partner. As soon as the contest was over, he took Lorimer aside and announced, "I've competed around the world, but someday I am going to stop competing. I am going to go into promoting bodybuilding, and I am going to raise cash prizes to over $100,000. And when I retire from competing, I am going to come back to Columbus and ask you to be my partner." It is a testament to his ability to think ahead as well as to the firmness of his will that, exactly five years later, on his retirement from bodybuilding, Arnold did return to Columbus and ask Lorimer to become his business partner. And that today, almost twenty years since their first meeting, the prize money for the Arnold Cup, an event staged by Arnold and Lorimer, amounts to $150,000.

Immediately after his Columbus victory over Oliva, Arnold went to dinner with him and, in a friendly voice, confided to his rival, "I could not have beaten you tonight if you had been, say, fifteen pounds heavier!" Two weeks later, on October 3rd, the day of the 1970 Mr. Olympia contest, Sergio Oliva, the current Mr. Olympia, arrived at the New York Town Hall weighing fifteen pounds more than he had when Arnold had beaten him in Columbus.

Half an hour before the contest Franco and Arnold watched Oliva pump up backstage. Then Franco suggested they go out to eat. Obligingly, Arnold suggested that they get some French fries and ketchup. In amazement, Oliva dropped his weight, in a bemused voice asking the duo if they really planned to eat so close to contest time. Didn't they, he asked, want to pump up before the contest? A scornful Arnold informed him that if he wasn't in shape now, he never would be.

Olivia, until then the king, always treated with reverence by other bodybuilders, was shattered. But there was more to come. As the Olympia drew to a close, only Sergio and Arnold were left posing onstage. Suddenly Arnold whispered something to Sergio, who then walked off the stage. The audience started booing. Arnold next assumed his most striking pose. Two thousand fans yelled his name. He was crowned Mr. Olympia.

Rick Wayne reports that Arnold told him that after the posing off with Sergio both he and Sergio were tired. According to Rick, Arnold told Sergio that he was ready to quit if Sergio was. Sergio replied that he had had enough. Said Arnold, "Fine, lead off." But unfortunately, for Sergio at least, the crowd misunderstood, believing that Sergio had abdicated. Meanwhile, when the booing started, Arnold naturally changed his mind and stayed onstage to win the Olympia.

He had won bodybuilding's triple crown, in the same year capturing the titles of Mr. Universe, Pro Mr. World, and, most important of all, Mr. Olympia. Arnold Schwarzenegger was now truly king. No other bodybuilder would ever beat him again.

Arnold settled into his rule over his bodybuilding realm with the ease of one who had been preparing for kingship since the age of thirteen. No prince has ever ascended to the throne with more assurance than twenty-three-year-old Arnold Schwarzenegger.

With his consort Barbara Outland beside him, his court jester Franco, and his coterie of wise older advisers, led by Weider and Joe Gold, his royal retinue was complete.

Gold's Gym was the inner sanctum and the arena where he could, literally, flex his muscles and demonstrate

the full extent of his power. And to ensure the loyalty of
his subjects Arnold employed his old Munich tactics, asserting his power by focusing on a luckless few, using them
as targets for his practical jokes.

Fellow bodybuilder Wil McArdle, who says he witnessed Arnold forcing a fan to do what he terms "a Heil
Hitler march," says of Arnold, "His right arm held light,
his left arm held darkness, and he liked to play with it. He
hates fans that are weak, that give themselves up to him so
completely. He almost punishes them for not being themselves. He respects himself because he did everything his
way. And he is going to make you into an asshole every
time you give yourself up to him. I think his practical jokes
were enlightening to the victims.

"Arnold was also sharing with us this art form he has
of intimidating people. At the same time, he wasn't intimidating us. He showed what he could do to others—and
what he wasn't doing to us. That implied a closeness."

During the seventies Arnold entertained his followers
by enacting the following scenario. An aspiring bodybuilder and fan, plucking up his courage, approached Arnold, asking for his advice on how to become great in the
sport. Arnold's answer was to obligingly produce a bottle
containing something that he described as special oil that
was flown in regularly from Austria exclusively for his
benefit. He told the bodybuilder to strip, then rubbed him
all over with his "special oil." Once the victim was thor-
oughly oiled, Arnold instructed him to assume various
poses. Then he cautioned him not to wash the oil off but to
get dressed. That way, Arnold explained, his muscles
would attain definition. Fully dressed, his clothing
smeared with Arnold's special oil, the victim would leave,
feeling blessed by his idol, unaware that Arnold's "special
oil" was, in fact, motor oil.

On May 20, 1971, Erika Knapp, the mother of Meinhard Schwarzenegger's three-year-old son, Patrick, woke
up at four in the morning, unable to sleep. Normally a

heavy sleeper, this weekend she was overexcited, happy, but restless. As she tells it today, after a stormy five-year relationship with Meinhard, they had finally agreed to get married. She says that the wedding was to be held in a month's time.

Although she had suffered from her own parents' disapproval of her for having given birth to an illegitimate child, Meinhard's mother, Aurelia, was kind to her, treating Erika as if she were already her daughter-in-law. And Meinhard's father, Gustav, had been her first visitor in the hospital, just hours after Patrick's birth.

He had been an eight-month baby, and Gustav, who loved plump women, insisted that Erika try to gain weight, primarily because he was worried about her health. As soon as she was able to get about, Gustav, overflowing with Old World charm, goodwill, and concern, escorted the mother of his grandson from restaurant to restaurant, ordering all manner of delicacies, hoping to tempt her to eat.

Although Gustav had always treated her with courtesy and kindness, she was acutely aware that there had been recent conflict between Gustav and Meinhard and had rarely seen them together. But now, just a month before the wedding, she had finally reconciled herself to Meinhard's drifting ways and fervently hoped that his parents would do the same.

This weekend, however, she had met with disappointment. She had asked her boss in Munich to give her time off so she could spend the weekend with Meinhard in Kitzbühel. But he had refused. So now she lay there, in Munich, unable to sleep, suddenly awake after experiencing a strange sensation that she couldn't quite pinpoint.

That evening Erika's mother phoned and broke the news to her. Depressed and alone, Meinhard, after drinking himself into a stupor, had gone for a drive. Smashing into another car, he was killed instantly.

According to Erika, dressed only in a T-shirt, she ran out of her house, not knowing where she wanted to go or what she wanted to do. Blindly she stumbled into a local

guesthouse and, to the amusement of all the drinkers surrounding her, ordered a double schnapps. She cried until
she had no more tears.

A day or two later, Gustav, whom she called Opa,
came to see her in Kufstein, where she was staying with her
parents. Deeply shocked by Meinhard's death, he ran
through the streets of Kufstein, clutching his older son's
blood-spattered watch. He gave Erika the watch and
Meinhard's other belongings and then began to cry bitter
and terrible tears.

He told her that he wanted to bury Meinhard in
Kitzbühel, where he had died. Erika agreed. Then they
waited, mother, father, and fiancée, for Meinhard's younger
brother, Arnold, to attend the funeral. But he never came.

Arnold does, indeed, hold the darkness in one arm and
the light in the other. The darkness is reflected in various
episodes of his life, including his failure to attend his
brother's funeral. The light, however, shines through
strongly in a story that, to his credit, Arnold has never
publicized.

Arnold has said of Meinhard, "Deep down, I expected
something to happen, because he always lived more on the
edge than I. . . . Now I wish he were here to enjoy all this
with me. Back then, I just brushed it off." That wasn't true.
For once, Arnold has undersold himself.

After Meinhard's death Arnold discovered his brother's
joke: he, Arnold, had been Patrick's godfather since his
birth, three years before, but had never known it. After
Meinhard's death Arnold wrote to Erika, offering to help
her if she ever had any problems or needed anything.

As Erika couldn't afford to bring Patrick up herself,
the boy went to live with her parents, who brought him up
in Kufstein. When Patrick was ten, Erika wrote to Arnold
and asked for his help. From then on Arnold sent her
money, paid for Patrick's high school in Lisbon, where
Erika had gone to live with her new husband, and later
offered to pay for Patrick's education and life in America—
an offer that Erika thankfully accepted.

Patrick, as all who see him agree, is the spitting image of his father, Meinhard. Tall, blond, and handsome, today he trains at World Gym in Venice, California, where he lives in a house belonging to his uncle, Arnold. He plans, like Arnold, to study business management and may go into politics. In 1988 Erika visited Patrick and Arnold in Los Angeles. One morning she sat by the pool with Arnold, ate strawberries, and talked about old times, noting that he seemed happy and more able to show his feelings than in the past. She thanked him for having been there for her whenever she needed him. And he replied that he was proud that Erika had sent him a half Schwarzenegger to look after.

There is, however, another, darker side to the tragic story of Meinhard Schwarzenegger, one that Erika may not have known. While Arnold's horizons had expanded, those of his brother had become smaller and filled with sadness. In the year and a half before he died Meinhard had worked for the Grabner publishing company in the Kitzbühel area and lived in a room he had rented from a young couple not much older than himself, named Maria and Johann Hautz, who lived in a house in St. Johann, on the outskirts of Kitzbühel.

Eighteen years after his death Maria Hautz remembers Meinhard with great affection and is upset that she can't find his obituary. Whenever she is in Kitzbühel, she visits his grave by the little San Andreas Church and thinks of the troubled young man who once lived with her and her husband: "Meinhard was charming and generous, but he lived beyond his means. He talked to me a lot. He seemed completely alone. He never phoned his parents, and they never phoned him.

"He showed me magazines with pictures of Arnold in them, but he never heard from him or talked to him all the time he was with us. He admired Arnold but was a little bit jealous of him. Secretly he wanted to be like him. He envied Arnold all his money. I think that was what made him desperate to make a big score."

Desperate and susceptible to alcohol as his father was,

Meinhard's desire to equal his brother led him astray. Although German police records from the 1960s have been destroyed, two independent sources have confirmed Maria's story: "He told me he did criminal things in Munich. Then, one day, he assaulted an old lady when he had been drinking. She called the police, they arrested him, and he spent at least a year in prison."

Maria says, "I never knew that he had fallen on bad ways again until two policemen came to visit me. They told me he had been driving without a license."

Maria remembers Meinhard as a womanizer and says that girls loved him and that, although Erika was his steady girlfriend, he had many others. "One of them, an older woman, lived in Kirchberg, where she ran a guesthouse," says Maria. "It was her car he was driving when he died. She had lent it to him, and after it was wrecked Arnold paid to replace it.

"In the last weeks before his death Meinhard was away a lot, and I had the feeling that he was planning something. He was drinking more than ever, and I only wish I could have talked to him more.

"His mother and father were at the funeral, but the atmosphere was very cold and without feeling."

Meinhard had started out as the golden boy, the favorite, and had ended up the black sheep, the outcast. Before he died, Meinhard told Maria that Arnold had been his father's favorite and that he, Meinhard, had been unloved. Perhaps he was talking about Arnold the bodybuilder, Arnold the athlete, but certainly not Arnold the boy of ten whom Meinhard had dragged into trouble and who was eclipsed by his charisma. Now the tables had turned; Arnold, not Meinhard, was famous, and that fame had brought him his father's love.

Both brothers had been misfits and bullies and, judging by Meinhard's history, had the potential to drift into criminality. But now there was only one brother left. And it was almost as if Arnold had switched souls with Meinhard, had exchanged destinies with him, taking the best that had been his brother's, making it his own. For it was Meinhard who had started out with the charm, the looks, the strong, well-defined body, and, above all, his parents' love. Now Arnold had it all. He had worked for it, fought for it; now it was his. Meinhard, dead and buried, lying in peace in the Tyrolean Alps, was merely what Arnold might have become.

8
Success, Death, and *Stay Hungry*

IN THE SUMMER OF 1971 ARNOLD AND BAR-
bara traveled to Kufstein to visit Erika. For a few moments
Barbara and Erika were alone, and Barbara confided that
she would die if anything happened to Arnold. She was
deeply in love with him, and eyewitnesses say that he had
affection for her, visibly melted in her presence, and seemed
genuinely in love.

From Austria they went to London, where Arnold had
planned to compete in the NABBA Mr. Universe. However,
the IFBB had passed a new regulation banning bodybuilders from competing in both the NABBA Universe and the
IFBB Mr. Olympia. Serge Nubret, organizer of the Mr.
Olympia, held that year in Paris, refused to bend the rules
for Arnold. Arnold didn't enter the NABBA Universe and
instead defended his Mr. Olympia title in Paris.

Bill Pearl won the NABBA Universe. Arnold's victory
in the Olympia was a foregone conclusion. As always, his
main challenge was Oliva, but as Oliva had chosen to enter
the Mr. Universe rather than the Mr. Olympia contest,
Arnold didn't have much serious competition, winning the
Mr. Olympia title for the second time.

Back in America, Arnold and Barbara settled into
their domestic home life. She was used to him by now,
accustomed to his domineering ways and insatiable ambition. For the past two years, each New Year's Eve she had
watched him compile a list of his ambitions for the year to
come. By the end of that year each ambition had been
fulfilled.

Barbara's ambitions, however, were not so easily satisfied. A conventional girl, she felt that she was destined to marry Arnold. Arnold, however, had different ideas, making it obvious to his bodybuilding comrades that he was far from faithful to the long-suffering Barbara. (Looking back later, Arnold said he had never planned to get married until past the age of thirty.) Meanwhile, his life with Barbara was congenial and as close to mundane as Arnold would ever come.

Barbara didn't just provide secretarial services for his mail order company. Arnold had enrolled in Santa Monica College, taking general courses, and Barbara also helped with his research. Although never a great reader, Arnold was a bright student and, in 1973, transferred to UCLA extension, where he went to night school and took non-matriculated courses. And even though there are those who saw them together and concluded that Arnold used Barbara, the relationship wasn't a one-way street, as he helped put her through school.

In September 1972 Arnold met George Butler, the son of a British army officer, at the Mr. America contest at the Brooklyn Academy of Music. Butler, a photographer on assignment for *Oui* magazine, had been an oarsman and a soccer player first at Groton and then at the University of North Carolina. As a sportsman he was also at the contest to research the upcoming book on which he was collaborating with author Charles Gaines, tentatively entitled *Pumping Iron*. From the first, Butler was riveted by Arnold. "It was clear that Arnold was a star," he recalls. "His presence was just incredible." He determined to make Arnold the focal point of *Pumping Iron* and to feature him extensively in the film of the same name that he and Gaines were planning.

The 1972 Mr. Olympia was held at the Handelshof in Essen, Germany, at the end of September. Competing against Arnold were Franco, Frank Zane, Serge Nubret, and the ubiquitous Sergio Oliva.

Arnold and his fellow bodybuilders arrived in Essen on the Sunday before the contest, with another guest, Arnold's father, Gustav, on hand to see his son compete. Over dinner Frank Zane, one of the few bodybuilders who rivals Arnold in savoir faire, stood up and toasted Gustav's health. Gustav, a broken man since Meinhard's death and not in the best of health, was highly gratified, telling Arnold afterward that he liked Frank Zane because of his friendly gesture.

According to Serge Nubret, who was with him, Arnold made a gesture of his own in Essen, taking a prostitute to his room, having sex with her, and then refusing to pay her. The girl, he announced to Serge, should instead pay him.

Once again Arnold was voted Mr. Olympia. Rick Wayne interviewed him after the contest, and Arnold confided, "In Germany Sergio [Oliva] was stupendous. His physique was flawless. But I knew better than to look for physical weakness in Sergio. I knew exactly where to find his Achilles' heel." Rick defines that weakness: "Arnold admired Sergio for having the greatest body but discovered that he was vulnerable. He knew Sergio had a chink in his armor because of being black. Arnold discovered that Sergio didn't have the confidence to go with his physique because he didn't have the white world behind him."

Indeed he didn't. Although no one has alleged that the Essen 1972 Olympia (or any other Olympia for that matter) was fixed, bodybuilding is a sport of opinion. There are no absolute standards. Veteran bodybuilding journalist Peter McGough explains, "You can influence the results of a contest by saying, 'I think X looks good this year.' All the judges come from bodybuilding, and they don't want to be left out."

Understandably Arnold's explanation of how he won the 1972 Mr. Olympia title was different. He told Rick Wayne that although he had been three pounds overweight at Essen, he saw an opportunity to gain an advantage in the judging. The room in which the preliminaries were to be staged had not yet been agreed on, and as no one was prepared to make a decision, Arnold took charge and chose the room himself. "I was far more interested in the [dark background] paint," he confided to Rick. "It hadn't occurred to Sergio that my white body would stand out against the dark wall behind us, while his would blend right in. To this day I believe that was how I got the edge. In a nutshell, the judges saw more than I actually had that day in Germany. Sergio suffered for his blindness."

On December 11, 1972, two months after the Mr. Olympia contest in Essen, Gustav Schwarzenegger died of a stroke at Graz Hospital. He was sixty-five years old. Some say that he died of a broken heart, still shattered by Meinhard's death. Whatever the cause, he was buried a week after his death, on December 18th, at Weiz Cemetery, just a few miles outside of Graz. More than a hundred members of the Gendarmerie Musik were present and played Chopin funeral dirges in tribute to their deceased colleague. They also placed a memorial notice in the *Graz Kleine Zeitung* citing Gustav's long membership in the Musik, ending with the sentiment that they would remember him. Arnold, however, was not present at his father's funeral. He had stayed home in America.

In *Pumping Iron* Arnold shocked his audience by saying that he didn't go to his father's funeral because he was deep in training, adding that he couldn't help his father as he was now dead. Art Zeller today corroborates that statement.

Later Arnold changed his story, attributing his *Pumping Iron* remarks to a French bodybuilder. And later still, he said that he couldn't go to Gustav's funeral because he had been in the hospital with a leg injury. Most recently Arnold reportedly said that the real reason was that he was not notified in time.

Arnold's three versions of why he didn't attend the funeral are all open to question. First, although Arnold was naturally in the habit of training year-round, his father died in December, a full nine-and-a-half months before the next Mr. Olympia contest. Second, though he had indeed suffered a knee injury during an Australian contest, he was accustomed to pain and could probably have endured the flight to Austria. Third, Barbara Outland confided to Ken Waller, Arnold's co-star in *Pumping Iron*, that Arnold's comment, as well as his failure to attend his father's funeral, had really upset his mother—and presumably Aurelia would not have been upset if she herself had failed to inform him of his father's death.

He was later to say of his father's death, "I would pay anything for my father to be alive again for just one hour to see what I'm doing today." He also said, "I took it badly, because I knew how much he had done for me. . . . My father saw my progress—that I was developing in my sport and was smart in business—but he never saw the full circle."

The full circle was, in fact, seen by those at Gustav's funeral, who had truly known him and noted Arnold's absence. Gustav had created him. He was what Gustav had made him.

In 1973 Barbara and Arnold moved to a new apartment on 6th Street in Santa Monica. There was now no question that he was at the pinnacle of his profession. Wayne de Milia, a top IFBB official, met Arnold during this period and observed, "Arnold studied everyone's physiques and knew their weaknesses better than they did. He knew he was stronger than they were and was able to play with them."

Unequivocally the king, he gave a posing exhibition in Hawaii with Franco and Art Zeller, staying in a hotel on Waikiki Beach. In 1973, too, a new element entered Arnold's already full life. An actor named David Arkin knew of him and mentioned him to director Robert Altman, then casting *The Long Goodbye*, a motion picture based on the Raymond Chandler novel, with Elliott Gould as Philip Marlowe.

Altman remembers, "David said, 'I've got this big, strong guy for you. His name is Arnold Strong, and he's a weightlifter who just came over from Germany.' " Despite the fact that details about Arnold were garbled, Altman hired him sight unseen. He played one of five hoods who worked for a gangster who was set on terrorizing Marlowe. Although Arnold just stood there, without saying a word, looking big and belligerent, Altman says, "He was a likable guy. He didn't push himself forward at all. And I would never have forecast his success. But I never thought Jack Nicholson would make it either."

Nineteen seventy-three was also the year when Arnold, as a favor, drove Art Zeller to the airport. On the way he suddenly turned to Art and announced, "Big things are going to happen to me." Art asked what made him think so. His answer was short and to the point: "I can feel it. I can smell it. It's in the air. I just know it is going to happen." And, as was usually the case with Arnold, he was right.

Pumping Iron was published in November 1974 and was largely ignored by established reviewers but, nevertheless, became an underground classic, finally going into an amazing fifteen printings. Bodybuilding's time had come. That trend was reflected and reinforced by a *Sports Illustrated* article, published the same year, which lent credence to the entire sport. At the 1974 Olympia Arnold posed for two minutes in front of five thousand besotted New Yorkers at the Felt Forum, who all went wild with passion, screaming his name in a frenzy.

Arnold beat the imposing twenty-two-year-old newcomer, Lou Ferrigno, who at six foot five and 265 pounds had been considered a serious challenger. Lou Ferrigno was the first man bodybuilders believed might have a chance of dethroning the mighty Arnold. Twice voted Mr. Universe, Lou was stupefyingly big and equally determined to trounce Arnold and to replace him.

On the Friday before the contest Arnold had appeared with Franco on a morning TV show and said of Ferrigno that he was probably watching his television appearance, deciding whether or not he should compete against him. Arnold's appearances were now becoming more frequent, and he used them to hone his ability to seduce hosts and audiences alike. Again and again he would tell his life story, redolent as it was of the American dream, flashing a look that combined innocence and mischievousness, then breaking into a stirring speech extolling the virtues of America and all it promised.

The boy from Thal who had grown up without a television was quickly conquering the medium. Again using the Weider principles of forced repetition, he reiterated both his life story and the benefits of bodybuilding, sticking to a strategy that was masterful in its simplicity as well as in its instant appeal to Americans during the swinging seventies.

In a summation of his habitual theme, Arnold explained to *Playboy*, "I think I made the sport more acceptable when I promoted bodybuilding in the mid-seventies. . . . In the old days bodybuilders talked about eating two pounds of meat and thirty eggs a day, how they had to sleep twelve hours a day and couldn't have sex, and so on. And I said to myself, 'Who the fuck wants to be part of that kind of sport?' First of all, it was not accurate; and second of all, if you want to make people join a particular activity, you have to make it pleasant-sounding. It's like promoting anything. You make it fun. I talked about diet—but I said I eat cake and ice cream as well. I said I stay out nights and I have sex and do all the things that everyone says you shouldn't do. I said all you have to do is train three times a week for 45 minutes to an hour and you will get in shape."

There are those who insinuate that Arnold was lucky in that his attempt at promoting bodybuilding coincided with the jogging boom as well as new medical evidence of the benefits of exercise for the cardiovascular system. Yet luck or no luck, it is undeniable that Arnold changed the face of bodybuilding and brought to it charisma and star-quality appeal.

While watching Arnold's appearance on "The Merv Griffin Show," the great comedienne Lucille Ball was captivated by Arnold's charm. Using a line that would later become famous, Arnold announced that bodybuilding was the way to a good time and that pumping was as good as humping, which made Lucy laugh. She promptly phoned Arnold and invited him to appear on a live TV special with Art Carney, called "Happy Anniversary and Good-bye."

Arnold played an Italian masseur, dressed in tank top and shorts, who was called in because Lucy's girlfriend felt she needed to get into shape. Before the show Lucy arranged for Arnold to have a week's acting lessons and directed him herself during shooting, coaching him on how to project himself. Arnold's charm had opened yet another door.

At the end of 1974 it seemed clear that the film *Pumping Iron* would soon be a reality. The cards were stacking up in Arnold's favor. Yet fate had even more aces in store for him. Bob Rafelson, who had directed the classic *Five Easy Pieces*, was in the process of casting *Stay Hungry*, based on the book of the same name written by Arnold's new friend, Charles Gaines. To Gaines, who knew and appreciated him, Arnold was ideal for the part of bodybuilder Joe Santo, so he suggested him to Bob Rafelson.

Gaines recalls, "There was a good deal of resistance on his part to using Arnold. His attitude was 'No way. We are not going to use some know-nothing Austrian body-builder as a main character in a major motion picture.' When I brought Arnold over to Bob's house—Arnold can charm the socks off a snake—Bob started to see the possibilities."

He certainly did, immediately calling his *Five Easy Pieces* star Jack Nicholson, asking him to suggest an acting coach for Arnold. Nicholson recommended Eric Morris, a respected teacher and author of four books on acting. Morris remembers, "Bob told me that Arnold was perfect for *Stay Hungry* but that he wasn't an actor. He asked me to help him, and we agreed that I would give him twelve weeks of private lessons. Bob set up a meeting for me with Arnold. We decided to rendezvous in a parking lot. Before I hung up, I asked Bob how I would recognize Arnold. There was a long silence, then he said, 'Eric, you just will.' "

Arnold arrived at the meeting in his latest acquisition, a silver BMW. Eric took to him immediately, booking Arnold for daily lessons lasting two or three hours each. The lessons were to continue for twelve weeks, but it was only during the ninth week that Arnold was allowed to tackle the *Stay Hungry* script.

From the start Morris was deeply impressed by him. "He is a sharp, sharp, sharp guy," says Morris, "He is one of the smartest people I have ever met. Very few people realize how talented he really is. If he got it into his head that he wanted to become a fine actor, Arnold could do it. He could compete with any of them."

True love, however, couldn't possibly compete with Arnold's acting ambitions. Barbara Outland, now an English teacher at Lincoln High School, West Los Angeles, while happy about Arnold's making a documentary like *Pumping Iron*, didn't want him to become an actor. Still pressing for marriage yet aware that Arnold, riding on the rainbow of his dreams, wasn't the least bit receptive, she capitulated and decided to end their relationship. Shortly after, commenting that "Arnold is the most goal-oriented person I have ever met. . . . Whatever he does must be useful to him in some way, in the direction of whatever goal he has set," she bowed out of his life.

Some people claim that Arnold suffered over his breakup with Barbara. To others, like Rick Wayne, he assumed a mantle of macho bravado and reportedly cracked, "Ricky, a woman is like a car. After five years, you change her." Barbara, sadder but wiser, eventually married, published a book called *Reading, The Success Formula,* and watched as the man she had once loved transcended anything of which she had ever dreamed during their life together.

If Arnold was suffering as a result of his breakup with Barbara, as he left California in April 1975 for Birmingham, Alabama, and the set of *Stay Hungry,* he didn't show it. Armed with Eric Morris's acting techniques, he was also conscious that Rafelson had done all in his power to make Arnold's debut a success. Arnold's part called for him to play the fiddle, and Bob Rafelson, knowing that Arnold would be miming to the music, had arranged lessons for him with Byron Berline, a fiddle player with his own bluegrass group who had recorded with such luminaries as Linda Ronstadt, Bob Dylan, and the Rolling Stones.

According to Berline, "Arnold took to miming the fiddle right away, learning the moves so well that during filming one of the old-timers watching him in Alabama turned around and said, 'That big ole boy can really play the fiddle'—even though he wasn't really playing at all!"

Making friends with Berline, Arnold went to bluegrass shows, taking with him Aurelia, who was in America on a visit. He also told the thirty-one-year-old Berline that he would be perfect for one of the *Stay Hungry* parts. True to his word, Arnold arranged a meeting between Berline and Rafelson. But when he arrived on the set, Berline was greeted by gales of laughter. The part for which Arnold had recommended him was that of a seventy-year-old man. One thing, however, led to another, with the meeting resulting in Byron's eventually doing the *Stay Hungry* music.

Arnold's character, Joe Santo, was a bodybuilder, a Mr. Austria who had come to Birmingham to compete in a contest. There he meets Mary Tate, played by Sally Field, an attractive woman who runs the gym where he trains. He also makes friends with a southern aristocrat played by Jeff Bridges. The eternal triangle that develops culminates in Arnold's losing Field to Bridges.

Arnold enthused, "I tapped a new well I had never tapped before. When Sally Field holds you, looks into your eyes and hugs you one last time before she leaves, you believe this, and it shows in your face. You don't have to act, you only have to be yourself."

Arnold soon discovered that learning to be an actor wasn't that simple. An old friend who worked on *Stay Hungry* as an extra revealed, "Arnold told me that he was afraid of acting. But he said that, at the same time, in confronting his fear and controlling it he was more intense and better. In bodybuilding he was one hundred percent comfortable. Now, in acting, he was a novice. He said he felt like an adult who had gone back to being a child. Suddenly everybody had to tell him what to do. Suddenly he was out of control. And he was no longer king."

9
Filming *Pumping Iron* and Retirement

ARNOLD'S FILM CAREER HAD JUST BEGUN. But he knew success was only a matter of time. Before filming started, friends had advised him to make sure he was billed as Arnold Strong, not Arnold Schwarzenegger. He refused, telling them, "Someday the world is going to know who I am—just by hearing my first name. Arnold." Then he observed that if his name was hard to remember, it should prove even harder to forget.

His performance held promise, with Rafelson calling Morris one day from the set and telling him that he had done wonders with Arnold, that Arnold was terrific.

Barbara visited him in Birmingham, but it was clear that the relationship was over. He would remain footloose and fancy-free until July 1977, dallying with all the many females available for his pleasure. He avoided involvement, commenting, "Y'know, the more your mind is complex, the less you can focus on sex. Many times, while I was getting laid, in my head I was doing a business deal."

Once filming of *Stay Hungry* was completed, Arnold returned to Los Angeles where, in anticipation of his next role, in *Pumping Iron*, he continued his acting lessons with Eric Morris. Sometimes he took part in group sessions, which, according to Morris, involved a certain amount of self-disclosure. Once he stood up in front of the class and ruefully declared, "I can't get an agent. The agents in this town say I've got too big a body, too heavy an accent, and they don't like my name. I can't get an agent."

Aware that in *Pumping Iron* he had found a vehicle

127

through which to project his star quality, Arnold began to set his intensely focused sights on an acting career, studying those he hoped one day to emulate—performers, as opposed to conventional actors. Discarding Reg Park as a role model, he turned to Elvis Presley, whose personality he admired, observing his stage presence in live performances whenever possible. He also studied Muhammad Ali and read Ali's biography by Wilfred Sheed.

Coincidentally, Butler and Gaines had flown to Paris and over a three-day period filmed Serge Nubret on his home ground. They asked him if they could use the footage in *Pumping Iron* for a fee of $1,000, telling him that they planned to present him as an Ali-style adversary, pitting him against Arnold. Nubret scuttled those plans by refusing to take a salary and demanding instead the French distribution rights to *Pumping Iron* in exchange for using the footage of him in the film. Butler and Gaines wouldn't agree to his demands and altered their original concept.

Shooting was under way by June 1975, Butler and Gaines having found a co-producer, a San Francisco cinema owner named Jerome Gary. From June until November 1975, in an attempt to portray bodybuilding as a self-contained universe and to explore the dream of physical perfection and the agonies bodybuilders go through to attain it, over a hundred hours of film were shot. The climax of the film was centered around the Mr. Olympia contest, scheduled to take place in Pretoria, South Africa, on November 8th.

Arnold once said, "I wanted every single person who touched a weight to equate the feeling of the barbell with my name." By 1975, on the eve of the Olympia in which Arnold was to defend the title he had already won five times, that was how it was. His supremacy is evident upon leafing through a 1975 issue of Weider's *Muscle Builder*. Naturally he is on the cover, in three different poses. On the inside cover he is featured (along with Larry Scott, Franco Columbu, and Ken Waller) in an advertisement for a Joe Weider course. On page 4 he is seen advertising "Joe

Weider's 'Arnold's super-arm blaster' and kambered kurling bar."

Page 58 features an article, written by Franco, on the filming of *Stay Hungry*, including an interview with Arnold. On page 60 his picture appears again in connection with an advertisement for Weider's "kambered kurling bar." On page 62 there is another advertisement, complete with photo, for Arnold's "super-arm blaster." On page 65 Arnold is found advertising Joe Weider's "strong arm bracelets"—complete with the word *power* engraved on the links. The ad, which suggests that two bracelets should be purchased, one per arm, also asks the question, "Are you man enough to wear them?"

On page 67 a subscription pitch naturally features Arnold's pictures. Page 70 finds Arnold, in living color, advertising Weider's protein supplements. Again, on page 74, Arnold is pictured advertising Weider's "wildcat" protein powerizers. On page 78 Arnold is seen advertising Weider's "powerful weight-supporting belt." Bodybuilders wishing to buy the product are invited to send in an order form that begins with the words "Dear Joe: I'm tired of coasting and waisting [sic] work-out time—I want to start blasting up my upper body with heavier weights like Arnold does! Enclosed is $19.95 as full payment."

On page 80 Arnold advertises Weider's "New fitness jogger," on page 81 the Weider training belts and competition belts, and on page 85, posed with a blond female model, Arnold proclaims, "I'm wearing 'The Panther' suit and I'm not even fat yet!" This time Arnold is selling " 'The Panther' Slimming Suit, for the Man Who Doesn't Want to Be Alone and Remain a 'Fat Cat.' " The rest of the magazine contains yet more Arnold—Arnold advertising a formula for rapid weight gain, flab fighters (special suits à la Panther), and last, but not least, Arnold's own training courses, which promise "Arnold's Shortcuts to Massive Muscularity" and offer readers the chance of yet further joys: "Buy the complete set and I will autograph in ink The Arnold Album." Signed A.S.

The same issue also features a column entitled "Ask

the Champ," in which Arnold, in answer to a letter from a reader desperate for his help, announces his new body-building seminars, explaining, "I believe that I must personally talk with the trainee who needs help." The seminars, he continues, will be made up of no more than thirty-five bodybuilders and will take place over two days. Arnold's seminars, sometimes costing thousands of dollars for a four-day session, would become another important ingredient in his booming financial empire. And if in 1975 bodybuilding really was a self-contained universe, Arnold, backed by the vast propaganda machine of Joe Weider, was definitely its master.

Apart from holding seminars, Arnold also made personal appearances, guest posing at contests all over the country. On October 18, 1975, just a few weeks before the Olympia, he was guest star at the Mr. Pacific Coast and Mr. San Francisco Muscle Show at the California Hall in San Francisco. Admission was $5 and two thousand people bought tickets. The following report of the contest captures the allure and the power, the omnipotence and the sway that Arnold held over his universe of fans:

> The emcee, Jimmy Payne, a Mr. America from 1950, spurred them on through the evening by shouting, "The more you use your body, the better it's worth!" . . . "He's backstage, pumping up," Denny Holmes told them. . . . The roof should have caved in at that point. The theme from "Exodus" exploded from the sound system . . . ARNOLD-ARNOLD-ARNOLD! the crowd screamed. Holmes clutched the mike, looking stage right. "He's coming! He's coming down the steps now. Here he comes! Ladies and gentlemen, the biggest man in bodybuilding, probably the greatest ever to come into the world of bodybuilding, our Muhammad Ali of bodybuilding, MISTER ARNOLD SCHWARZENEGGER!" The Austrian Oak went

through his posing. Women wept. Men openly cov-
eted.

Yet with all that, Arnold, the adventurer, Arnold, the
brave, was moving on, primed for another challenge. His
audience was growing; *Pumping Iron* was on the horizon.
A film career was the next step in his master plan. But
before he stormed the silver screen, he had the 1975 Olympia ahead of him. For the first time, partly as a result of
Arnold's influence, the contest was being held in South
Africa. He had made friends with Sports Minister Piet
Koornhof's son, who subsequently introduced him to his
father. Koornhof confided that his main ambition was to
hold a Mr. Olympia contest in South Africa. Money was no
object. Arnold promised to discuss the proposition with
Ben Weider.

A discussion with Koornhof, Weider, and Mrs. Lolly
Bester, secretary of the South African Amateur Body Building Union, followed, after which Weider received a letter
from Koornhof assuring him that all athletes, regardless of
race, would be received on an equal basis and treated as
friends. Many bodybuilders were surprised that the IFBB,
whose official line was to condemn racism, was holding its
most important event in South Africa. Yet Serge Nubret,
himself black, had traveled to South Africa to spend a week
as Koornhof's guest to assess the racial implications of
holding the Olympia there. After a week of being wined
and dined in Pretoria restaurants where apartheid restric-
tions had been miraculously lifted for his benefit, Nubret
concluded that the 1975 Olympia should, indeed, be held in
South Africa.

The participants in the 1975 Olympia traveled to
South Africa on South African Airways, stayed at the first-
class, five-star Burgers Park Hotel in Pretoria, and were
also given a chance to visit the famous Kruger National
Park Game Reserve. The government paid all expenses.

Two days before the contest, black bodybuilder Robby
Robinson, while enjoying the South African sunshine with

his fellow white bodybuilders, was thrown out of a public
park by a Pretoria policeman who was apparently unaware
that apartheid had been temporarily suspended. And although the *Pumping Iron* crew wasn't on hand to record
the Robinson episode, it did document the subsequent
Olympia contest in full.

In fact the *Pumping Iron* cameras caught every nuance
of the backstage and precontest action. Onstage they recorded Arnold's predictable victory, first over Serge Nubret
and Lou Ferrigno and then over Franco Columbu, winner
of the under-two hundred pounds category. Reg Park, a
ghost from Arnold's past, the man with whom it all began,
presented him with the trophy. Then there was a further,
surprise development. With the *Pumping Iron* cameras
rolling, filming the historic moment for posterity, Arnold,
in an almost deadpan fashion, announced that he would
no longer compete, though the sport had been a beautiful
experience for him and that he would never stop bodybuilding. He had now officially retired. He was twenty-
eight years old. The bodybuilding world would never see
his like again.

From South Africa, Arnold visited his mother in Graz,
going by way of Vienna. Christmas found him driving a
metallic silver Mercedes 450SE, complete with black fur
seats, a gift from health club promoters in Vienna. The
retired hero was finding himself the lucky recipient of
many gifts from adoring fans and sharp businessmen hoping to attract his attention. The gifts, ranging from alarm
clocks to bed sheets, tape recorders, statues, and even
checks, poured in from all over America. So did the fan
letters, many from men and women begging to be allowed
the opportunity to do unspeakable things to his hallowed
body.

The first part of 1976 was, in essence, a waiting game
for him. The release of *Pumping Iron* had been delayed for
another year, and it was not projected to be released before
January 1977. And although *Stay Hungry* was scheduled to

open in June 1976, Arnold was aware that his role was not
a major one and would probably not garner him the attention that he expected to receive from *Pumping Iron*. Not
that he was lacking the spotlight. On February 26, 1976, he
demonstrated his star quality at New York's Whitney Museum of Art, along with two other bodybuilders, who took
part in a seminar entitled "The Articulate Muscle: The
Male Body in Art." The exhibition attracted a standing-
room-only crowd of twenty-five hundred, most of them
clamoring to see Arnold. Suddenly he appeared, posing on
a revolving platform, while Candice Bergen, on assignment
for the "Today" show, photographed the event. When asked
how he felt about being reduced to a sex symbol, Arnold
admitted, "I'm in heaven. I feel like a king."

Far from abdicating his throne, he had only expanded
his kingdom, adding to it his new partnership with Jim
Lorimer, with whom, as he had promised five years before,
he was promoting the 1976 Olympia. Aware that he was
finally poised on the threshold of cinematic stardom, Arnold worked hard on his image. George Butler had initially
found Arnold to be touchingly unsophisticated. "There
were just a lot of things he didn't know," Butler recalls.
"He didn't know how to dress. How to order from a menu
and stuff like that." Arnold asked Butler's advice on what
hotel to stay at when he was in New York and, on hearing
that Butler favored the Algonquin, promptly made a reser-
vation for himself there, along with eighty other bodybuilders, who were in the Big Apple for an event.

Clothes had always been a problem for him. His suits
had to be custom-made, as did his size 54 short-sleeved
cotton shirts and his size 38 jeans, which, at $150 a pair,
came from Nudies in Hollywood. His shoes, size 12, he
says, were not a problem. But, eschewing the tight T-shirt
look so beloved of the average muscle man, he sought the
services of New York tailor Morty Sills. Ushering Arnold
into the fitting room in his East 53rd Street atelier, Sills
transformed the outsized king of bodybuilding into a fashion plate, dressing him in conservative clothes and preppy

looks. The casual look appealed to Arnold, who had also
developed a fondness for cowboy boots and western wear as
well as a taste for country-and-western music.

All of his preparations for the future hadn't, however,
obliterated his sense of humor. He and Frank Zane went to
Mexico City together to do a posing exhibition. But everything went wrong. No one was there to pick them up, and
they had to wait at the airport for six hours. There they
were accosted by a Hare Krishna who came up to Arnold
and said, "I'd like to give you this book." It was the Bha-
gavad Gita in Spanish. Taking the book, Arnold said,
"Thank you very much. I really appreciate it." The man
said, "How about giving me some money now?" And Arnold said, "No, you gave me this book as a gift, and I am
going to keep it." Then he and Frank Zane walked away,
with the irate Hare Krishna in hot pursuit. Later, in Mexico City, Arnold bought two marble bookends for the book.

In June *Stay Hungry* was released, and although the
film didn't open to much critical acclaim, Arnold emerged
relatively unscathed and was even nominated for the Hollywood Golden Globe Award for the most promising newcomer of 1976. A critic would later write that he "came
across as a gentle giant, large and cumbersome, always
having to be careful not to step on anybody. He even had
some funny lines which he delivered ably, and you ended
up liking him in an uneasy kind of way, as you might a
panther that didn't kill you after all."

In 1976, too, he posed for famed photographer Francesco Scavullo—who shot photos of him in the nude for a
Cosmopolitan centerfold. Scavullo observed, "He was nude
and very charming and very cooperative and very easy to
photograph. Then he changed his mind and decided he
didn't want the photos published. I put them in a bank and
gave a guarantee that I would never publish them."

At first sight it seemed that Arnold was not, at that
stage, taking any chances. But that wasn't true. According
to Kurt Marnul and Karl Kainrath, who were at the Montreal Mr. Universe contest with him, after a particularly

fun-filled evening Marnul got a 2:00 A.M. call from Arnold, begging him to come downstairs and help him. Apparently Arnold was in bed with one of Weider's employees, a girl who adored him and was totally acquiescent to any demands he might make of her. But, as he told Marnul, "I can't get it up. You have to come down and save the honor of Austria." Marnul eagerly complied, but, amid laughter from Arnold, found that he also was unable to perform. Luckily, a third Austrian friend of Arnold's stepped in, saving the day and, in the bargain, the honor of Austria.

Arnold saw his old friends from Austria in a more conventional context later in the year when he invited fifteen of them, including his childhood playmate Franz Hormann, out to dinner in Vienna. Now a movie star, he was there to promote the Austrian release of *Stay Hungry*, but he remembered them all and always would—the farmers' sons, the firemen's sons, the clerical workers, and the peasants whose Austrian dialect reminded Arnold of the countryside and the cow dung he had worked so hard to escape. In Arnold's often tender heart, there remained room for everyone.

Now Arnold was a businessman, launching his career on September 18th by producing the Mr. Olympia contest in Columbus. The contest, held at the 3,944-seat Veterans Memorial Auditorium, was a sellout at $20 a ticket. As one journalist noted at the time, "It was as if a retiring Miss America had turned around and hired the band, the hall and Bert Parks." His income, by then, was over $200,000 a year, and he also owned an apartment building at 1108 19th Street in Santa Monica, where he lived in one of the units.

Stay Hungry opened in England on October 3rd. Before the premiere Arnold gave an interview at his home in California to the prestigious *Sunday Times* of London. His apartment, they noted, was furnished with pieces made from gnarled timber that had once held up the local pier. Arnold offered the reporter coffee in a handmade mug the size of a vase. The apartment, a duplex, housed his collection of guns and pictures of himself with Aurelia. "I was born to be a leader," he confided to the *Sunday Times* reporter, and revealed that as a boy he had dreamed of either becoming famous or becoming a dictator or a savior "like Jesus." In the apartment, too, was a plaque bearing the legend "Without bodybuilding there's no NATION BUILDING."

By the end of 1976 it was obvious that Arnold had, indeed, built himself, if not a nation, certainly a personal empire, where he ruled unchallenged. In 1977 the world would see him, in *Pumping Iron*, playing his greatest role yet, one he had been preparing for throughout his entire life—that of Arnold Schwarzenegger.

10
Stallone, *Pumping Iron,* and Sue Moray

THE HOLLYWOOD GOLDEN GLOBE AWARDS, at the beginning of January 1977, were timed fortuitously, just days before the long-awaited opening of *Pumping Iron*. Sponsored by the Hollywood Foreign Press, the thirty-fourth Annual Golden Globe ceremony was held at the Beverly Hills Hilton. Among the winners were Jessica Lange (best female acting debut in a motion picture, *King Kong*), Laurence Olivier (*Marathon Man*), Faye Dunaway (*Network*), Barbra Streisand (*A Star Is Born*), and Arnold Schwarzenegger (best acting debut, *Stay Hungry*). But the man of the hour, although he didn't win the best actor award (which went to Peter Finch for *Network*), was Sylvester Stallone, whose *Rocky* won the award for best motion picture.

That night it was clear that Stallone was the sensation and Arnold merely the newcomer to films. Yet the two men were, in many ways, strikingly similar. Both were the sons of dominant fathers who had driven them to strive for fame and fortune. Stallone's father, Frank, known for his violent temper and his prowess with polo ponies, was also something of a ladies' man. Like Gustav with Arnold, he was a demanding father, never satisfied with his son's achievements, always pressing for more.

Stallone's mother, Jacqueline, the daughter of a Washington-based attorney, was a glitteringly beautiful show girl. An ex–"Long Stemmed Rose" in Billy Rose's legendary Diamond Horseshoe Club, she was willful, intelligent, and overflowed with charisma. Yet like the very different,

137

far more conventional Aurelia Schwarzenegger, she too
experienced marital difficulties while Sylvester was young,
finally divorcing Frank Stallone. All in all, both Arnold
and Sylvester grew up in stormy homes, with tyrannical
fathers who did their best to dominate them and yet, by
putting iron into their respective souls, set the stage for
their overwhelming ambition to succeed.

Both men had wild and lusty youths and pushed their
bodies to the limit, in the process making a great number
of sexual conquests. They were both unconventional and
iconoclastic, strong-willed and rebellious. Each of them
had, in his own way, been inspired by Muhammad Ali.
Arnold, with his brilliant capacity for self-promotion, had
modeled his image on Ali—like him, constantly proclaiming to the media that he was "the greatest." Stallone, as an
out-of-work actor, had seen the Ali-Wepner fight in which
the underdog Chuck Wepner—a latter-day David—went the
distance with Ali/Goliath. Inspired, Stallone rushed home
and wrote *Rocky* in three-and-a-half days.

All through 1976 the American media had been saturated with the romantic rags-to-riches story of how Stallone
was swept from the back streets of New York to Hollywood
and a gutsy confrontation with big-time moguls who had
wanted to buy his script but discard Stallone himself. Determined to star in *Rocky*, Stallone—broke and on the
verge of starvation—turned down $300,000, held his
ground, and finally won the part of Rocky. The story of
Rocky Balboa soon became inseparable from that of Stallone, merging within the mind of the great American
public, capturing the imagination of the country.

Stallone's astounding success could not have gone unnoticed by Arnold. Now, as flashbulbs exploded, Arnold
was meeting the toast of Hollywood in person, a man who
was only one year older than he was, yet who had not only
scripted but had also starred in his own film. As they
exchanged glances it must have galled Arnold that Stallone, who had pumped iron and had also made physical
fitness an integral part of his life, was now being pro-

claimed the best. However powerful Arnold was in body-building, however auspicious his film debut, in the movie industry, next to Sylvester Stallone he was nothing—a nobody. It is highly likely, given Arnold's competitive personality, that at this, their first meeting, he resolved that one day in the future he would dethrone Stallone.

There was no time for conversation that night at the Beverly Hills Hilton. But they had met, and the extraordinary relationship between the world's most famous muscle men had begun. They were not then aware that they had a great deal in common, far beyond the platitudes spewed out by their respective studio bios. But fate had put them on a collision course. Within nine years Sylvester Stallone and Arnold Schwarzenegger would share an experience that would initially galvanize and then almost destroy them both.

Pumping Iron opened at New York's Plaza Theatre on January 18, 1977. Five hundred bodybuilding fans as well as Carly Simon, James Taylor, Carroll Baker, and Tom Wolfe turned up for the invitation-only premiere. And although the film was billed as a documentary study of bodybuilding, there was no question whatever that it was, in reality, a showcase for Arnold Schwarzenegger.

The film begins with Arnold and Franco taking ballet lessons from dancer Marianne Claire. As she explains a particular move, we see Arnold's concentration, his eagerness to learn reflected on his face. Later the film cuts to Gold's Gym, where Arnold is "working the room," shaking hands, patting backs, already the consummate politician.

It is 101 days before the 1975 Mr. Olympia and Mr. Universe contests in South Africa. We are given Arnold's age, twenty-eight, and his height, six foot two, and weight, 240 pounds. We see him examining himself in the mirror, coolly, without passion. In these early scenes he is low-key, patiently explaining bodybuilding to his audience.

Then the film cuts away from the gym to Arnold alone, lounging back in a chair, relaxed and in total com-

mand. Tongue in cheek, in a remark that—given that it is
1977, pre-AIDS America, and right in the middle of the
sexual revolution—is perfectly placed, he says of pumping
iron, "It is as satisfying to me as coming is—you know, as
having sex with a woman and coming. So can you believe
how much I am in heaven? I am like getting the feeling of
coming in the gym. I'm getting the feeling of coming at
home. I'm getting the feeling of coming backstage when I
pump up. When I pose out in front of five thousand people—I get the same feeling. So I'm coming day and night."
He leans back, luxuriantly, having made his point: he's
king. And what's more, he isn't gay either.

We next see Arnold at a federal prison in Terminal
Island, California, where he often makes charity appearances. Standing surrounded by a crowd of male and female
prisoners, a female inmate helps him as he peels off his
shirt like any stripper might. He kisses the girl as wolf
whistles echo all around him and then almost apologizes
for doing it (rather like a small boy who is insinuating that
"girls are soppy").

Another prisoner, this time male, calls out, asking for
a kiss. Arnold smiles, pauses for effect, then raises an
eyebrow, saying that he knows about male prisoners, and
jokes that he'll give him a kiss. He lifts his arms in triumph, in perfect control of the situation.

Later we see Arnold in a serious and paternalistic role,
helping a young bodybuilder pose. Next there is a sequence
on bodybuilder Mike Katz in which Katz emerges as an
obvious nonthreat to Arnold. The film will go on to focus
on Lou Ferrigno and Franco Columbu, emphasizing their
weaknesses, lingering on the grimaces they make when
working out, their maliciousness, their lack of star quality.
Basically all the participants in *Pumping Iron*, with the
exception of Arnold, are diminished. Indeed, if Arnold had
hired the top PR firm of Rogers and Cowan and invested
$1 million to have a film made promoting him, they prob-
ably couldn't have improved on *Pumping Iron*.

The next sequence features Arnold in a photo session,

posing as professionally as any *Vogue* model. He then tells his life story—or rather an encapsulated version of it—in voice-over narration, culminating in Arnold's earnestly confiding his belief that his destiny always lay in America and that he had dreamed of coming to America since the age of ten.

Joe Weider appears for a brief moment, directing Arnold and several bathing beauties during a photo session. Next there is a sequence of shots (in many ways reminiscent of Stallone as Rocky on the steps of the art museum in Philadelphia) of Arnold posing triumphantly on a mountain, to the sound of an anthemlike chorus, "Everybody Wants to Live Forever." Arnold's image is that of a god enshrined on Mount Olympus.

Then, in sharp contrast, the film cuts to the suburban scene of Lou Ferrigno having breakfast with his family. The message is clear: Arnold is triumphant on the mountaintop, while poor Ferrigno is having breakfast in Brooklyn. We have already heard the story of how Arnold, at only ten, courageously planned to come to America; now we are confronted with the spectacle of poor hard-of-hearing Lou still living at home at twenty-four.

The film sets Lou up in the role of child. His father, Matty, embarrassing in his zeal, tells the story of how he took Lou to see Arnold's first American show and then went backstage with him and watched Lou being spellbound by Arnold, then vowing to become Mr. Olympia.

Matty Ferrigno, an ex-cop, is intensely involved in a quest that anyone who has seen the first part of the film knows is useless. To emphasize that point the film cuts to Arnold emerging from the sea, the picture of health and supremacy. Faking sleep on the beach, he virtually ignores a bodybuilder who tells him that he is about to go to New York to see Lou. Does Arnold have any messages for him? Smiling, like a well-brought-up little boy, Arnold sends greetings to Louis and his father and comments that Louis needs a lot of help. And then he winks—a wink that is both innocent and nonchalant, sweet and simultaneously malicious, and that would win him the hearts of his audience.

The sequence switches from Lou agonizing over his training to Arnold training, showing grace under pressure, studied, smooth, like a well-oiled machine. Then there is more of Lou, with his father getting increasingly desperate as the Olympia gets closer. Back at Gold's, Arnold is seen lackadaisically chewing gum. Then he explains his training philosophy, stressing his endurance and commitment, adding that even when he faints or throws up it's worth it.

By this point in the film Arnold has been established as sexy, patriotic, heterosexual, paternalistic, self-confident, and now macho and dedicated. At this late stage Franco is profiled in a sequence that evokes the circus strongman acts of another, prebodybuilding era, with Franco lifting up a car, then blowing up a hot water bottle until it bursts. Cut to Arnold helping Franco with his training.

Later, sitting back in his chair, exuding relaxation, Arnold says that if Lou arrives at the contest in good shape Arnold will spend the night with him. He will confuse him by booking them into a hotel room together. Louis, says Arnold, will never forget that night. He will emerge from it confused and set to lose the contest. Arnold will convince him of that. All in all, boasts Arnold, Lou's condition is irrelevant, for his own tactics will overcome everything.

Then he is asked about his other adversary in the Olympia, his best friend, Franco. In the future Arnold would often maintain that *Pumping Iron* was scripted, that much of the dialogue was created by Butler and Gaines. Gaines's previously cited comments regarding the admiration of Hitler that Arnold professed in the original uncut version of *Pumping Iron* contradict this. Whatever the case, Franco was devastated by Arnold's comment that he, Franco, was a mere child, a child who would ask Arnold for advice. And, Arnold confided to the camera, his advice would naturally be wrong.

Cut to South Africa, where Arnold is interviewed by a female reporter who tentatively asks him to describe his special woman. Reinforcing his image as Tom Jones, Henry Fielding's picaresque hero who romps from bed to bed, Arnold replies that he likes every kind of woman, just so long as she has personality and charm.

Next, in a poolside sequence, Arnold laughingly tells the story of the practical joke he played on "Power Mike," the Munich bodybuilder whom he told to scream while posing. As he tells the story, he is endearingly funny, winningly sly, mockingly charming. It is virtually impossible not to like him.

On the day of the contest Arnold is seen eating breakfast with the Ferrignos. He starts out gently patronizing the entire family. Then, switching to another tack, telling Lou he looks worried, he adds sympathetically that the contest timing was wrong for Lou, that he needed another month and might as well retire, never having been Mr. Olympia. Then, with a radiant smile, he says he has already informed his mother that he has won the Mr. Olympia title. His charm and chutzpah are breathtaking.

Later he tells the story about how he didn't go to his father's funeral because he was in training. He is smooth, almost penitent, confessing his sins, yet citing them as evidence of his dedication, his machismo.

After he is voted Mr. Olympia, the film cuts to an ecstatic Arnold dressed in a T-shirt emblazoned with the words ARNOLD IS NUMERO UNO. He is smoking something that appears to be grass.

Pumping Iron doesn't finish with Arnold's victory, though. It rams home the message of his immense superiority and brilliance at manipulation with a final scene on the airport bus, as Arnold magnanimously informs Lou that, now that he has beaten him, he will come to his house to eat spaghetti, meatballs, and strudel. After which he tells Lou that Lou's mother is going to fix him, Arnold, up with Lou's sister. A bemused Lou smiles, grateful for the attention. The audience, though, understands Arnold's fi-

nal coup de grace; he isn't satisfied with just screwing
Lou—Lou's sister is next on his agenda.

The audience loved Arnold. So would America. He
was a charmer, a champion, an endearingly arrogant
winner, and, above all, a self-parodying villain who se-
duced victims and audiences alike.

Just a few days after the *Pumping Iron* premiere,
Jimmy Carter was sworn in as president of the United
States, ushering in a gentler, kinder, and more puritanical
America. In theory, at least. Interestingly, however, the
media would fail to mirror the new churchgoing puritan-
ism of the Carter era, making a cult hero first out of Arnold, who had proclaimed that his father's funeral was less
important than the drumbeat of his own ambition, then
out of a certain Mr. J. R. Ewing.

"Dallas" would premiere on April 2, 1978, fifteen
months after *Pumping Iron* unleashed Arnold, the lovable
con man, the ruthless winner, on the American psyche.
And, in a way, Arnold, through first the film, then his talk
show appearances, was a precursor to J. R. Ewing. Eleven
years after the program first aired, actor Larry Hagman,
who played J.R., wrote that his fictional character served as
a role model for Americans: "He realizes there are no hard-
and-fast rules, that it is a jungle out there and that the weak
perish. It is not corruption in which J.R. is engaged; that's
not what they call it anymore. It's called 'getting things
done.' J.R. makes up his own laws as he goes along; whatever works—and it usually does." Men and women alike
admired J.R.'s power and ability to get away with anything. And as Larry Hagman says of the lovable villain he
created, "J.R. is the man America secretly emulates."

So, too, it seemed, was Arnold Schwarzenegger, and
the film critics loved him. Nik Cohn, in *New York* magazine, wrote, "[Schwarzenegger] lights up the film like neon
every time he comes on-screen. . . . His physical power is
balanced by great humor, prodigious charm, that same

mixture of sweetness and sass, mock arrogance and mock innocence, that Ali once possessed."

The Soho Weekly remarked, "[Arnold Schwarzenegger's] charm and wit, combined with a kind of infernal arrogance, are irresistible." Richard Schickel in *Time* magazine proclaimed that if the movie took off, Arnold could become "a multi-media presence of some force," adding, "A cool, shrewd and boyish charmer, he exudes the easy confidence of a man who has always known he will be a star of some kind. . . . Arnold has a gift that cannot be acquired no matter how hard an athlete trains, no matter how many pep talks—replete with references to Michelangelo's sculpture—he absorbs. It is, of course, the gift of charisma, something capable of magically compelling his opponent's collapse and the judges' favorable votes."

On February 19th, as the film was due to be released in Washington, *Washington Post* critic Gary Arnold's judgment of Arnold was prophetic: "He carries that phenomenal physique so nonchalantly that one can't help feeling charmed and reassured. . . . It is difficult to foresee what direction Schwarzenegger's movie career might take. . . . One would need to devise a format that accommodated Schwarzenegger's obvious intelligence and wittiness. It might be fun if he and Woody Allen could be brought together on some pretext, perhaps as devastating ladies' men, illustrating utterly contrasting styles of sexiness."

If one substitutes Danny DeVito for Woody Allen, Gary Arnold's comments prefigure Arnold's hit movie *Twins*.

Top New York PR man Bobby Zarem was employed to promote *Pumping Iron*. His masterly campaign naturally was centered around Arnold. And its success is reflected by the comments of British film critic Alexander Walker: "This week, all New York really cares about is Arnold Schwarzenegger. He's everywhere—in all the papers and magazines, all the gossip columns. No dinner is complete without a new, mouthwatering detail about Arnold. In fact, if Robert Redford were to walk into the same room as Schwarzenegger, he would probably be in analysis for years recovering from the shock to his ego."

Suddenly he was the darling of high society, filmed for CBS's "Who's Who" program while posing for Jamie Wyeth, feted at Elaine's, and admired by Diana Vreeland herself, who said of Arnold, "Charming, he's simply charming." Fiat heiress Delphina Ratazzi threw a party for him, attended by Charlotte Curtis, Andy Warhol, Scavullo, and Arnold's future aunts by marriage, Pat Lawford and Jacqueline Kennedy Onassis. According to Arnold's publicist, Jackie begged to be allowed to edit Arnold's next book after *Arnold: The Education of a Bodybuilder,* which was due to be published in 1977.

Aurelia, naturally, had flown in from Austria for the premiere, armed with the English sentence "I am Arnold's mother." Not that she needed much else, for fortune was certainly smiling on her and her son; Arnold was staying at the Park Lane Hotel, carried only $100 bills, and both Mercedes and BMW offered him free cars. Austrian Airlines even volunteered to fly Arnold and fifty of his closest friends to Austria for a skiing holiday. The boy from Thal who could afford to eat meat only on Sundays was now the toast of New York, wined and dined at the famous "21." The boy who had wanted to be somebody now definitely was. And for Arnold, a dreamer whose dreams had come true, the effect was intoxicating.

Arnold had become an accomplished TV performer. On the "Today" show, Barbara Walters had invited only Butler and Gaines to guest on the show and reportedly was dismayed when they brought Arnold with them. According to George Butler, Barbara said quite pointedly that she wished they hadn't brought the hulk along. Butler recounts what happened next: "We sat down, and she was hostile to Arnold, and the first question she asked was 'Do you take steroids?' She expected him to say no, but instead Arnold eloquently explained that to be a champion one couldn't rely on steroids, but that, yes, he did take them." Then Arnold offered Walters his arm, which she grabbed, squealing, "It's soft." According to Butler, "From that moment on, Arnold had her in the palm of his hand. It was as if she felt his humanity. That's the kind of gesture he's capable of. His spontaneity is so acute—a real gift; that's why he's so good."

Respected columnist Liz Smith too was not immune to the Schwarzenegger charm. At lunch with Arnold she felt his arm and later wrote, "It was one of my proudest moments in journalism."

Butler and Gaines were also proud of the new star they had helped create, with Gaines later conceding, "Arnold is like the Matterhorn—we didn't discover him, we just noticed him first. Arnold already knew he was going to be famous. It was in the way he walked, the way he held himself. . . . Mentally and spiritually, he was one of the most acquisitive people I'd ever met."

His fans were definitely eager, as it were, to acquire him. Once, during a Detroit promotion, a woman asked Arnold to take off his shirt. He retorted that he would take his shirt off if she would take off hers. She did. Admitted Arnold, "I used that line a lot, but that's the last time."

He remained in the limelight right through the spring of 1977. In May he flew to Vienna, where he planned to screen *Pumping Iron* for his friends, gym owner Bernd Zimmermann and his wife, Erika, a former Miss Austria who shared her birthday with Arnold. At first the film company didn't want to lend him a print of the film. Always the master strategist, Arnold retaliated with the threat that he would boycott the upcoming Cannes Film Festival, where he was scheduled to appear at a *Pumping Iron* screening. The film company sent him the print.

He and Bernd and Erika celebrated at the Hauermandl in Grinzing, on the outskirts of Vienna, where they ate Leberknödel soup, Wiener schnitzel, and strudel. In Vienna, at the Intercontinental Hotel, he sat on the jury at the Mr. Austria contest.

Next it was on to the Cannes Film Festival, where he assured film critic Alexander Walker, "No Tarzan roles for me. The ape-man really wasn't a muscle man, you know. Anyhow, I want roles in films that express more emotion than swinging around the branches like monkeys."

By July 1977 the spotlight had begun to dim slightly. It was time for Arnold to turn his attention to his private life. Barbara Outland had been Arnold's first love, a woman who had catered to the side of him that sought a mother. His next love, Sue Moray, in contrast, appealed to other instincts, satisfying the side of Arnold that needed excitement, drama, and, of course, a great deal of sex. Twelve years later, now a redhead, married, and with a baby daughter, Sue is outspoken and attractive, with cornflower-blue eyes and a good figure.

They met on Venice Beach in July 1977. Then a blond, Sue, an athletic twenty-five-year-old, was on roller skates. It was, she says, "lust at first sight." She was with a girlfriend. Both had seen *Pumping Iron* and recognized Arnold immediately. They put on a roller-skating show for him and began flirting, trying to get his attention. Arnold had an entourage of guys with him, and he started flirting with Sue, simultaneously keeping an eye open for the other pretty girls strolling along the beach. In the end Sue flirtatiously announced, "You are really a whore, Arnold, a beach whore." Surprised for a moment, he countered, "I am not a whore; a whore is a prostitute."

"A whore doesn't do it for money," said Sue, "a prostitute does." Decisively seizing the moment, Arnold said, "I think you should come over to my house. I have a dictionary, and we can look it up in that." Sue refused and instead went to look up the definitions at a local bookstore. Then she came back and informed Arnold that he had, in actual fact, been right. Arnold liked that.

He asked for her phone number, writing it in a little book. She noticed that he wrote "roller skates" next to her

The house at 145 Thal-Linak where Arnold grew up. *(Stephen Karten)*

Arnold's boyhood school in Thal, which has been rebuilt since his days there. *(Stephen Karten)*

Gustav Schwarzenegger (second from the left), resplendent in his
police chief's uniform—the one that young Arnold loved to try on.

Gustav leading the Graz Gendarmerie Musik. (*Courtesy of Willi
Kalcher/Graz Gendarmerie Musik*)

Above: Arnold in 1963 with Kurt Marnul, the man who discovered him but whom Arnold soon eclipsed. *(Courtesy of Kurt Marnul)*

At right: The teenage Arnold competing in his first contest at the Steirer Hof hotel in Graz, flexing for the edification of the young ladies. *(Stefan Amsüss)*

The victor at the 1967 Mr. Universe contest. Arnold was the youngest
Mr. Universe in history. *(Arax-Hankey)*

At right: Mr. Universe, 1969.
(Arax-Hankey)
Below: Arnold tangling with his
number-one bodybuilding
nemesis, Sergio Oliva, in 1972.
(Benno Dahmen)

Arnold with his idol Reg Park (second from the right) at the 1970 Mr. Universe contest. In a few hours Reg would be vanquished by his disciple. It would be Arnold's fifth Mr. Universe title. *(Arax-Hankey)*

Arnold taking it easy in January 1977. *(Gummere/New York Post)*

Sue Moray, photographed
just after she and Arnold
broke up in 1978.
(Courtesy of Sue Moray)

A meeting of "the Arnia" (from left to right): Paul Graham, Wag
Bennett, Joe Weider (men to whom Arnold owes a lot), and Dianne
Bennett. *(Kevin Horton)*

Arnold in 1982 clowning around with Sandhal Bergman, his leading lady in *Conan the Barbarian. (Dan Brinzac/New York Post)*

True love: Arnold with Brigitte Nielsen at a December 1984 party at Bernd Zimmermann's fitness studio in Vienna. *(Norbert Kössler/ Pressefotografie)*

Arnold and his bride, Maria, acknowledge the crowd outside the church on their wedding day, April 16, 1986. *(Peter Carrette/Outline)*

On facing page: The wedding party. The bridesmaids are, from left:
Renee Meier Schink, Charlotte Soames Hambro, Sydney Lawford
McKelvey, Courtney Kennedy Ruhe, Linda Potter, Theo Hayes,
Roberta Hollander, Wanda McDaniel Ruddy, Alexa Halaby,
Caroline Kennedy. The ushers, standing, from left, are: Timothy
Shriver, Bobby Shriver, Anthony Shriver, Sven-Ole Thorsen, Patrick
Knapp, Albert Busek, Karl Schwarzenegger. Seated, from left, are:
Mitsuo Kawashima, Neal Nordlinger, Mark Shriver, Jim Lorimer,
Franco Columbu, Bill Drake, John Ruddy, and Al Ruddy. *(AP/Wide
World Photos)*
Above: The women behind the man: Aurelia and Maria in
attendance to Arnold at the clock tower in Graz, 1985. *(Christian
Jauschowetz)*

Arnold visits Kurt Waldheim in 1986 at Waldheim's summer home near Salzburg. *(Courtesy of the Press Office of the President of Austria)*

Arnold having lunch in 1986, just before he stood up and threatened *New York Post* photographer Michael Schwartz (5′10″, 135 pounds) for taking his picture. *(New York Post)*

Arnold, Aurelia, and Maria visit the Anderwald family, who live in Arnold's childhood home in Thal. *(Courtesy of Helga Anderwald)*

An aerial view of Arnold and Maria's Pacific Palisades mansion. *(David Hogan/Syndication International)*

At left: Arnold in Styrian national costume during the filming of *Red Heat* in Austria. He was soon to learn of his stuntman's tragic death. *(Christian Jauschowetz)* *Below:* A proud Aurelia Schwarzenegger visits her son in Budapest, where he was filming *Red Heat. (Gino Molin-Pradel)* *On facing page:* Arnold, the movie star, surveys the scene in Budapest. *(Gino Molin-Pradel)*

"Conan the Republican" with his candidate at a campaign rally in a Chicago suburb during the 1988 presidential race. *(AP/Wide World Photos)*

name. In the heat of their sexual relationship he showed her his book again, pointing out other entries in it that didn't merely include women's phone numbers but also notations next to their names, like "big breasts" or "black hair," so he wouldn't confuse one woman with another.

They went out on their first date four or five days later, Arnold taking Sue out to dinner at Yesterdays in Westwood. Subsequently she discovered that his most recent fling was still working there as a waitress. It was Arnold's modus operandi to flaunt his new girlfriend in front of the last. One day Sue herself would suffer the same fate.

"Ours was a lusty encounter," says Sue, confiding that Arnold was a great lover who could alternate between tenderness and kinkiness. Sue threw herself into the affair with gusto. The daughter of a Beverly Hills–based attorney, she was not a classic all-American girl like Barbara, but more passionate, less compliant. Arnold, however, would soon change that.

At the time of their meeting she was working as an assistant at Vidal Sassoon's Beverly Hills salon. Arnold told her that he wanted a woman who would devote herself to his career and not put too much emphasis on her own. He found Sue a job as a stylist at the Palm Salon in Venice, situated conveniently close to Gold's Gym, where he trained.

Sue was athletic, worked out, and was a good runner as well as a roller skater. She loved dancing—an activity during which, she says, Arnold became a child, hedonistic and relaxed. Their relationship was fun and, in Sue's words, "We really clicked."

Not knowing anything about Arnold's family background or his father's politics, Sue mentioned to Arnold that she was half Jewish, her mother having converted to her father's religion. Arnold's reaction was to announce that he was an honorary Jew.

In a matter of days after their first meeting, Sue and Arnold were living together at his apartment on 19th

Street. She had no plans to give up her own apartment, aware that Arnold would soon be going out of town on a promotional tour.

Before leaving, he made a proposal to Sue regarding the future of their relationship. The deal was this, remembers Sue: "When he was in town, he would be committed to me and I would live with him and go to work from his house. We would be faithful when we were both in L.A., see each other exclusively, and not go out with anyone else. But when he was out of town, we were free to do whatever we wanted and to date anyone else we wanted."

On the surface Sue appeared to be poised and confident. Yet looking back, she believes that Arnold, with his ability to sense vulnerability and weakness, fathomed the reality that behind her poised facade she was insecure and overwhelmed by him, took advantage of that knowledge, correctly assessing that she would agree to his proposal that they have an open relationship. Ultimately, Arnold was even able to convince Sue that she herself was the architect of this new and unconventional element in their love affair and that she had suggested it to him herself.

Before leaving on his trip, Arnold asked Sue to yield to yet another condition. While he was away, she could, he said, date anyone she wanted. With one exception. No bodybuilders. Sue, who didn't really want to date anyone except Arnold, agreed. Eventually, "as a defense," Sue says she did go out with other men. And Arnold was tormented. "He was hurt that I wasn't trying to duplicate him while he was gone. He said, 'All the women I go after, they remind me of you, they look like you, or they have your body type. But the men you go after never look like me.' I asked how I could possibly find anyone who looked like him!"

As with most things in life, the first step, for Sue, was the most difficult. Soon, however, she and Arnold were comparing notes, discussing details about whom they had been to bed with and what they had done with them. "It was," admits Sue, "part of the turn-on for us. He would tell me. Then I would tell him. But when I did, he got really mad."

In theory their relationship was open. So it was with a complete lack of guile or secrecy that Arnold returned home from New York carrying a poster of the Robert F. Kennedy Tennis Tournament, which had just been held at Forest Hills on August 28th. As he tacked the poster to the wall of their bedroom, he also mentioned to Sue that at the tournament he had met John F. Kennedy's niece, Maria Shriver.

11
Maria

THESE WERE HEADY DAYS FOR ARNOLD. He was now the focus of the attention he had always craved. There was no doubt in anyone's mind that he was a personality—a film star, the mention of whose name could gain him admission to social events from which the average bodybuilder would normally be barred. Naturally he took full advantage of the situation, so that when *Pumping Iron* publicist Bobby Zarem arranged for him to be invited to the Robert F. Kennedy Tennis Tournament at Forest Hills, he accepted eagerly. That invitation led to another, to Hyannis Port and a weekend with the Kennedys.

Arnold had spent years diligently educating himself to be a gentleman, a 1970s version of Charles Dickens's Pip Pirrip, bettering himself in accord with his "great expectations." Now, dressed like an Ivy League graduate, an art collector (courtesy of Joe Weider), no longer a country bumpkin but comfortable with upper-middle-class American mores (thanks to Barbara Outland), and, as a result of his own thirst for knowledge, a student of politics, he was, of course, not only a bodybuilder but also an accomplished all-around athlete able to swim, sail, water-ski, and compete with the best of them. And although he claimed, "I felt like I was going into the unknown," it was as if he had spent his entire life preparing for this weekend at Hyannis Port.

The invitation seems to have been issued jointly by Maria and her brother Bobby. For once it appears that Arnold may have been on the receiving end of a practical

153

joke. Maria had assured him that there was no need to bring special clothes since everyone there dressed informally. He arrived at the Kennedy compound in Hyannis Port without a tie or a jacket, just as members of the Kennedy and Shriver family were leaving for church. Bobby came to his rescue by lending him some clothes. Arnold later recalled that, despite the clothes being too small, he felt completely at ease during his three days in Hyannis Port.

According to Arnold, Teddy Kennedy and Sargent Shriver spoke German and so did Rose: "Rose Kennedy was great. She speaks perfect German; so we spent the whole weekend talking to each other in my native tongue. We went for several long walks together and talked about Austria at length. The odd thing was that she knew everything about my country. Music, art, opera, books, even history! I was on my toes every second with her." The image of the frail matriarch striding around Hyannis Port with Arnold does—at first—seem a trifle incongruous. Yet anyone delving beneath the surface might conclude that Arnold probably didn't experience great difficulty in impressing Rose Kennedy, who was eminently susceptible to powerful and ambitious men.

Rose's husband, Joe, who had died eight years before Arnold first arrived at Hyannis Port, is an American legend, a multimillionaire with a buccaneer's spirit and a highwayman's ethics, who imprinted his creed on his family as firmly as did Gustav Schwarzenegger on his. In fact Joe's oft-quoted comment, "We want winners. We don't want losers around here," was eerily similar to the beliefs that Gustav had drilled into Arnold. Arnold himself once confided to *Time* magazine's Denise Worrell that he was impressed by Joe Kennedy.

Joe and Gustav possessed another similarity. In March 1938, eleven days after Hitler marched into Austria, Joe Kennedy, then American ambassador to Great Britain, cabled President Roosevelt that Hitler was bluffing. State Department documents on German foreign policy claim that after meeting Joe Kennedy, Herbert Von Dirksen, the

German ambassador to England, cabled Berlin to the effect
that Joe Kennedy had accused the American press and the
president of being influenced by Jews and that he understood Germany's Jewish policy and had cited Boston clubs
that banned Jews from becoming members. In short, inas-
much as an American was able to be pro-Hitler, Joe
Kennedy, like Gustav Schwarzenegger, ostensibly favored
Nazism.

Like Arnold, Joe was a master of public relations, a
genius at manipulating the press in favor of his only
clients, the Kennedy family. Once, when her brother Jack
was discussing the possibility of running for Congress,
Eunice asked Joe if he really thought Jack could be a con-
gressman. Joe's answer was "You must remember—it's not
what you are that counts, but what people think you are."
Arnold, never slow to project an image that wasn't always
a totally accurate reflection of reality, would probably have
applauded Joe Kennedy's answer. And it was an artistic
stroke of fate that brought Arnold—an adventurer, a
winner, a manipulator, and a latter-day Joe Kennedy—into
the life of Maria Shriver, Joe's granddaughter.

Had she come from the South, Maria Shriver might
well have been a model for Margaret Mitchell's heroine,
Scarlett O'Hara. Her looks are classically Irish, with a
determined jaw, catlike green eyes, and cascades of rich
dark brown hair. Despite having been born into a life of
privilege, she also exhibited the fighting spirit and strong
will of a woman destined to carve her way in the world.
Although Maria, with her Kennedy/Shriver blood, was
never compelled to do a great deal of carving, her brother
Bobby claims, "Once Maria decides she is going to get
something, she does. She is an absolute mule."

It is often said that the majority of women marry men
who remind them of their father. Maria, on the other hand,
seems to have reversed that axiom by marrying a man who
had much in common with her mother, Eunice Kennedy
Shriver.

Born in 1921, a practical joker who once attended a

party thrown by her brother Jack dressed as a pregnant nun, Eunice was a bright, optimistic girl who was known as the family cheerleader. Although not beautiful, she was an accomplished athlete. While she was at school in England, she shocked the "proper" British schoolgirls at the Sacred Heart Convent in Roehampton with her aggressive play during a field hockey match, shouting "hey, hey" as if she were playing in a rough touch football scrimmage. Indeed, Eunice was so aggressive that her father, Joe, was heard to comment, "If that girl had been born with balls she would have been a hell of a politician."

Eunice had not only tremendous drive but compassion as well. Always very close to her retarded sister, Rosemary, each summer she invited fifty or sixty retarded children to Timberlawn, the summer place she rented, giving them love and attention.

Ironically, like her future son-in-law, she delayed getting married for as long as possible. Once linked with Senator Joe McCarthy, Eunice met Sargent Shriver over dinner at the St. Regis Hotel through a friend, Peter Houget. Shriver, the well-born son of a prominent Baltimore family that had lost everything in the Depression, was an intellectual, a scholarship boy at Yale, who then worked as assistant to the editor of *Newsweek*.

Courting Eunice with a dogged persistence over seven years, Shriver finally gave up and started dating other women. However, once Eunice heard that he was thinking of marrying one of them, she dashed back from Europe, confiding to a friend that Shriver wasn't marrying anyone but her. They married in 1953, and Maria, their only daughter, was born on November 6, 1955.

Maria has talked often of her upbringing, emphasizing her mother's influence, once explaining that her mother is tough and independent and brought Maria up to believe that winning is essential. She also said that, because of her energy, her mother reminds her of Lucille Ball.

She was not, however, brought up entirely in the

Kennedy mode, for her father did his utmost to exert his influence on his children. Unlike the Kennedys—or, for that matter, Arnold—he was uneasy with an ethic that sacrificed feeling to action. As Peter Collier and David Horowitz related in their book, *The Kennedys*, once, when one of his children fell down and received the admonition "Kennedys don't cry," he scooped the boy up and told him, "That's okay, you can go ahead and cry. You're a Shriver."

For the most part, however, Eunice's ethics ruled unchallenged. Rose Kennedy's spiritual influence on her daughters, in particular, had been strong, with Eunice astounding her schoolmates at Sacred Heart with her displays of piety. Like Arnold's mother, Aurelia, Eunice Kennedy Shriver is an extremely religious woman—and Maria, unlike Arnold, has never rebelled against her mother's ardent Catholicism. She prays daily, has been known to keep her rosary beads on her desk at work, and is a firm believer in the Judeo-Christian ethic.

Her parents' marriage provided a healthy and happy example for their children. Maria has said of her parents, "Their marriage was a religious union. They are daily communicants." She has also observed, "Both my parents are workaholics, but their interests are very varied. They're always working either on a specific job, or with their kids, or with their friends. I've watched that and I've learned that people who do really well work at it. That to me is very important, to work at it."

Maria was nearly as well schooled in competition and sibling rivalry as Arnold. Growing up with four brothers, she required constant proof that she was as tough as they were, that she, as it were, was the best. She once remembered, "When you are the only girl, you really have to knock yourself out just to get a chance to play. There was no way to fool those guys. If I didn't hold up my end, I was O-U-T of the baseball or football game. Did I cry? Not a chance. They'd have drummed me out of the corps mercilessly. That's how I got tough."

Part heiress to the estimated $35 million to $50 million

fortune that Joe Kennedy left Eunice, Maria should, in theory, have grown up in an insulated, secure world. Despite her parents' efforts to shield her, the ill-fated Kennedy history did, however, darken her youth. She was eight years old and a third-grader at the Sacred Heart School in Washington when JFK was assassinated, was twelve at the time of Bobby's assassination, and was often pressed to comment on both her uncles' deaths and the tragedy that seemed to stalk her family. Invariably she refused.

When Lyndon Johnson named Sargent Shriver ambassador to France, the family moved to Paris, where Maria's bedroom overlooked the Eiffel Tower. Always keen to avoid keeping Maria in a gilded cage, the Shrivers sent her first to school in Paris and then, for a short time, to a kibbutz in Israel. However, she eventually ran away to join her parents at Jerusalem's King David Hotel because "All I wanted was a hot shower. I was the only woman in that kibbutz. It wasn't a kibbutz so much as it was a camp to train Israeli soldiers. I was living in a room with seven men."

Determined to broaden Maria's horizons further, Eunice lectured her on the need to have a career. Maria recalled, "When people used to say to my mother, 'Oh, your daughter's pretty,' she'd say, 'Well, what about her brain?' She'd always say to me, 'Don't think that your looks are going to help in the long run. Because you'll be pretty today and someone else will be prettier tomorrow. Make sure you improve your brain because that in the long run will make you interesting.' "

In 1972, when she was sixteen, she traveled with her father, who was George McGovern's running mate, in the campaign for vice president, spending most of her time with the press corps. Although she was shy, she found that she felt at ease with the press and noted the importance of the TV journalists. Her father started his career at *Newsweek*; her grandmother, Rose, for a time hosted a TV show; and her uncle Jack, of course, was a great communicator. Journalism, then, was an obvious choice of profession for Maria, and she made up her mind that when she graduated from college she would aim for a career in television journalism.

Meanwhile the Shrivers guarded their princess, watching her like a hawk and, when she went out on dates, insisting that she be home by midnight. Nevertheless she managed to have two boyfriends, one in high school, the other in college.

At Georgetown University she majored in American studies, writing her thesis on Jack Kennedy's 1960 West Virginia primary campaign. She graduated from Georgetown on May 22, 1977, just three months before Arnold Schwarzenegger walked into her life.

The weekend at Hyannis Port was a great success. Arnold, the Austrian peasant who was now a sophisticated Americanized gentleman, passed muster with flying colors. Always adept at dealing with the older generation, he played tennis with Sargent Shriver, gracefully losing the match. Eunice took him for a ride in her twenty-five-foot boat. Maria's brother Bobby confided, "I think she wanted to see how tough he really was. He swallowed about a gallon of water." Arnold was able to impress Bobby quickly, an easy task as Bobby had seen *Pumping Iron* and, as a result, already admired him.

Most important of all, Maria was captivated by Arnold, later commenting that when she met him at the family tennis tournament it was as "a human being, not a bodybuilder." That Arnold was a self-made man and had what she termed "a strong sense of family and religion" appealed to her. Said Maria, "I am absolutely fascinated by people who overcome whatever limitations they might have had to achieve their dreams."

One can only guess at the effect Maria had on Arnold. As George Butler perceived, "I'm not sure Arnold was deprived, but he came from quite primitive origins. And I think that this has always played on him." And although Arnold, the diplomat, naturally didn't mention it, even a saint, coming from Thal and poverty as Arnold did, would

have been thrilled with Maria's purebred "Kennedyism."
Maria's approval must have symbolized his acceptance in
his brave new American world. Publicly, of course, he
usually avoided the issue and has said, "She was filled with
all kinds of dreams and ambitions. . . . I was taken with her
sense of humor and absolute joy," and "I knew instantly
that Maria was *the* woman for my life, she was so *full* of
life, so *very* beautiful! I loved her drive to succeed, among
her other great qualities."

After the weekend, back home in California, Arnold
told his friends at the gym about his latest conquest. Rick
Wayne, in California at the time, remembers, "We all
thought he had scored with Maria. It was like a notch."
There are those who, in later years, would accuse Arnold of
courting Maria merely because she was a Kennedy, to benefit his image, increase his visibility, and feed his ego. In
contrast his defenders maintain that Maria's attraction for
Arnold was that she was, in her own right, beautiful, viva-
cious, intelligent. To top that, from the moment she met
him, she was extremely devoted to him.

The talented British author Muriel Spark, in her novel
The Prime of Miss Jean Brodie, created a heroine, Edin-
burgh teacher Miss Jean Brodie, whose motto was "Give me
a girl at an impressionable age and she's mine for life."
Like Miss Brodie, Arnold too was adept at finding girls at
an impressionable age and making them his for life. Both
Barbara Outland and Sue Moray, though pretty, educated,
and from affluent homes, were naive and easily led. An
excellent leader, Arnold naturally made an indelible impression on both Sue and Barbara.

Although Maria was born to a magnificent heritage
and at twenty-one reflected that heritage magnificently, she
was, at heart, no different from Barbara and Sue before her.
She was more than pretty, exquisitely educated, but also,
despite the outward appearance of rebelliousness, extremely impressionable.

Maria once stated that she was impressed by Arnold

because he was different. To her he was unique, and he understood that from the start. The girl who had wanted to join her brothers at sport and be one of the boys had found in Arnold a man who could beat the Kennedys and the Shrivers at their own game—and on her behalf. He was charming, bright, competitive, and knew how to handle a woman.

There was only one hitch: Sue Moray, three thousand miles away in California. Though Maria was unaware of it, from the beginning of her relationship with Arnold, she was sharing him with another woman. Maria was not the first Kennedy woman to share her man. This was the first time she would share Arnold with another woman. But it would not be the last.

12
Maria and Sue

IN AUGUST 1977, ALTHOUGH APPARENTLY Maria Shriver didn't know about Arnold's relationship with Sue Moray, Sue, from the start, knew about Maria. Arnold described their meeting to Sue, intimating that his relationship with Maria was not physical, that she was young and "just a friend." Sue, who knew Arnold well, didn't believe him.

In the meantime their relationship progressed, with Sue spending her time at Arnold's home and playing a part in all areas of his life. Sometimes, however, she would rebel. Arnold was a hot property, often approached by entrepreneurs anxious to capitalize on his body and his name. Once a businessman proposed launching an "Arnold Hamburger," and although Arnold wasn't the least bit interested, he nevertheless accepted the businessman's invitation to dinner, taking Sue along with him. She recalls, "Arnold kept turning to me and saying, 'Well, what do you think?' Like, 'Hey, what a good idea!' I knew he was going to turn the guy down, and I just couldn't play him along, so I said I had no comment."

They were continually surrounded by autograph seekers, businessmen, and other bodybuilders. But when the pressure was off, and they were skiing or trapshooting, Arnold relaxed. At such times, according to Sue, he was very loving. However, knowing he was in contact with the formidable Maria Shriver, Sue sometimes became objective, concluding, "He had a good heart, but he was so incredibly ambitious. There was definitely a terrible ruthlessness. Yet he also had the ability to be like a little boy."

163

After one of his weekend trips Arnold came home to Sue and gave her gonorrhea. "I was outraged," remembers Sue. "Arnold just said, 'Look, what if I came and gave you a cold—would you be outraged? You know I sleep with other people.' He turned it on me, telling me that I was outrageous even thinking there was anything wrong about getting gonorrhea from him."

They traveled a great deal, always, however, staying on the West Coast, as the East Coast was fast developing into Maria Shriver's territory. Arnold bought a jeep in Oregon, and he and Sue drove up there to pick it up. Along the way, Sue, an avid skier, was reading *The Book of Skiing*, and Arnold, ever the auditory learner, asked Sue to read it to him. She wasn't surprised; often when she recommended a book to him he would beg off, asking her to read it to him instead.

Aurelia came to visit, and Arnold and Sue took her to Palm Springs, then skiing with them in the Mammoth Mountain Ski Area of California. However, Sue and Aurelia didn't take to each other. Sue remembers, "Aurelia's vacations with us were extremely long. She was devoted to Arnold. She kept giving me the camera and asking me to take photographs of the two of them so that she could show them to her friends back in Austria."

It would soon transpire that Aurelia had more than mere photographs with which to impress her friends back home. Arnold's relationship with Maria, who had, in September 1977, started working as a trainee at KYW-TV in Philadelphia, was beginning to develop on more serious lines. Aurelia, much to her delight, found herself accompanying Maria to church.

Arnold spent Christmas Eve 1977 with Sue Moray, inexplicably choosing to take her to visit Barbara Outland's parents. Barbara too was there, without a boyfriend. Two-and-a-half years had passed since her breakup with Arnold, yet she still hadn't really gotten over him. Sue liked

Barbara but would have been less than human had she not experienced a frisson of self-satisfaction that she, not Barbara, was now the reigning queen in Arnold's life.

Any satisfaction Sue may have felt, however, was swiftly wiped out when Arnold informed her that Maria was coming out to California to spend the New Year's Eve weekend with him. Telling her, in effect, "She's coming; you're out of here," Arnold nonetheless assured Sue that Maria, contrary to appearances, was merely a friend.

Arnold and Maria spent New Year's Eve at a restaurant in Santa Monica together with his former adversary and friend, Frank Zane, and Zane's wife, Christine. Describing the restaurant to Sue as the kind of establishment where waiters and waitresses sing and dance between courses, Arnold managed to present the entire evening to her as if it had been a church outing. Sue, though slightly mollified, was far from feeling secure.

She began to eavesdrop, listening at doors, trying to discern snatches of telephone conversations. She made an effort to project happiness, but it wasn't always easy. She remembers, "Arnold brought out this humor in me, initially. Then it became a requirement. Even when I didn't feel like being funny or keeping things light, he got mad. He used to say, 'You just aren't fun anymore.' He wanted to be entertained all the time. I felt all this pressure to do that in order to keep his love."

In the New Year, Arnold, while promoting *Arnold: The Education of a Bodybuilder*, which had made the top ten of the *New York Times* bestseller list, took Sue with him to Denver, then on a skiing trip to Aspen. It was his first visit, so Sue, who knew Aspen well, showed him around town. Later she heard Arnold on the telephone telling Maria about his Aspen trip, how great the skiing was, and studiously omitting the fact that he hadn't been alone but had taken Sue with him.

Soon Maria came out for more weekends on the West Coast, with Arnold reiterating to Sue, "She's young. I don't sleep with her; she's just a friend." Sue was on the West

Coast, Maria on the East Coast, and Arnold wanted them both. So when Maria came to L.A., he lied to Sue about the purpose of her visit, simultaneously convincing her to move out of his apartment for that particular weekend.

With other people Arnold was open about his double life. Amazingly, Bobby Shriver, then working part-time at the *Los Angeles Herald Examiner*, often dropped over to Arnold's house while Sue was there. Arnold was so close to Bobby that, according to Sue, Arnold fed him negative stories about Gold's Gym, whose current owner, Ken Sprague, had sued Arnold for libeling his gym. Arnold, secure in his male camaraderie with Bobby, made no attempt to hide the truth about his relationship with Sue from him. If Maria ever questioned Bobby about the intimate details of Arnold's California existence, it is highly likely that her brother stuck to the Kennedy code of *omertà*, reacting as did Teddy Kennedy, who had denied the truth when his sister Eunice asked him if Jack Kennedy really was a womanizer.

By April 1978 Sue and Arnold were fighting bitterly about Maria. During one fight Sue threw her keys at him, and in another she jumped out of the car in the middle of a freeway. Ever cool and mindful of the importance of maintaining the relationship's balance of power in his favor, Arnold proceeded to drive home, leaving Sue standing on the freeway.

Sometimes, however, Arnold's cool did desert him, once affording Sue a privileged glimpse into the secret recesses of his heart. Nine months after they first started going out together, almost at a breaking point due to his duplicity, Sue announced to Arnold that she was leaving him. True to her word, she packed up all her belongings, put them in her car, and drove off. After a few blocks, thinking of Arnold alone at home, she softened and drove back. What she saw convinced her that, no matter what, Arnold did love her. "When I walked into the house, I found him there, crying. I've never seen a man cry so hard. He was just like a baby, crying and crying. We hugged and held on to each other tight. Then he stopped crying, and I said, 'I am not going.' " At that moment she knew he loved her, that he was vulnerable, and that his vulnerability was a fear of abandonment.

Arnold was a restless sleeper, tossing and turning, once even accidentally whacking Sue in the face while he was sleeping. Afraid of growing old, he was prematurely gray and had begun to dye his hair. Steroids too were still a part of his life. So, of course, were his bodybuilding cronies.

Peter Schachtschneider, one of Arnold's old friends, came to visit him in America, and he, Arnold, and Sue went river rafting together. "Suddenly," remembers Sue, "Arnold started treating me as if I were some meaningless whore he had brought along. We'd been together for quite a while, but around Peter he couldn't treat me respectfully. I was a little bit overweight, and they began to make fun of me in German. I understood what they were saying, and I was very hurt. But I didn't stand up for myself. Arnold can be very unkind. It broke my heart, and it killed part of the love I felt for him."

Arnold's double game lasted until August 1978, one year after his first meeting with Maria. The ultimatum, however, came from Sue, not Maria. Arnold, probably aware of the repercussions and prepared, as it were, to bite the bullet, told Sue that he was going on vacation to Hawaii with his Austrian friends, Bernd and Erika Zimmermann. Sue, however, was not invited.

She knew he was planning to take Maria, and so, telling him that she wasn't going to put up with the situation any longer, Sue, this time, did in fact move out. Maria, Erika, and Bernd went to Hawaii with Arnold, and it seemed as if Maria, a year after she had first met him, finally had Arnold to herself.

Things were not, however, quite what they seemed. Two months after the breakup, Sue and Arnold were still meeting secretly whenever, as Sue says, "it was convenient."

Their sexual attraction was still strong, and they continued to act on it. But then one day Arnold happened to see Sue having lunch with a black male friend, whereupon she says he informed her, "Sue, I want you to know that I am not going to sleep with you anymore. I can't risk giving Maria any diseases."

Nevertheless, their relationship, in a new and different form, managed to endure. Sue, who had gone into therapy after their official breakup, often saw Maria in Santa Monica with Arnold, who, as was his pattern, persisted in taking her to the same places he had taken Sue. Once Sue and Maria even met at the same gym, the Sports Connection, where they both worked out. The meeting was cordial.

Sue, who today is happily married, lives near Arnold and, in the years since their breakup, has sometimes encountered him in Venice or Santa Monica. In 1985 they had lunch together at Chinois on Main Street in Santa Monica, and Arnold gleefully confided to Sue all the details of his latest steamy liaison. It seemed to Sue that his excitement about the love affair was heightened by its clandestine quality. They also reminisced about their own relationship, with Sue reminding Arnold of how hurt she'd been. "Oh, no, we had the greatest relationship," responded Arnold. Sue smiled, then said, "Maybe *you* did. I was a very insecure person who put up with a lot of things I wouldn't put up with now." "Oh, no," insisted Arnold, adamantly adding, "You had a great time." With that he changed the subject, thus ending the conversation.

In August 1978 Maria, who had been advised by Barbara Walters not to tackle the New York job market prematurely, moved from Philadelphia to WJZ-TV in Baltimore, set on advancing her television career. Arnold too continued to be successful, producing bodybuilding contests and mulling over film offers.

On September 15th Arnold and Maria were in New Orleans for the Spinks-Ali fight at the Superdome. Arnold had never been to New Orleans, so their guide was bodybuilding great Boyer Coe, a Louisiana native. After a day's sightseeing Boyer took Arnold and Maria to dinner at the Caribbean Room in the Pontchartrain Hotel.

There he ordered the hotel's special dessert for them to share; Mile High Pie, which measures a foot high, is an enticing mixture of spumoni topped with meringue and smothered in thick chocolate sauce. Smiling in anticipation, Maria was about to eat a mouthful when, suddenly, Arnold grabbed her by the back of the neck and pushed her face right into it. Maria, niece of a president, granddaughter of a multimillionaire, and one of America's princesses, found herself covered in mounds of meringue and rivulets of chocolate sauce.

Boyer says that Maria was, to say the least, surprised. Arnold, of course, having captured the attention of the entire Caribbean Room, was delighted. He reportedly played the pie-in-the-face joke on Maria and other friends a number of times. In a July 1988 interview with *Cable Guide* he boasted about a variation on it—telling a waitress that the cream is off, inviting her to smell it, then pushing her face into it. In another interview Maria, when asked by a journalist which of Arnold's qualities she liked, declared, "his sense of humor." And when the journalist, who had done his homework, asked, "You mean the sour-milk-in-the-face trick doesn't appall you?" Maria answered, "No." Persisting, he asked, "Not even in your own face?" "No, of course not," came the reply.

Maria may, no pun intended, have been saving face. However, there are those who, surmising that Arnold's sense of humor might not always be appreciated, have attempted to conceal his pranks. Arnia member Wag Bennett, when asked about Arnold's cream/milk/pie-in-the-face antics, denied them. "Arnold wouldn't do a thing like that," Bennett maintained. "That would be taking liberties. And Arnold isn't a liberty taker."

In public neither the Kennedys nor the Shrivers have ever made any negative comments about Maria's relationship with Arnold. In the early days there were those who

declared that he was the Kennedys' worst setback since
Chappaquiddick, an accusation based not on any evidence
but purely on speculation. As it was, Arnold, officially at
least, has always done his best to fulfill his role as the man
in Maria's life.

Eunice Shriver, the closest of all her family to her
retarded sister, Rosemary, put that closeness and empathy
into practice. Besides having Rosemary spend summers
with her and her family, in the late sixties she launched the
Special Olympics, a nonprofit sports organization for people with mental retardation, run under the auspices of the
Joseph P. Kennedy Foundation. Eunice is chairman and
Sargent Shriver president.

Arnold's relationship with the Shrivers led to his involvement in the Special Olympics, an association that
illustrates what Sue Moray, who loved and lost him, terms
"Arnold's good heart." Soon after his first meeting with
Eunice, Arnold became Special Olympics honorary weightlifting coach, a post that he still holds. He was instrumen-
tal in developing the Special Olympics' entire weightlifting
program, traveling around the country, holding demonstrations, and helping to raise money for weightlifting
equipment. He explained, "[Weightlifting is] most popular
among the kids because it's easy to improve and they can
see progress. Maybe it's only two pounds to start with, but
then they can lift five pounds. It gives them immediate
satisfaction."

Later, when he was a major international star, Arnold
worked with eighteen-year-old twins Mark and Mike
Hembd, who suffer from Down's syndrome. Their experience with Arnold, as recounted by their mother, Sandra,
sums up the positive effects wrought by Arnold's good
heart in action: "I think they feel that [Schwarzenegger]
will be their personal friend. He was real sincere, and
[Mike and Mark] pick up on that. They don't know his
title, if he's a governor or a movie star, but they think they
can call on him at any moment."

Today Arnold always makes himself available for the

Special Olympics' International Games, which are held every four or five years. He took part in the 1988 Special Olympics Christmas TV special, and the premiere of his film *Twins* was held in aid of the Special Olympics. He is obviously sincere about the charity and its importance in his life.

Long before the advent of the Shrivers and the Special Olympics in his life, Arnold, in the mid-seventies, was doing charitable work in prisons throughout the country. As soon as he became famous as America's leading body-builder, letters began to pour in from prison inmates eager for training tips. According to Arnold, "I found an enormous need for prisoners to have something positive to focus on while they're in there, something to continue with when they're released. There are so many ways for people like me, with some celebrity and certain specific skills, to be useful to society. I want to keep expanding that part of my life, too."

To that end he spent a lot of time in prisons, working as a trainer and consultant to inmates, believing, he said, that "weight training helps make prisoners less violent. It makes them release some of their negative tension and energy in the gymnasium, and it gives them a better self-image."

Those aware of his sadistic practical jokes and often cruel psyching out of opponents might find the concept of Arnold's charity incongruous, but then Arnold, neither in his personality nor in his actions, has ever conformed to conventional expectations. Capable of cruelty, he is also capable of great kindness and commitment to a cause greater than himself.

In October 1978 Arnold went to Tucson, Arizona, to work on Hal Needham's film *The Villain*. He was paid $275,000 for his part as "the handsome stranger"—a cowboy who was shy with women. Upon reading the film script he had realized that, unlike the immensely popular *Cat Ballou*, this western spoof, in his words, "was not interesting." Still he accepted the part, he says, because he would be working with Ann-Margret and Kirk Douglas and hoped to learn from them.

Hal Needham remembers, "Arnold was an absolute delight to work with. He's very funny and is a nice guy. He is professional and eager to learn. He played a straight man to Ann-Margret with all that cleavage. I think he did that very well." Arnold too was impressed by his co-stars, saying that Kirk Douglas "is very muscular and lean and in great shape. I've never seen him step onto a horse, he jumps." Of Ann-Margret, who weighed 93 pounds next to his 215, he commented diplomatically, "Ann-Margret can run six miles without breathing hard." However, despite the physical fitness of all three stars, the film, released a year later, proved to be the archetypal bomb. One acerbic film critic quipped something to the effect that neither Arnold's facial expression nor his acting was equal to that of the horse's. At the time Arnold actually conceded that he was hurt. Later, having achieved superstardom, he would forget his hurt and pin the offending *Villain* review on his office wall, giving it pride of place.

Eunice Shriver had wanted to take Maria on vacation with her to Kenya over Christmas 1978. But Maria was completely committed to Arnold and refused; instead she went to Vienna with him. It must have been a difficult choice for the Shrivers' only daughter, who at the time of their first meeting, according to Arnold, had been an extension of her family. Her decision not to travel to Kenya with her mother testifies to Maria's growing independence.

In Vienna Arnold took Maria to the famed Stefanskirche, and she blushed when his friend Erika Zimmermann pointed out that weddings were held at the Stefanskirche and that if Arnold and Maria got married there she and Bernd would pay for the wedding.

Arnold, still training rigorously, worked out at Zimmermann's gym, taking Maria to the Hauermandl for strudel afterward and for drinks in the taverns of Grinzing on the outskirts of Vienna. They also went on a day trip to Budapest, ending their European stay by skiing in Lech Am Arlberg. Next it was back to America and the last part of their vacation, a visit to Hawaii.

Combining business trips with pleasure had always been Arnold's style. In May 1979 he took Maria with him to Cannes, where he made an attempt to promote the hapless *Villain*. Next he went on to Vienna and then Graz to visit his mother.

It was obvious that Arnold, whose horizons had always far outreached those of his mother, had expanded himself even more. On November 10, 1979, he graduated from the University of Wisconsin in Superior with a general business degree (individually designed) in the international marketing of physical fitness.

On the film front, however, although his *Pumping Iron* success had seemed to herald the beginning of his stardom, so far his film career had proved a disappointment. He turned down $200,000 to endorse tires, protesting that he didn't want to project the image suggested by his proposed lines, which were "Hi, I've been building my strength for the past fifteen years, but I'm still not half as strong as these tires. . . ." He also wisely declined the part of one of Mae West's muscle men in the film *Sextette*.

Not that he was totally averse to playing the role of a bodybuilder yet again. Perhaps through his acquaintance with Kirk Douglas, whose son Michael was playing the lead, he made a brief, clichéd appearance on "The Streets of San Francisco" as a European bodybuilder who had come to America after winning some important contests. As the story unfolded, it emerged that the bodybuilder, unable to endure rejection, killed any woman who dared refuse his advances.

Arnold too would prove to have his breaking point. Bodybuilding was still very much a part of his life, and in the fall of 1979 he did commentary for CBS at the Mr. Olympia contest, held in Columbus, Ohio. There he watched as Frank Zane won the Mr. Olympia title for the third time. After the presentation, Arnold, in his role as commentator, asked Frank the classic question "How does it feel becoming Mr. Olympia for the third time?" Frank, intoxicated by his victory, felt like king of the universe as had Arnold before him, and, with a twinkle in his eye, answered, "Arnold, it feels even better than it did the last time I beat you!"

Frank Zane, secure in his friendship with him, aware that Arnold was an arch practical joker, prone to making the barbed remark or clever riposte, had unwittingly committed *lèse-majesté*. For Arnold, in bodybuilding, if not in life, was more than just a king. He was a god. A cruel and jealous god. A god who would never, under any circumstances, tolerate disloyalty. Frank Zane had made fun of him. Frank Zane had reminded a national television audience that Arnold had once been vanquished by him and was mortal. Frank Zane would pay.

13
Australia and the Comeback

SINCE THE MID-SEVENTIES ARNOLD HAD been aware that a businessman named Edward J. Pressman had bought the film rights to *Conan the Barbarian*, and he was determined to play the part of Robert E. Howard's cartoon superman. Knowing that Pressman planned to cast him as Conan, he bided his time but, in anticipation of a call from the film's producer, Dino De Laurentiis, was not idle, taking acting lessons and trying to eradicate his Austrian accent.

De Laurentiis had met Arnold before—a meeting that the diminutive producer had definitely not forgotten. Summoning Arnold to discuss the possibility of casting him as Flash Gordon in the film of the same name, De Laurentiis was stunned by Arnold's full frontal tactics. When he walked into the room, Arnold took one look at De Laurentiis seated behind his desk and wondered aloud, "God, why does a little man like you need such a huge desk?" A sputtering De Laurentiis tried to explain that he needed the desk to accommodate his paperwork, and then, after exactly one hundred seconds, terminated the meeting. Arnold, rejected for the part of Flash Gordon, had nevertheless made an impact.

De Laurentiis had originally wanted a big-name actor for the part of Conan, and when Arnold's name was mentioned, De Laurentiis, calling Arnold "a Nazi," refused to consider him. However, director John Milius explained to De Laurentiis that as Arnold was the world's best-built man he would have to commission someone to make a

replica of Arnold if he didn't cast him in the part. Consequently, De Laurentiis relented, albeit grudgingly, and cast
him as Conan.

Overjoyed, Arnold believed the part of Conan would
be his own personal Rocky Balboa, the part that would
propel him to international stardom. He announced, "I've
never been wrong yet with my instincts, and they tell me
this is going to be a really big film, a whole new phenomenon. I don't care what it takes; I don't care if I have to take
one year out of my life and be an animal. I know this film
is going to be unbelievable for me." Shooting was slated to
begin in Spain toward the end of October 1980. Arnold
began to train harder than ever.

Maria's television career too promised great things.
She was quick to explain that some of Arnold's self-confidence had rubbed off on her, helping her achieve success in
her chosen profession. Citing his ability to visualize goals
and reach them, Maria said, "He sets a very positive example for me, as I set out to reach my goal as a journalist."

Originally she had planned to be a producer. She now
had revised that ambition, fixing her sights on becoming
an on-air talent and setting the goal of becoming an anchor by the age of thirty. She spent hours watching anchor-
women on TV, studying them and thinking to herself,
"This is my dream job. This is who I want to be."

Maria was professional, goal-oriented, and won the
respect of other journalists who dealt with her. Of course
being a Kennedy did not, in theory at least, hurt. Yet she
assiduously avoided interviewing any of her family and
apparently considered her Kennedy heritage somewhat of a
liability, raging, "All those commas—the daughter of, the
girlfriend of, the granddaughter of, the niece of—I hate
them!" She continually strove to prove her professionalism
as opposed to her Kennedyism.

Based, as she was, in Baltimore, Maria and Arnold
were rarely together on a permanent basis, although she
visited him in Los Angeles and Arnold was often in New

York, squiring her to functions such as Jerry Rubin's "The Event," a New Age conference that featured Buckminster Fuller, "est" guru Werner Erhard, and sex therapists Masters and Johnson.

Although there were rumors that Maria wasn't fond of the large group of bodybuilders with whom Arnold surrounded himself, he made few concessions in his lifestyle for Maria's sake. He continued to structure his life around his friends, his work, and his ambitions rather than the woman he professed to love.

Later he explained that Maria's family background has made her understanding about the demands of public life, and he pointed out, "Maria comes from a family where women have always been supportive of the guys." Rather than holding him back, Maria and her family have been helpful to him, said Arnold, who added, "That's why I love her so much."

Their liaison, understandably, had attracted a certain amount of media attention. At "The Event," Arnold, in Maria's tow and looking uncomfortable stuffed into his clothes, at first glance had the air of a queen's consort. Yet that definitely was not the case. He was fiercely independent, standing alone, not in Maria's shadow. From the start he manifested a perverse pride in proclaiming his political affiliations, which definitely were not to the Democratic party. His political point of view, he boasted proudly, had not changed since he was eighteen years old. He was ardently anticommunist and believed in the death penalty, conservative economics, and minimal government intervention. In short, he was a die-hard conservative Republican.

Through the years both he and Maria have taken great pains to express tolerance for each other's political point of view. Maria has said that she respects Arnold's point of view. "Arnold has specific opinions on issues that he really thinks through and supports by facts," she said. "Listening to him, I learn how the other side thinks. Before him, I never really knew a Republican."

Arnold, although never conceding many points to the Democrats, commented, "The advantage of being a liberal is that you're open-minded. And they [the Kennedys] are. There's no animosity. I never argue politics with Maria, because I totally understand that for her to be Republican, having grown up as she did, would be very unusual."

Cynics might add, with perhaps a touch of disappointment, that it is quite usual and only too predictable for Arnold, son of Gustav Schwarzenegger, to be extremely right-wing himself.

Neither Chappaquiddick nor the tales of Jack's womanizing had destroyed the Kennedys. Nor would the romance between Arnold, the arch Republican, and Maria Shriver. And Arnold's liaison with Maria patently wouldn't harm him either. Politics appealed to Arnold, as he confided to the German magazine *Stern* in 1977: "When one has money, one day it becomes less interesting. And when one is also the best in film, what can be more interesting? Perhaps power. Then one moves into politics and becomes governor or president or something." The Kennedys were, in a strange way, beyond politics. His connection with them could only enhance, lending him prestige and power, lifting him high above the crowd, transcending bodybuilding, Hollywood, and even his past.

In August 1980, Arnold, now known in the bodybuilding community chiefly as CBS commentator and, along with Jim Lorimer, producer of bodybuilding shows, attended the Miss Olympia contest at the Philadelphia Sheraton. Rick Wayne, there to cover the show for a Weider magazine, interviewed Arnold afterward.

Casually Rick asked Arnold, who had now been retired from bodybuilding for five years, if he would ever consider making a comeback. "No," Arnold said firmly. "No amount of money could tempt me out of retirement." The only reason he had been training, he told Rick, was that he was rehearsing for his part as bodybuilder Mickey Hargitay in the upcoming *The Jayne Mansfield Story*. As an aside he mentioned that he was planning to be in Australia for the 1980 Mr. Olympia contest, having just been signed by CBS as commentator for the event. Rick, ending the interview, believed every word that Arnold had said.

Meanwhile, back on the West Coast, the reigning Mr. Olympia, Frank Zane, had suffered a severe setback. Eight weeks before the contest in which he expected to win his fourth Mr. Olympia title, Frank met with a terrible accident that almost killed him. After a spell in the hospital, on the verge of withdrawing from the contest, Frank approached Arnold and asked his advice. The accident, he said, had weakened him, interrupted his training, and left its mark. Should he still compete in the 1980 Mr. Olympia or back out of the whole thing? Arnold, whom Frank habitually viewed as a friend and coach, thought for a moment, then said that he strongly believed that Frank should go to Australia and defend his Mr. Olympia title. As an afterthought, Frank, a man who is nobody's fool and had been Arnold's friend for more than twelve years, casually asked him if he planned to compete. No, said Arnold. He was going to Australia to do commentary on the Olympia for CBS—that was all.

Frank Zane wasn't the only man who had his heart set on winning the 1980 Mr. Olympia. Mike Mentzer, a Philadelphia-born bodybuilder of Italian and German descent, four years younger than Arnold, was convinced that 1980 would be his year. In 1976 he'd won the IFBB Mr. America and in 1978 the IFBB Mr. Universe, whereupon Joe Weider had invited him out to California. There he soon became the subject of several articles in the Weider magazines, in which he was projected as the new great hope of bodybuilding. In 1979 he narrowly missed beating Frank Zane in the Mr. Olympia contest. Now Mentzer was certain that this year the Mr. Olympia title would be his.

Mentzer, who had studied medicine in Washington, D.C., before moving to California in 1976, had developed a new training system that dramatically cut the time required for training. Mentzer believed that shorter, more intense workout sessions, followed by greater rest time, would ultimately result in more muscle growth than traditional training methods would. Under Mentzer's system, a bodybuilder would work very hard on all body parts during ninety-minute sessions for no more than four days a week. Mentzer believed that the body recovered from strain first and grew muscle second, and his "high-intensity" training system simply allowed more time for muscle growth.

Mentzer's method was gaining acceptance and winning popularity among the new breed of bodybuilders who had risen to prominence since Arnold's retirement. Arnold, not one to lose touch with any facet of his roots, was aware of Mentzer's rapidly increasing role in bodybuilding. Mentzer, it transpired, had made a fatal mistake. Not a cautious man, he had, within the incestuous, tightly knit circle of champion bodybuilders, expressed a distaste for Arnold's own training methods, claiming that they were dated and far inferior to his own. In short, Mentzer was declaring publicly that he, not Arnold, was the best. Arnold didn't like hearing that. He didn't like hearing that any other man thought that he, not Arnold, was the best. It had been that way since he was ten years old.

Two weeks before the 1980 Mr. Olympia Arnold fell ill, losing ten pounds. That didn't deter him from giving an interview to Austrian journalist Roman Schliesser, who wrote about Arnold on a regular basis in his column "Adabei" for the Viennese paper *Die Kronen Zeitung*. And if Mentzer, Zane, *et al*, had subscribed to *Die Kronen Zeitung* and had been fortunate enough to understand German, they would not have been at all surprised by the events that took place subsequently in Sydney, Australia. For Arnold had quite openly revealed to Schliesser, "On October 4th the next Mr. Olympia will be chosen in Sydney. I'm a sports commentator for CBS television. But I'm doing it. I've trained for six weeks. . . . I'm competing against Frank

Zane who was Mr. Olympia three times, but they will all cry when I win again." Schliesser's article was published on September 28th, just six days before Arnold dropped his bombshell on the 1980 Mr. Olympia contest.

Maria Shriver accompanied Arnold to Australia, although initially she had been against the idea of his making a comeback. Far better, she suggested, for him to learn a new language. After all, he had been Mr. Olympia six times. But his mind was made up, so naturally she was there to support him.

The contest was promoted by one of Arnold's closest friends, IFBB official Paul Graham. Whether or not he was aware that Arnold was competing, Paul had arranged for a film crew to be on hand to record the event. The result was *The Comeback*—by no means *Pumping Iron*, but a rather biased account of the 1980 Mr. Olympia.

The contest was held at the Sydney Opera House, and although professing to be nervous for the benefit of Graham's cameras, Arnold strode into the opera house exuding self-confidence. When asked what music he was using for the contest, with a carefree toss of his head he replied scornfully, "Music? What music? I came with muscles. Put on any music you want." Naturally all the other bodybuilders who hadn't yet seen his body believed that Arnold, the surprise contestant, was in great shape. Later Serge Nubret, who had known him for years, observed, "I am sure that Arnold, being Arnold, had already inspected the hall on his own, listened to his music, and made sure that everything was right."

The night before the contest Boyer Coe discovered that Arnold was planning to make a comeback. After watching Arnold strip down, he took Frank Zane aside and, with a degree of concern for Arnold, wondered out loud, "Why is Arnold doing this to himself? He doesn't have a prayer." Not only had he been out of competition for the past five years; bodybuilding had also changed. In Arnold's day only three or four other bodybuilders had come close to approaching his standard. Now there were many. Moreover, the level of competition was far higher and the bodybuilder's routines were less haphazard and more choreographed.

Later that night Arnold approached Zane and asked if he wanted to share a dressing room with him. Frank replied, "Arnold, are you trying to psych me out?" "Oh, no," replied Arnold. "I wouldn't try and do that." The truth, however, was that that very same night, he was about to take part in one of the greatest psych-outs of his entire career.

The IFBB had just made a crucial revision in the regulations governing the Mr. Olympia contests. Before 1980 the Mr. Olympia contest had been divided into two separate weight classes. First the men weighing over two hundred pounds would compete. Next the men weighing under two hundred pounds competed. Then the winners of the two classes competed against each other. The victor of that contest was then awarded the Mr. Olympia title. Boyer Coe, on various grounds, had put forward a proposal eliminating the two weight classes, with the final contest being among the six best bodybuilders. The governing council of the IFBB had accepted Boyer's proposal, and the new regulation was implemented.

Although the high point of the Mr. Olympia contest is normally the show, the results are determined mainly during the private prejudging meeting. At the 1980 prejudging, Arnold, the eleventh-hour contestant, violently objected to the new IFBB regulation. He preferred the old-style contest, insisting that the original rules be reinstated. Boyer Coe patiently explained to him that the new rule had already been agreed on.

Arnold protested. Mike Mentzer shouted him down. Whereupon Boyer sprang to Arnold's defense, telling Mike that they should listen to Arnold's point of view. Arnold, never one to need a defender, turned on Coe, shouting, "Boyer, why don't you act like a man?" Then, turning to Mentzer, he delivered a zinger to the young upstart who had dared question both his supremacy and his training methods: "Mike, what you have to learn is to keep your big fat gut from hanging out. The reason why you lost the contest last year was that you are just too fat. You looked like hell, and you don't look any better today."

Mike Mentzer went for Arnold. And if Bill Pearl and Ben Weider hadn't separated them, Arnold, who was sitting down, might have had his famous head smashed to pieces by Mike, who was standing above him and, in a blinding rage, was prepared to lash out and pulverize Arnold. Instead, Arnold, with a few well-chosen words, had ultimately pulverized Mentzer. For by now Mike Mentzer had forgotten about the contest. Once again Arnold had psyched out his opponent.

From then on, as far as Mike Mentzer was concerned, Arnold had the upper hand. Whenever Mentzer walked past Arnold, his entire body began to shake. Onstage, every time Arnold managed to catch his eye, he winked at Mentzer, who became so angry he forgot to flex.

Frank Zane was Arnold's next target. A year later Arnold described his tactics in an interview: "I knew Frank Zane would be tense at the moment of the competition, because he hadn't laughed once in the last six weeks. So if I could crack him up with a good joke, all the laughter that he had stored up would come out in a torrent.

"So I prepared a joke and told it to him during the prejudging. He cracked up so much that he leaned back and bent over. And of course the judges are always looking and making notes. They probably thought, 'He is not taking this seriously.' After five years away from competition it was wonderful to use psychological warfare again."

In interviews filmed for The Comeback, conducted before and during the contest, Arnold would allege that he was insecure about stepping onstage for the first time in five years. But as he began to pose to the strains of "Exodus," he enthused that nothing had changed. Waiting for the results, he was exultant: overflowing with enthusiasm and self-confidence, impatient to hear the outcome of the 1980 Mr. Olympia, convinced that he had won.

As Dan Howard, one of the 1980 judges, says, "Arnold beats people before they go onstage." He was right. Although Arnold had trained for only eight weeks, while all the other contestants had trained for a year, he was nevertheless declared the 1980 Mr. Olympia. The audience went wild. Though not in the way to which Arnold was accustomed.

Paul Graham, executive producer of *The Comeback*, with the help of film editor Geoff Bennett, didn't include in the film's sound track the subsequent eruption that greeted the announcement of the 1980 Olympia winner. In the words of an eyewitness, "The audience was furious, throwing things, swearing. A great chorus of 'Rigged, rigged, rigged' flared up. There's never been anything like it in any bodybuilding contest ever. Everyone in the place was booing Arnold, shouting 'bullshit,' and brawling in disgust. Arnold was enraged and went red in the face."

Seething with anger, Arnold stormed out of the Sydney Opera House with a group of reporters in hot pursuit. Almost running toward the exit, he avoided answering their questions, tossing his head in a combination of anger and disdain. Close to the exit, he suddenly realized that Maria, far from being by his side, was talking to some reporters behind him. According to Helmut Cerncic, at the top of his voice Arnold screamed, "You stupid bitch, I'm waiting for you. Come here." Witnessing the scene, Helmut, who had known Arnold since he was a teenage misfit all those years ago in the Athletic Union, thought to himself, "This boy from Austria, who never had a penny, couldn't speak English, now knows someone from the Kennedy family and speaks to her like that. It was amazing."

The attitudes toward Arnold's Olympia victory were many and varied. Some declared that he had been out of shape, that his legs wouldn't even have won him a Mr. Australia title. Others felt that, compared to the rest of the contestants, yes, Arnold had been in shape, but he had been far below his own best form. Then there were those who said that during the contest Franco had tipped the scales in Arnold's favor by marching onstage, in full view of the judges, and toweling down Arnold's body, which, the critics said, made it easy for Arnold to hold his poses.

Among the more serious allegations was the one claiming that all the judges of the 1980 Mr. Olympia either were Arnold's friends or had business relationships with him. And although no one accused the IFBB of having fixed the contest in Arnold's favor, it seemed as if the judges had had eyes only for him.

One of the judges, however, hadn't been taken with Arnold. Surprisingly, his old friend Dan Howard had actually placed him fourth. Dan, not wanting Arnold to hear the truth from anyone else, confronted him and told him how he had voted, explaining, "I didn't think you were the best." Dan's words could not have been more upsetting to Arnold, and he refused to talk to Dan for a year. When he finally relented, almost like a hurt child, he said, "I don't believe that you, a friend of mine, would put me fourth."

The controversy raged on, with Arnold doing all in his power to refurbish his reputation. A month after the contest Jack Neary, one of Joe Weider's top journalists, was at home in Calgary, about to write his report of the 1980 Olympia. Out of the blue, Arnold called, inviting him to lunch, explaining that, just by chance, he was in Canada, nearby in Alberta, holding a seminar. Jack had lunch with Arnold, who tried his best to determine what line Jack was taking in his article. Meeting with failure, he reverted to his elder statesman mode, exhorting Jack, "Let's have a positive report on the contest. This is no time to be airing dirty laundry." Jack assured Arnold that he would be fair. When the article was published, complete with a full report of the contest, Arnold, to Jack's face, called him a whore.

The fallout from the 1980 Olympia was extreme, spilling over into Arnold's next contest, the Pro-Mr. Universe, which he and Jim Lorimer produced a month later in Columbus, Ohio. Arnold had promised that the new Mr.

Olympia would guest pose at the contest, unaware then that he himself would win the title. When the time came, with the crowd expecting Arnold, the new Mr. Olympia, to pose, he adamantly refused. And the Pro–Mr. Universe crowd, like the 1980 Olympia audience, retaliated by subjecting him to vigorous boos. The mighty Arnold was beginning to fall.

It wasn't until six months after the contest that Frank Zane had his moment of confrontation with Arnold. Frank believed—and still does—that Arnold's unexpected participation in the 1980 Mr. Olympia was due partly to the remark Frank had made on winning the 1979 Olympia. "I knew that revenge was part of his motive," says Frank. "He definitely led me into competing. And he didn't say anything about his intentions until he arrived at the show with his gym bag."

So, when Frank and Arnold, like the old friends that they were, had breakfast together half a year after the Sydney event, Frank broached the subject of the contest. Arnold's explanation was this: "If Jimmy Carter went to Ronald Reagan and said, 'This is my plan for beating you in the next election; this is how I plan to win,' Reagan would naturally take advantage of his knowledge. The relationship between Carter and Reagan isn't friendship. They are competitors. So it is strategy." The truth, for Arnold, was that when it came to contests and competition, friendship meant nothing.

Frank and Arnold did remain friends. Yet the stigma of Arnold's last-minute entry into the Mr. Olympia and the accusations surrounding the results clouded his victory and reverberated through the bodybuilding world. Arnold too, with typical bravado, added fuel to the fire, gloating over his 1980 Mr. Olympia title in the revised edition of George Butler and Charles Gaines's book *Pumping Iron*. His purpose in entering, said Arnold, was "to have a good time," to surprise his rivals, to "see them freak out and have diarrhea, you know? And be confused and be upset about it, and have a career that they had planned for themselves go down the tube in two seconds."

As a result of the 1980 Mr. Olympia, Arnold might have endangered his position and eventually relinquished his bodybuilding crown. The last word, however, goes to Arnold himself, who, during a visit by Rick Wayne shortly after the contest, said, "I know I am getting a hard time for this now, but give me a year—six months to a year—they will all have forgotten all the fuss. And I will still have won the Olympia seven times." And so it was.

14
Jayne Mansfield and
Conan the Barbarian

ON OCTOBER 29, 1980, *THE JAYNE MANS-field Story,* in which Arnold played the part of Mickey Hargitay, was aired on network television. Loni Anderson, who played Jayne, performed sexy love scenes with Arnold, engulfing the set in what some perceived as a steamy atmosphere. According to one report, Anderson surprised the director by prematurely ending a love scene with the word "Cut," whereupon Arnold turned bright red. Later Anderson told Arnold, "Thank you. If I ever get divorced, I'll look you up." Be that as it may, when the CBS film aired, Arnold projected a charm and sweetness equaled only in his *Twins* performance eight years later.

He had met Mickey Hargitay before shooting began. Mickey, who had won the NABBA Mr. Universe title in 1956, just eleven years before Arnold, typified the old-time bodybuilder who had achieved fame before the days when, partly thanks to Arnold, bodybuilding had attained respectability and become a big-money sport.

Mickey Hargitay's story underlined the immense strides made by bodybuilders as well as the fate that could have befallen Arnold had it not been for his intelligence, shrewd strategy, and masterful self-promotion. As the film portrayed, Mickey met Jayne when he was appearing at the Latin Quarter in New York as one of Mae West's boys, who, like all bodybuilders, were then regarded merely as outsize pieces of meat. That attitude is reinforced as Jayne takes her new boyfriend to meet Conway, the head of her studio.

Seeing Mickey, as played by Arnold, he coldly ob-

189

serves, "I suppose this strapping young man is your bodyguard, Mickey Hargitay." Although the scene occurred
during the fifties, Conway's assumption that bodybuilders
were destined solely to be bodyguards was not foreign to
Arnold. He had himself encountered similar disparage-
ment during the early seventies.

The studio head's attitude that Mickey, a bodybuilder,
would be bad for Jayne's image had also only recently been
eradicated. As shown in *The Jayne Mansfield Story*, the
bodybuilder was persona non grata. All in all, the Mickey
Hargitay segments of the movie in which he is treated as a
cross between a chorus boy and a big lug, emphasize the
change in the status of bodybuilding and the bodybuilder.
After all, bodybuilders were now accepted not only by studio heads but by Kennedys as well.

Arnold immersed himself in Jayne Mansfield's life
story and was later to say that he had learned a great deal
about show business from studying the blond bombshell's
career. Indeed Jayne Mansfield's story, of a woman who
started her career as merely a great body—albeit with a
higher than average intelligence—provides a parable for
what might have become of Arnold and his own career.

As portrayed in the film, Jayne, with her 162 IQ and
virulent ambition, decides to exploit her body until she
becomes famous, hoping to become known for her intelligence once she becomes a star. Like Arnold, she is intensely
publicity conscious, and like him, analyzed the appeal of
all the Hollywood stars, concluding, as Arnold might,
"They aren't so much actors as personalities frozen."

Known as the most fabulous body in the world, like
Arnold, she accepts mediocre parts in third-rate films—
equivalents of *Hercules Goes to New York*—convinced that
she will have to do so only "till I become a household
name; then they'll have to give me the scripts I want."
Later Arnold would say of Jayne Mansfield's story, "I
learned that you have to establish yourself in an area where
there is no one else. Then you have to create a need for
yourself, build yourself up. While their empire goes on,

slowly, without their realizing it, build your own little fortress. And all of a sudden it's too late for them to do anything about it. And *they* have to come to *you*, because you have what they want. Because you're stable and your films always make money for the producer or the studio."

Sadly, Jayne Mansfield's movies, with the exception of *The Girl Can't Help It,* failed to make enough money for the studios, and she fell into the trap of alcohol and high living. Arnold would not make the same mistake.

There is, however, another eerie echo of Arnold's own life in *The Jayne Mansfield Story.* As Mickey Hargitay, he muses of Jayne, "It really mattered to her, the whole business of being a success. I always wondered what it replaced in her life. What needs it fulfilled." Then, recalling that Jayne's father died when she was three, he answers his own question: "After that, there was never enough love for her."

In late 1980 Arnold had lunch with Rick Wayne and told him that he was going to make a million-dollar movie. Rick assumed that the film's budget was $1 million until Arnold enlightened him: "Oh, no, I am talking about me making a million dollars from a movie." That movie was *Conan the Barbarian.*

Conan the Barbarian tells of a brawny superman who lived in the mythical Hyborean age twelve thousand years ago. Conan, as depicted by author Robert E. Howard, is "afire with the urge to kill, to drive his knife deep into the flesh and bone, and twist the blade in blood and entrails." However much drenched in blood and guts—or perhaps because of it—Howard's Conan stories have always had a cult following.

A sickly only child, Howard built his body up to two hundred pounds and then, starting in 1932, went on to write twenty-one Conan stories. Howard's philosophy, as espoused by Conan, is a highly colored potpourri of macho sentiments exemplified by Conan's words: "Let me lie deep while I live, let me know the rich juices of red meat and stinging wine on my palate, the hot embrace of white arms, the mad exultation of battle when blue blades flame crimson, and I am content. Let teachers and priests and philosophers brood over questions of reality and illusion. I know this: If life is illusion, then I am no less an illusion, and being thus, the illusion is real to me, I live. I burn with life, I love, I slay, and am content."

In 1936, at the age of thirty, on hearing that his mother was on her deathbed, Howard shot himself. His books were published posthumously, and by 1982 the original Conan books had sold an amazing four hundred thousand copies apiece. Now Conan fans from all over the world were eagerly awaiting the spectacle of their beloved character come to life.

The actual budget for the film was $19 million. Arnold, unimpressed, noted that De Laurentiis had allocated $24 million to *King Kong*, his remake of the classic that, despite introducing Jessica Lange to the American public, had bombed. The Conan budget remained a sore point for Arnold throughout filming, during which De Laurentiis exhibited a constant concern about production costs. A contemptuous Arnold would later charge, "Those are the things which are important to Dino. The biggest gorilla in a movie or the longest snake."

John Milius, the film's iconoclastic director, also clashed with De Laurentiis. His solution was to buy a statue of Mussolini and take it to his meetings with De Laurentiis, instructing him, "Dino, while you talk to me, *look at this.*"

Milius, who shared the screenplay credit for *Conan the Barbarian* with Oliver Stone, was born in St. Louis in 1944. Rejected for military service because of his weak lungs and chronic asthma, he confessed that he felt guilty for years. He worked on *Dirty Harry*, wrote the original script for *Magnum Force*, co-wrote *Apocalypse Now* with Francis Ford Coppola, and directed *Dillinger* and *The Wind and the Lion.*

Calling himself "a zen fascist," Milius claims, "My

politics are strange. I'm so far to the right, I'm probably an anarchist." Milius also had his own motorcycle gang of friends, aptly named Mobile Strike Force Paranoia. And according to one source, on set, "Aides come and go with clicking heels and mock Nazi salutes." Working on a Milius film was a unique experience. Said Arnold, "He runs a set like an army. So that's the feeling everyone had—that this wasn't a movie, it was a battle. I felt like I was once again an army tank driver back home in Austria. . . . It *was* a high-spirited set and Milius took it all very well—the Nazi salutes, the drills, 'General Milius' written on the back of his director's chair." An interesting choice of director for Arnold's mainstream film debut, Milius soon became a firm friend of Arnold's.

Conan the Barbarian began shooting in Segovia, Spain, in subzero temperatures. Later the unit moved to Almería, where they endured oppressive heat and a plague of mosquitoes. Undeterred, Milius and his crew soldiered on, determined to re-create the Hyborean age.

Arnold, who had taken sword-fighting lessons, did all his own stunts, the Milius philosophy being "Pain is only temporary, but the film is going to be permanent." Having promised Arnold that during the shooting he would have to deal with pain and dirt, Milius was true to his word.

Minimally dressed, Arnold was run over by horses, bitten by a camel, and smashed all over the room during a snake-wrestling scene, in the process pulling the ligaments in his knee.

Prepared to endure all manner of macho experiences in the interests of his art, Arnold declared, "John wants to bring to the screen as much reality as possible. If you're attacked by a vulture, he wants a real vulture. If you fight with broadswords, he wants real swords that weigh ten pounds. Which, of course, puts you in danger as an actor."

Unafraid, Arnold would later describe his *Conan the Barbarian* exploits in terms that ring with heroism: "Sometimes you have to do what frightens you. . . . In the first scene I had to be attacked by four live wolves. They let the wolves out of their cages too early. I ran back and fell off the rocks and split my back. They rushed me to the medical trailer, a doctor stitched the wounds.

"The second day, I had to be attacked by twenty horses. The third horse charges at me and I fall! But I get up again, yielding [sic] my sword. You cannot imagine the joy of not feeling afraid. I don't care if I'm wounded physically. I am inspired by not being afraid of fearful things." In the same vein he later enthused, "John is a true leader on the set. He brings such joy and energy that it really makes you just do anything he tells you to. He talked me into jumping forty feet into boxes, which I don't think anybody else could do. You feel that to ask for safety measures would be 'pussying out.'" In short, Milius, often himself labeled "Mr. Macho," had obviously found in Arnold the right man for the part.

But if Arnold, as always, was unbeatable in the macho stakes, Milius was not so sure about his abilities in the acting department and voiced his doubts. "He's not a natural," he said. "He'll learn, and he'll improve, but he's not an actor." Milius zealously set about remedying the situation, taking Arnold skeet- and trapshooting, all the while talking about Conan's character. At the same time, he memorized Arnold's facial expressions and then called for the identical expressions on camera.

However much Milius strove to help him, Arnold still experienced difficulties during his love scenes with co-star Sandahl Bergman. Given Arnold's legendary boldness with women and his ability to literally embarrass them into bed, his sudden reticence is difficult to explain. Yet he insisted, "The love-making scenes, they were very, very difficult. It's so strange when you're used to doing these things within the privacy of your own four walls, and then all of a sudden here we are naked with 120 horny Spanish guys breathing down our necks, and we're not even sure who they want to get a look at, Sandahl or me.

"Before nobody had asked us whether we wanted something to drink between takes, and now every other minute here are five guys saying, 'Arnold, do you want some orange juice?' while they're looking up and down. That was kind of uncomfortable, and laughter was the only way we could get through it. Sandahl would sit on top of me and go 'Unnh,' and I would look at her and say, 'Oh, is this the way you do it?' Also, when we shot those scenes it was silent; the sounds were dubbed in later. So we'd hear John saying, 'Arnold, roll over now. Kiss her. Feel her breasts.' And all this time Sandahl would be making faces at me."

Sandahl Bergman, who was romantically involved with *Conan's* stunt coordinator, Terry Leonard, also found the love scenes amusing: "They didn't want to show a lot of flesh. That was nice, but it meant you'd hear things like, 'Sandahl, get the pillow . . . quick, get the pillow. Now, cover Arnold's butt.' We both got hysterical to the point of tears. Maria was worried that Arnold and I were going to have a mad passionate affair."

Although Sandahl and Arnold had private nicknames for each other—Hansel and Gretel—on this occasion Maria didn't have anything to worry about. Arnold's concentration was focused entirely on making *Conan the Barbarian* into a great success. And his efforts were not in vain.

Conan the Barbarian was released in the United States on May 14, 1982. Some reviewers, like critic Peter Rainer of the *Los Angeles Herald Examiner*, were not enthusiastic about Arnold's performance. "In 'Conan' he's not given much opportunity to demonstrate anything except his physique—" Rainer wrote; "he's about as emotive as a tree-trunk. When he's supposed to show love for Valeria, he might as well be staring at a hunk of burlap." Yet *Conan* grossed $9.6 million in its first weekend and was the hottest film of the summer, taking in over $100 million world-wide.

One of Arnold's major strengths has always been his ability for self-promotion. "I'm a salesman," he claimed. "I know exactly what it takes. . . . You want to be one of the

people, rather than coming off like a stiff guy preaching
down. You know what you get from talking down to people. You lose. If you make yourself one of them, you win."
Now, with the entire resources of Universal's publicity
department behind him, he set about applying his vast
talents to promoting *Conan*.

Arnold's publicity campaign, which included a prestigious spread in *People* entitled "Arnold Schwarzenegger
Conquers as Conan and Maybe as a Kennedy In-Law,"
stressed his business savvy, mentioning that he was currently negotiating to sell a square block in downtown
Denver for more than $10 million. At the same time, Ar-
nold took care to mention his University of Wisconsin
degree and his art collection and generally to project the
image of a Renaissance man.

His interviewer also emphasized the fact that Arnold
already owned all the trappings of a full-fledged movie
star—a $300,000 Spanish-style house, complete with Ja-
cuzzi, guesthouse, and a silver Mercedes in the garage.
Then, naturally, there was the Kennedy element, with
Arnold explaining that the Kennedys had totally accepted
him but that marriage, as yet, was not in the cards.

In the meantime Maria's career had zoomed after one
or two setbacks. Sticking to her decision to become an on-
air talent rather than a producer, she approached a Hollywood agent and asked him to represent her. According to
Maria, she was shocked when the agent told her she was
overweight. So shocked, in fact, that she did exactly as he
suggested—losing weight, improving her diction, and
learning to stop using what she called her "big Irish family
hands" when she talked. Her diligence won her a job in
Los Angeles, hosting "PM Magazine." But although she
and Arnold were now based on the same coast, marriage
was still a long way away.

In August Arnold traveled to London to promote *Conan the Barbarian* and joked, "Maria is well-rounded and
gorgeous. I tell her that, if we marry and have kids, with

her body and my mind they'll have some real winners in the family."

Gone was the bodybuilder of yore, replaced by a film star, subtly fielding questions about his romance with Maria Shriver, sophisticated and assured. Now known as an international star, a businessman, an art connoisseur, and a man of property, Arnold Schwarzenegger had made it, in all senses of the word.

15
Conan the Destroyer

NINETEEN EIGHTY-THREE DID NOT BEGIN auspiciously for Arnold. His mother, often sick, suffered a serious health scare, and toward the end of January he flew to her side, visiting her in Graz Hospital.

If he had suffered neglect as a child, had been overshadowed by Meinhard, and had felt unloved, his childhood experiences weren't reflected in his behavior toward his mother. Aware that she missed him, he invited Aurelia to visit him in America for at least six weeks a year. Giving his mother her own room in his house, he watched in amusement as Aurelia, ever the proud Austrian housewife, insisted on polishing his shoes and washing the dishes. He usually spent either Christmas or New Year's Eve with her and thrilled her by taking her with him to the set of whatever film he was currently shooting.

Although he had now been in America for fifteen years, Arnold had not lost touch with his Austrian roots, explaining, "I had a European mentality and now I have an American mentality. Still, with a European upbringing, the European's still in me and will never go away, and I'm happy about that." And, although applying for American citizenship, he turned to his old mentor, Alfred Gerstl, now a powerful politician in Graz, and asked whether Gerstl could arrange for him to retain his Austrian citizenship as well.

Dual Austrian and American citizenship is unusual, but Gerstl, calling on the Styrian governor, Josef Krainer, arranged for Arnold to keep his Austrian citizenship. Never

could it be said of Arnold that he forgot a favor. Eventually,
during the Austrian elections that followed, he thanked
Gerstl by campaigning for him, appearing on television
commercials on his behalf, proclaiming that he owed his
career to Gerstl. He would also indirectly reward Krainer
for his help by subsequently inviting him to his 1986 wedding to Maria Shriver. It may say something about the
nature of his political ambitions that Arnold, in the very
near future, was to forge even stronger links with another
leading Austrian politician.

On September 16, 1983, at the Shrine Auditorium in
Los Angeles, Arnold became an American citizen. With his
showman's instinct for the dramatic possibilities of the
occasion, he played the moment to the hilt, dressed in a
blue and white striped suit and wearing a red tie. Clutching
a small American flag, he held it tightly while singing the
national anthem and, with his hand on his heart, along
with two thousand other immigrants, recited the Pledge of
Allegiance to the flag "and to the republic for which it
stands." When the ceremony was over, he kissed Maria and
informed the group of journalists who had been summoned to witness the historic event, "I always believed in
shooting for the top, and becoming an American is like
becoming a member of the winning team." Then he and
Maria disappeared into their waiting limousine.

Now an American citizen and aware of the publicity
value of flag-waving patriotism, Arnold never missed an
opportunity to advertise his belief in America and the
American dream of which he was a product. He told *Time*
magazine, "In Europe people will have a million reasons
why you will never make it. . . . Americans have such a
wonderful history of growth. When I came here to America, it was like heaven. It was the most pleasant experience
I've ever had. All the great things have happened to me
since I came here."

Again and again he was to make similar admirable
and effective pronouncements, none of which would dam-

age his image. Explaining that he had always wanted to be financially successful, Arnold said, "That's why I came to this country. America is known for being a country of opportunity. When you come over here as a foreigner, this country is heaven because there is no one here that creates obstacles for you to hold you back from making money.

And earlier he had said, "My dream was to end up in America. I felt it was where I belonged. I didn't like being in a little country like Austria. I did everything possible to get out."

Arnold's last statement must have been news to Austrians to whom Arnold had proudly declared, "At heart, I will always be a Styrian." The American public, gratified by Arnold's patriotic statements, might perhaps also have been surprised by his refusal to relinquish his Austrian citizenship. But of course it was unlikely they would ever know about it, since in his press interviews Arnold rarely stresses his dual citizenship. More than a bodybuilder, more than an actor, he was, above all, a politician.

Rumors of Arnold's political ambitions sparked a debate as soon as he became a citizen. His friends too persisted in fanning the flames. Charles Gaines confided to *Esquire* reporter Lynn Darling, "When you think of the things that Reagan is putting his finger on: the new patriotism, the cheerfulness, the optimism, the voracious work ethic—I can't think of a person better placed than Arnold to capitalize on that."

His political ambitions, despite repeated denials, seemed apparent. In 1984 he attended the Republican convention in Dallas, giving a breakfast speech on how proud and pleased he was that he could, on his first opportunity to vote for president, vote for a man like Ronald Reagan.

Of the convention he would later enthuse, "I admire him [Reagan] very much. . . . Because he's done the impossible—he's never gotten beaten in any election. He's really in touch with the people—which is why he wins. . . . God, when I'm his age I hope I'm still alive. He's remarkable."

Always one for action, not just words, Arnold, now a

millionaire from a combination of films and real estate investments, made financial contributions to the Republican party. Lynn Darling observed of his political ambitions, "They are, in fact, of the rock-ribbed conservative Republican variety, ardently anticommunist, founded on a faith in free enterprise, and buttressed by generous contributions not only to Ronald Reagan's presidential campaigns, but to just about any California Republican running for an office higher than dog catcher."

It seemed just a matter of time before "Senator Schwarzenegger" was born. There was just one warning note, sounded by Arnold himself. When asked during one interview about the possibility that he might enter politics, throwing patriotism and lofty statements to the wind, he soberly commented, "I can't imagine the scrutiny."

Politics aside, Arnold's film career was moving ahead as planned. In the fall of 1983 he began filming *Conan the Destroyer*, the sequel to *Conan the Barbarian*. This time, however, Richard Fleischer, not John Milius, was directing. Initially he invited Fleischer to his house to see him in action with the sword master Yamasaki. According to Arnold, the demonstration proceeded perfectly. Then Fleischer stood up, announcing, "This is absolutely fantastic, the best I've seen any actor do. But, Arnold, could I talk with you a minute?" Tactfully taking him aside, Fleischer ventured, "This is a little difficult to say, but could you put on more muscles?" Arnold, slightly shocked, rose to the occasion, went to the gym, trained really hard for five hours a day, ate more protein, and put on ten pounds. Fleischer was delighted.

Things didn't go so smoothly in November, however, once shooting began in Samalayuca, Mexico, fifty miles south of the border. Arnold and the crew were staying at the Plaza Juarez Hotel. Soon after they arrived, *Diario de Juarez* society reporter Alicia Figueroa approached Arnold and seven other people while they were lazing around the hotel pool and asked if she could take some photographs.

Arnold said no. The other members of the group remained silent, so Alicia took their photographs, stopping only when one of them mooned her. Then Arnold sprang into action, demanded her film in what Alicia later described as "a strong voice," and removed it from the camera. And although Arnold gave her the token sum of $4 for her film, Alicia called Arnold "barbaric and mean" in her newspaper column and reported the incident to the Juarez Press Association, which then filed a complaint with the Mexican immigration authorities, seeking to have him thrown out of Mexico. Instead, one of the other crew members who had been at the pool was deported, and Arnold escaped from the situation unscathed.

The incident illustrates Arnold's discomfort when forced to deal with journalists in unstructured situations over which he is unable to exercise any control. For instance, in May 1987, while in Manhattan as he and Maria were making their way to the Regency Hotel, a photographer tried to take their picture, whereupon, the photographer alleged, "Schwarzenegger came up to me and twisted my arm behind my back, grabbed me by the back of my hair and pulled my head back, arching my whole body. . . . By the time I flagged down some police, the Schwarzeneggers had already gone into the Regency."

After being invited by the manager of the Liberty Cafe in Manhattan to take pictures there in 1986, New York photographer Michael Schwartz also encountered the full blast of Arnold's media-directed wrath. According to Schwartz, after he began taking photos of Arnold seated at a table, Arnold got up, walked over to him, and, pointing at him, said, "If you take my picture again I'm going to break your face."

On another occasion, in 1988, Arnold attended a National Rifle Association lunch honoring Texas senator Phil Gramm. The lunch was emceed by Charlton Heston, who asked him how he dealt with being both a Republican and a member of the Kennedy clan. His reply is not on record, but when asked by a journalist if he owned a gun, he appeared tense, snapping, "I'm not here to talk about guns. Write down 'Phil Gramm, Phil Gramm.' We are soul-mates."

Since his first British interview in 1968, he has always been far more at ease telling journalists what they should write, rather than letting them exercise their freedom to ask and, within the boundaries of truth and accuracy, write whatever they wish. At the 1988 Republican convention in New Orleans, that lack of ease spilled over into an encounter with a sixteen-year-old journalist, Adam Horowitz of the publication *The Children's Express*, who approached him to ask why he had attended the convention and was told "Get back" before being pushed aside by an irate Arnold.

Throughout his career he has made the mistake of believing that the press is his own personal sales tool—significant and worthy of respect only if utilized as a way of selling his latest film or promoting his newest venture. Demanding nothing but positive publicity, he is often outraged by negative media coverage. For example, if a publication publishes a photograph or an article that he considers unflattering, Arnold or his publicist sometimes contacts the publisher and complains. In 1988 Peter McGough, editor of the British edition of *MuscleMag International*, published in Nottingham with a British circulation of 35,000 and a U.S. circulation of 150,000, tired of the sometimes excessive adoration of Arnold that still dominates the bodybuilding media in Britain, played a joke on the master practical joker. In the fall issue of the magazine they advertised an upcoming article in the following way: "EXCLUSIVE; Arnold exposé; Arnold; Wild nights at Stallone's! Arnold; The Biggest Boozer! Arnold; the Cracks are showing! Arnold; The Banned Book! Arnold; Facts that will shock! The low-down on Arnold by *MuscleMag*'s Peter McGough who knows more about Arnold than any other journalist." Arnold, in fact, is a place outside Nottingham, complete with a disco called Stallone's. But however small the magazine, however insignificant it may be in the world scheme of the Arnold media machine, when the advertise-

ment was published editor Peter McGough still got a call
from Arnold's press agent, Charlotte Parker in Los Angeles,
saying, "This article could damage Arnold's private and
professional life," and threatening serious consequences—
although she had no information whatsoever about the
contents of the article. Insisting to McGough that his
sources, whoever they were, were lying, she hinted that
"something could be arranged" in exchange for not publishing the offending article.

In the fall of 1989, Arnold said "I realized as time went
on that that's what is great about America, that the people
have freedom to express themselves"—a statement that
sounded a trifle hollow to journalists and writers who have
found themselves tangling with Arnold's attempts at cen-
sorship.

Although Arnold's interventions normally occur post-
publication, they nevertheless serve to reinforce the impression that "Big Brother" Arnold is always watching. It is an
impression that he relishes and makes no attempt to dispel.

By August 1983 Maria had attracted the attention of
the powerful Ed Joyce of CBS, who, after viewing a tape of
Maria submitted by her agent, Art Kaminsky, hired her as
CBS West Coast correspondent. Ostensibly hired to work on
"softer features" for "CBS Morning News," she shared her
beat with entertainment reviewer Pat Collins and, in New
York, former Miss America Phyllis George, who anchored
the program. Maria, with her strong determination and
professionalism, soon outstripped her competition, becoming known for her thoroughness and willingness to do her
homework. Her stories ranged from a straightforward chat
with bestselling author Danielle Steele to a funny item on
Madonna's wedding to Sean Penn, as well as an intimate
interview with "Dynasty" star Linda Evans.

Now twenty-seven, she adhered fiercely to the values
inculcated in her by her Catholic background, adamantly
refusing to ask Linda Evans about her love life, insisting,
"I'd never ask anyone about their sex life." Her background

continued to be a talking point in the media, eliciting the comment from Maria that "I am the person you see on the air. The Kennedy stuff is an illusion of birth. My parents brought me up to be like every other twenty-seven-year-old trying to make a name and profession for herself."

Maria and Arnold were fast gaining the reputation of being a classic workaholic power couple of the eighties. In Juarez, during the filming of *Conan the Destroyer*, Arnold got only five hours sleep a night. His sole Juarez diversion, a love scene with English actress Sarah Douglas, who played the villainess of the piece, ended up on the cutting room floor. Said Sarah, ruefully, "There was a lot of grease and sweat and flailing legs. It was a good raunchy scene." The film was rated PG and opened in America the following July to largely mediocre reviews but good box office receipts.

Nineteen eighty-three, however, ended as badly as it had begun. On December 29th UPI reported that Arnold and Maria had been involved in a car accident. Around midnight, on Interstate 10, ninety miles east of Los Angeles, Arnold lost control of the jeep he was driving, and the jeep rolled down a forty-foot embankment. Maria was slightly injured in the process. California Highway Patrol spokesman Greg Transu later said of Arnold, "His intent was to stop to allow Miss Shriver to drive. Apparently, he thought there was a lane south of where he had intended to stop, but he continued to roll across an asphalt berm down the shoulder and struck a fence bordering the freeway." Transu added that Arnold would be cited for driving without a license.

It is said that people drive the way they live, that their driving styles reflect the way in which they conduct their lives. And Arnold, no matter how much he professed to have planned every single step of his journey through life, was, inside, a breeding ground for rebellion and rashness. And although 1984 would begin with a New Year's resolution reeking of self-discipline—to get up at five each morning and read a magazine or book for an hour—it would ultimately end in lust, sexuality, and recklessness.

16
Gitte

ON MARCH 19, 1984, PRINCIPAL PHOTOGRA-
phy began in Los Angeles on *The Terminator*, the film that
was to win Arnold great acclaim. Arnold originally tried
out for the part of the hero, Reese, but he fell in love with
the part of the terminator, a cyborg killer of the future,
programmed to change history by committing a vital
murder. He got the part and threw himself into it enthusi-
astically, braving sleazy locations in downtown L.A. and
perfecting a deadpan expression as befitting a robot.

He loved the futuristic vehicles and laser guns used in
the film, as well as the Uzi submachine gun, guarded on
the set by two FBI agents. Speaking only five or six lines of
dialogue throughout the picture, he also scored a career
first by appearing fully clothed during most of the film.
His leather jacket and "terminator" sunglasses, as well as
his line "I'll be back," sparked a craze during the fall of
1984, when *The Terminator* was released. His audience
loved him as the villain, cheering wildly as he wreaked
havoc on a police station. One of 1984's top-grossing films,
The Terminator was also chosen as one of the year's ten best
films by *Time* magazine.

All through the spring and summer of 1984 Arnold's
star seemed to be in ascendance. The July release of *Conan
the Destroyer* increased his box office power, yet that film
was to be eclipsed by the success of *The Terminator*. In the
summer he released a fitness record album, which, along
with his bestselling bodybuilding books, further consoli-
dated his position in the health and fitness field. His media
visibility was enhanced by his attendance at the Republi-

can convention in Dallas. Maria too was making her mark in her chosen career, working hard for CBS as a television journalist in L.A. And their romance continued to excite the imagination of the American public. Fortune, as always, was working in Arnold's favor. Or so it seemed.

It all began when Dino De Laurentiis, while leafing through a pile of fashion magazines, first saw her face. She was twenty-one years old and blessed with what the French term *la beauté du diable*—the beauty of the devil. Her name was Brigitte Nielsen. She was born to dazzle, bewitch, and almost destroy two of the most charismatic specimens of masculinity that Hollywood has ever seen.

Had she been honest with you, Brigitte, in an English once faintly tinged with the inflection of her native Denmark but now inexplicably overlaid with the cadence of the Louisiana bayous, would have explained that she was moody, emotional, and extremely passionate. Then, flexing her voice in an attempt to project a power equaling that of her amazing body, she might have added, "But I've learned to live with it."

She had always been stormy, restless, and reckless, consumed by a desire to escape from her conventional background. Born to a middle-class family, her father was an engineer and her mother a librarian. The family, which also included her brother, Jann, three years her junior, lived in a chalet-style brick-fronted house in Herlev, on the outskirts of Copenhagen.

Years later her personality would enthrall even those who, aware of her reputation, were prejudiced against her. But at school she experienced difficulty in mixing with her contemporaries, who didn't seem to like her. Eager to please, she joined in, singing in the school choir and smoking grass with the other girls in the school bathroom, but nevertheless seemed out of place, out of sync with suburban Denmark.

Earning money had always been important to her. At the age of eleven she delivered mail, then took a part-time job selling bread in a bakery. Food, however, apparently was not vital to Brigitte; at thirteen she was five foot eleven and weighed in at an emaciated ninety pounds. Nicknamed "Giraffe" by her schoolmates, she had become hyperactive and was prone to erupting in startling explosions of energy.

Her teenage ambitions indicate a lot about Brigitte; she wanted, she says, to be a vet and to write poetry. And simultaneously aiming for worthiness and romance, she could never quite make up her mind whether she wanted to be Florence Nightingale or something altogether more glamorous.

Her father, Sven, instilled self-confidence in the gangling teenager, telling her, "Just be polite and don't ever be afraid to ask questions." Brigitte, as it turned out, never found it necessary to be too polite, for success, although initially not sought by her, came swiftly and easily.

At seventeen, while having a glass of wine at the Pederoxa Cafe in Copenhagen's Grabodretrov district, Brigitte was discovered by photographer Marianne Diers, who asked her if she had done any photographic modeling. Replying that she hadn't and insisting that she was too ugly to be a model, Brigitte confided to Marianne that she hated her life and used to spend her school days crying because she was too tall and skinny.

Realizing that although Brigitte was beautiful she was emotionally volatile and in desperate need of guidance, Marianne's solution was to persuade her to pose for photographs. That done, she sent the photographs to one of Copenhagen's top model agencies, run by Trice Tomsen. Says Trice, "I immediately knew she was special. But it took time for her to begin to believe in herself. I decided to cut her hair because it made her legs look even longer. She looked like a goddess."

Seeing her pictures, Brigitte suddenly was aflame with egotism and self-interest. According to Trice, "Brigitte finally realized what was happening to her, and her ambition grew. She was determined she was going to be somebody. Having lovers or relationships was not that important. Her ambition took over."

Bubbling with intensity and a newfound desire for success, Brigitte left home, still only seventeen, to work for Trice, who billed her as the face of the eighties. Following the model's classic route, she set off on that gilded road between Paris, Milan, and Rome, ricocheting from photo session to photo session.

When she was seventeen-and-a-half, she worked with photographer Monte Shadow, modeling for an Italian sportswear firm, and they spent three weeks together in the Seychelles. From the start, he was overwhelmed by her: "She was tall and strong, healthy-looking, and very sexy. She was a strange combination. On one hand, she was like a lost child. On the other, she was very wild and loved adventure. Four days after we arrived in the Seychelles, there was a coup. Brigitte insisted on looking around, although I told her to stay with the rest of the team. Instead she went off and, for a few hours, was taken hostage. She lived on impulse and never thought before she acted."

An individualist, Gitte, as those close to her called her, was nonetheless not a loner. For a time she basked in the sensation her Amazonian body was creating in Milan. According to Monte, "There were parties, and Brigitte was very exposed. She loved it when people talked about her and she was the center of attraction. She was the queen of the Milan discos—a star." Soon she was living with Milan-based modeling agent Lucca Rossi. He provided her with security while she waited for the success that she now believed was her birthright. A close friend, another Milan photographer, Riccardo Gay, says of the Brigitte of those early days, "There was never any doubt that she was going to be a somebody. There was a sensual, stylish magic about her. She was like a volcano just waiting to explode with temperament."

Before the explosion, however, there was a period of calm. In 1982 she met a musician named Kasper Winding and moved into his three-bedroom flat in Copenhagen's

Kronprinsessegade. Kasper was successful, he loved Brigitte, and a life of domesticity seemed inevitable. Soon they were married, she was pregnant, and the prospect of high-fashion stardom appeared remote. Her future, on the surface, seemed predictable, especially once she gave birth to a baby, Julian.

Later she would allege that she had wanted to name Julian Sylvester, after *Rocky* star Sylvester Stallone, but that Kasper, out of jealousy over her adolescent crush, had stopped her. However, it is highly unlikely that Kasper ever could have managed to prevent Brigitte from doing anything she wanted. She was willful and irresponsible and hungry for fame so that when the call came from De Laurentiis nothing, not even Julian, would stop her.

De Laurentiis had spent nearly a year searching for his Red Sonja, an Amazonian actress who would star in his proposed film of the same name, which told the tale of a female version of Conan. Traveling the world, he was set on finding a unique woman of fire and passion, capable of re-creating Howard's legendary swordswoman. Then luck intervened, in the shape of a fashion magazine with Brigitte Nielsen gracing the cover. Studying her photograph, De Laurentiis, no mean appraiser of female flesh, knew that he had finally found his Red Sonja.

Hailed as De Laurentiis's latest discovery, the embodiment of stars to come, and the find of 1984, Brigitte rushed to London, where she was to take sword-fighting lessons with expert Mike Finn. There she also gave her first English-speaking press interview. Victor Davis, a *London Daily Express* writer, found Brigitte "friendly" and "warm-hearted."

Then it was on to the Pontini Studios in Rome, where shooting was scheduled to begin almost immediately, on September 24th. American director Richard Fleischer projected that the shoot would last eleven weeks, including location work in Abruzzi, Italy. Fleischer enthused, "Brigitte had a lot of sparkle, had an amazing body, and is an incredible girl." The film was centered around Brigitte and her two co-stars: the ubiquitous Sandahl Bergman and the male lead, Brigitte's love interest, Arnold Schwarzenegger.

There are those who claim that Maria Shriver, perhaps filled with a sense of impending doom, had advised Arnold not to travel to Rome, not to play a part in De Laurentiis's latest extravaganza. Arnold had, indeed, attempted to back out, arguing that he didn't like the script, but was unable to break his contractual obligations to De Laurentiis. So here he was in Rome on the set of *Red Sonja*, face to face, for the first time in his life, with Brigitte Nielsen.

Each, in their own way, was accustomed to exercising charm, to captivating anyone who crossed their paths, but both knew that they had met their match. For in many ways Brigitte Nielsen was Arnold's doppelgänger, his female mirror image, his other self.

They both burned with an implacable ambition, Arnold's having launched him on an odyssey covering four continents, resting finally in Hollywood, and Brigitte's having led her to leave her baby son Julian with her soon-to-be-ex-husband Kasper in Denmark.

Both European adventurers were determined to conquer America. Their charm was unassailable, switched on and off at will, potent, and capable of enveloping any target in a cobweb of charisma from which escape was virtually impossible. Arnold had perfected every nuance of charm over his show business career. Brigitte, however, was another story, inexplicably at twenty-one already a world-class charmer.

Some say that charm is a dangerous gift from the gods that, while opening many doors, can far too quickly lead the charmer into realms with which he or she is unequipped to cope. Undeniably Brigitte Nielsen's charm brought her very far, very fast, earning her unparalleled media attention. Three-and-a-half years after the shooting of *Red Sonja*, in the course of that media attention, I interviewed Brigitte and thus gained some insight into the woman who was to enslave first Arnold Schwarzenegger and then Sylvester Stallone.

Interviewing her for an *US* magazine cover story in early 1988, I was confronted by Brigitte, dressed in a clinging Azzedine Alaïa outfit. Impishly, or perhaps out of habit, she was, for a woman who had recently and universally been lambasted as a gold digger, laden with gold: a bit of Bulgari here, a sparkle of Cartier there, a cluster of diamonds surrounded by yet another chunk of gold fashioned in intricate Italian design.

Although the interview was Brigitte's first American cover story since her divorce from Sylvester Stallone, she answered all questions nonchalantly, in a monotone, completely uninvolved, assuming an attitude as jaded as Gloria Swanson might have exhibited in *Sunset Boulevard* after decades of press interviews. She drank beer, chain-smoked Marlboros, and made it obvious that the interview held less interest for her than a rotting piece of chewing gum she might step over in the gutter. Until I mentioned astrology.

In passing I said that I had studied it, and she was transformed. I alluded to her sun sign, Cancer, and it became obvious that she was determined to extend the discussion and to have me interpret her chart. Suddenly I was plied with offers and attention. Did I want an amaretto? A little cognac? Perhaps a cappuccino? Or, as I was English, would a cup of tea be more appropriate? What a beautiful wedding ring I was wearing! How long had I been married? And was I happy? Her interest and concern were warm and all-embracing. All at once we were sisters under the Alaïa. While creating an atmosphere of intimacy and charm, she casually mentioned that she would really love to discuss her chart and astrological future with me. Anyone witnessing the scene might well have concluded that at that moment, to Brigitte Nielsen, in quest of her destiny among the stars, I was the most important person in the world.

During that interview, long after her first meeting with Arnold, when asked to comment on him, her answer, short and abrupt, was "Of course, I don't know Arnold that well." That, however, was not the truth.

Those first few days in Rome, Arnold made it clear to her that they were merely working together, that their relationship would remain on a purely professional level. He had not, as yet, realized that he and Brigitte had much in common, including one extremely striking similarity that was to play a vital part in their respective destinies: an extraordinarily strong will to win.

Remembering Arnold's decision to resist her charms, she later confided to her bodyguard, Mike Cantacessi, "No way. I wanted it, so I was going to go for it." Go for it she did. Sometime, somewhere, not long after they first met, Brigitte managed to seduce Arnold. Not that it was difficult. According to Arnold's one-time girlfriend Sue Moray, Arnold later compared Brigitte to Sue—sensual and uninhibited, willing to have sex anywhere, anytime, anyhow. She also worked out with him in Rome and was warmhearted, solicitous of his welfare, and flatteringly eager to learn from his superior wisdom.

By October 11th the rumors of their relationship were already so rampant that the *Vienna Kurier*, normally anxious to protect its native son's image, carried an item commenting on the blazing new attraction that had flared up between Arnold Schwarzenegger and Brigitte Nielsen.

In November Aurelia Schwarzenegger visited Arnold on the Roman set of *Red Sonja* and to her horror found him involved in a torrid liaison with a Danish bombshell named Brigitte Nielsen. After meeting her, Aurelia exclaimed to Arnold, "Just who is this stupid person?" Accustomed to the joys of churchgoing with Maria Shriver and anticipating the gratifying prospect of becoming grandmother to the Kennedy genes, Aurelia, a down-to-earth and far from unintelligent woman, took one look at the adventuress who had bewitched her son and was dismayed.

According to Sue Moray, who says Arnold told her the story, by the time the *Red Sonja* cast and crew had moved to Abruzzi for location shooting, Arnold had discovered that a suspicious Maria had charged spies in the unit to report his every move to her. Giving full rein to his recklessness, Arnold, according to Sue, refused to terminate his affair as he and Brigitte were sexually intoxicated with each other. She was obsessed with him. And Arnold, though virtually engaged to Maria Shriver, found himself falling in love with Brigitte.

It was undeniable that there was an excitement about her, a danger, which she almost openly courted. Arnold too must have relished the danger of discovery, something he had probably never really experienced before. Perhaps, given his father's propensity for applauding him for having girlfriends, he had never undergone the normal adolescent sexual rites of passage, had never shivered with a combination of fear and excitement, terrified that his sexual escapades might be discovered yet still excited by the prospect. True, he had lived with Sue Moray while courting Maria, but that had been at the start of their relationship. Now they had been together for more than seven years, with marriage almost inevitable. It was patently clear that he was her intended. Despite Arnold's awareness that Maria's spies were watching, Sue Moray says that when they had lunch together after his return from Rome, Arnold boasted to her about how he and Brigitte had evaded their clutches.

There is a byword among those who work in television and films, "On location it doesn't count," the subtext being that once the cameras stop rolling and the picture is over, the affair is over. Given Arnold's self-control and capacity for making the right moves in all areas of his life, combined with his opportunism, it was to be expected that his affair with Brigitte would stop as soon as filming ended and he left Rome. The Austrian media were hinting about the affair, but word had not yet leaked out to the American media. Maria too may have had reports from her "spies," but Arnold's infidelity was not yet public knowledge. In short, he had had what appeared to be a lucky escape. After all, disclosure of his love affair with Brigitte, who was basically nothing more than a starlet, could ruin his romance with Maria and send him hurtling out of Camelot, ruining his media image in the bargain.

Yet around December 9th Brigitte and Arnold flew to Vienna—together. Due to fog, their plane from Rome arrived half a day late. They checked into the Vienna Hilton. Next, throwing caution to the wind, Arnold took Brigitte to visit his old friend, Bernd Zimmermann.

The visit to Zimmermann's Kaiserstrasse Fitness Center was not a tête-à-tête but a party, lavishly attended by the Vienna press corps, some of whom took one look at Arnold and his Gitte and sized up the situation correctly. In an astonishing move, Arnold confirmed their suspicions by posing for photographs with Brigitte, holding her tightly. Standing together, visually they typify the Aryan ideal: strong, tall, and confident. Brigitte, with a smile as blindingly dazzling as Arnold's own, looks seductively into the camera, projecting herself with charm and sexuality, perhaps aware that together she and Arnold are the stuff of legend, a radiant couple who appear to have been matched up in heaven by the very gods themselves.

That Saturday night Zimmermann, whom Brigitte had probably charmed, invited her and Arnold to Hugo Reinprecht's Grinzinger wine bar, where they feasted on ham, eggs, and sauerkraut, accompanied by caraway-seed rolls, followed by Salzburger nockerln and strudel. Then it was back to the Hilton's Klimmt Bar, where they sat talking until two in the morning.

Arnold's business partner and mentor, Jim Lorimer, whether by accident or design, was in Vienna, and, cautious for a moment, Arnold left Brigitte behind at the Hilton while he and Jim had Sunday brunch with the American ambassador to Austria, Helene Van Damm. It is highly

likely, in the light of subsequent events, that Arnold confided details of his passion for Brigitte to his older mentor.
Yet if the relatively conservative Lorimer did, indeed, warn
Arnold to break up with Brigitte, Arnold ignored the advice. And although she was scheduled to depart from
Vienna that Sunday, instead Arnold took Brigitte with him
to Munich. The *Vienna Kurier*, apprised of that fact, commented on how well Arnold and Brigitte were getting
along.

On December 27th the ever-vigilant *Kurier* reported
that Arnold had recommended Brigitte to his agent, Lou
Pitt, at the influential International Creative Management
agency. Not content with that, according to the report,
Arnold also raved about Brigitte, enthusing quite openly,
"She is heavenly. If I could, I would have her in Hollywood
tomorrow."

So far the American press hadn't noted Arnold's apparent defection from Maria. But instead of thanking his lucky
stars, Arnold decided to push fate to the extreme by taking
Brigitte on his annual skiing holiday, a stag affair, from
which Maria was usually banned. This time Arnold took
Brigitte along with a group of three male friends: Eric
Holme, Bernd Zimmermann, and Munich fitness studio
owner Wolfgang Spieker.

They booked into a hotel owned by two of Arnold's
friends—Austrian ski champion Klaus Heidegger and his
American wife, Jami Heidegger, an aerobics teacher—in
Axams, a tiny ski resort twelve miles outside of Innsbruck.
Although Axams had played host to the Winter Olympics
on two occasions, normally it was a quiet, typically Tyrolean village—the perfect setting for a love affair that required privacy. Brigitte, however, never one for keeping a
low profile, soon alerted the locals to her presence in Axams by shopping for ski outfits in the boutique next door to
the hotel.

They stayed at Heidegger's for only two or three days,
enjoying themselves in the chalet-style inn, complete with
sauna. Heidegger's, today under new management and re-

named the Sonnpark, was fun, unpretentious, and unsophisticated, the kind of place to which Arnold would never
have taken Maria. During their trips to Austria she and
Arnold traveled in high style, staying at one of Graz's best
hotels or, once, at Schloss Fuschl near Salzburg, a luxurious resort frequented by kings and queens.

Maria and Brigitte, it was clear, were worlds apart—
Maria, the protected Kennedy princess, and Brigitte, the
flamboyant and worldly model. Ironically, however, although both women claimed to be ambitious, it was Maria,
the privileged, who worked hard at her career and Brigitte,
the streetwise adventuress, who, it would transpire, was the
dilettante, theoretically an actress, yet refusing to study
acting for any length of time. While Maria stoutly refused
to trade on her birthright, educating herself for success,
Brigitte, with her fabulous face and figure, insisted on
trading on that and little else.

On January 9, 1985, the *Tiroler Chronik* published a
picture of Arnold, Jami, and friends having dinner at
Heidegger's. Brigitte was absent from the group. But Arnold must have known it was only a matter of time before
his love affair was picked up by the American press. As it
was, he had tempted fate for long enough, perhaps, like
Senator Gary Hart after him, subconsciously yearning to
sabotage the gilded future that awaited him. Gary Hart
and Arnold both are men of power and potential who
apparently delighted in taunting fate, testing their power
by flying close to the sun, challenging the gods to destroy
them. The more scorching the danger, the more exhilarat-
ing the experience.

Arnold, in his arrogance, driven by desire, must have
believed that however close to the edge he ventured, he
would never fall. He once said, "I'd never ski down a safe
slope because that's no fun. I'm looking for the risk." He
had always valued ambition and worldly success above all
else. Yet for a short while he deviated from his destiny,

risking discovery, ridicule, and the end of his relationship with Maria Shriver.

Perhaps he took that risk because on some level he hoped his affair would demolish his relationship with Maria. Then again he may, indeed, really have been tempted to break off with Maria and instead link his life to Brigitte's. As he later confessed to Sue Moray, he was in love with Brigitte. Not merely sexually—although he is reported to have told others that sex with her was incredible—but because, somewhere deep inside, she was vulnerable and had let Arnold glimpse that vulnerability. And like him, she was reckless, carefree, and undeniably sensual.

Yet a warning voice inside him, one that had rarely failed him, must have told him that she was too much, too rash, too irresponsible. She was attractive because she had no limits and no sense of survival. And Arnold being Arnold, he must have sensed that Brigitte could be self-destructive, could destroy them both. In love or not, he would always remain a survivor. There was another factor, apart from his gut instinct, that disturbed him: Brigitte's attitude toward her baby son, Julian. Sue Moray said he later confided, "I loved her, but I didn't respect the fact that she just dumped her son. . . . And she was too reckless for me."

Around January 11, 1985, he flew back to America on the *Concorde*, alone. Wearing a brown leather jacket, he seemed pensive and sad. He may have thought that their star-crossed affair was over, that he had seen the last of her, that she would never enter his life again. But that wasn't true. For Brigitte was an uncontrollable force of nature and, like Arnold himself, devoured by ambition, was determined to win her heart's desire.

17
Arnold, Brigitte, Maria, and Stallone

BACK IN LOS ANGELES, ARNOLD BEGAN filming *Commando*, an action/adventure movie that was close in style and substance to Sylvester Stallone's phenomenally successful *Rambo: First Blood Part II*. Arnold played the role of a commando who wants to retire to spend time with his daughter but swings into action when she is kidnapped, undergoing untold ordeals until he rescues her.

Conceding the similarities between *Rambo: First Blood Part II* and *Commando*, producer Joel Silver would later say, "Of course *Rambo* and *Commando* have a lot in common. They are both larger than life stories about cartoon-like characters that take on enormous odds and win. I think, because of Arnold, *Commando* has a sense of humor that Rambo doesn't have."

When the film was released in October 1985, *Commando* was a big box office success, although it still didn't eclipse *Rambo* at the box office. Eight years had passed since Arnold first met Stallone at the Golden Globe Awards, and Stallone, not Arnold, was still on top. Through his relationship with Maria and the Kennedys Arnold had socially eclipsed his rival. But with *Rambo: First Blood Part II* Stallone had become a folk hero, an American legend welcomed by President Reagan at the White House. His private life may have been in shambles, after an extremely public separation from his wife, Sasha, but professionally Stallone was invincible.

It seems clear that Arnold made a decision to change that, for since 1977 Stallone had continued to command a far bigger salary and far more power in Hollywood than Arnold had. In short, Stallone, who had been trained by Franco Columbu for one of his film roles, was Arnold's Frank Zane, his Sergio Oliva, the man who had beaten him and who he, in turn, was now determined to beat.

Arnold, while publicizing *Commando*, began his campaign to dethrone Stallone. "I'd be angry at hearing my name mentioned in the same breath as Stallone's," he told journalist Ian Harmer. "Stallone uses body doubles for some of the close-ups in his movies. I don't. . . . We probably kill more people in *Commando* than Stallone did in *Rambo*, but the difference is that we don't pretend the violence is justified by patriotic pride. All that flag waving is a lot of bull. . . . I've made a better film than Stallone's and I'm happy to wait for time to prove me right." A spokesman for Stallone commented, "Sylvester doesn't want to get into a dispute over who is tougher."

Arnold had fired the first shot in the feud he had decided to manufacture. And perhaps he had been waiting for the opportunity since their first meeting. His *Commando*-related comments were the first of his moves that seemed designed to rile and undermine Stallone.

His second public move was made in a July 1986 interview with *GQ*, during which he observed, "I think Stallone, as far as I know him, is extremely intense all the time, even when he comes to the gym; it's continuous competition. If you're doing 120-pound curls, he will say, 'I can do 130.' He's obsessed, and that carries through in the way he dresses, how hard he tries to belong to a charity organization. It's all Rocky. It doesn't come from, you know,"—Arnold points to his heart. "There's no love there. And people see that. You can fake your way through for a year, but for ten years, that's hard. Eventually, it catches up with you. I think that's the difference between him and me."

Shortly afterward, according to journalist Pat H. Broeske, Stallone admitted that he phoned Arnold and informed him that if it hadn't been for him (Stallone), Arnold wouldn't even *have* an action-film career. "I told him there was room for both of us," said Stallone. "So why backstab?" Arnold replied that he had been misquoted by GQ.

Around the time of Arnold's GQ interview, Rick Wayne, then working for Flex magazine, was about to publish a photograph Art Zeller had taken of Arnold, Franco, and Stallone standing around a machine at World Gym. Then the phone rang. Says Rick, "It was Arnold. He asked me not to use the picture. At least not to have him in it. He said, 'Why should I be in a picture with Stallone?'— the impression being, 'Why should I help make Stallone?' That picture has never been used anywhere. Arnold stopped it from being used."

It seemed clear that Arnold had appointed Sylvester Stallone as his nemesis.

Brigitte Nielsen was determined to continue her affair with Arnold. Officially Arnold had told her it was over, presenting her with a watch that she later dismissed as being too inexpensive and unworthy of her. Nevertheless, deciding to ignore the significance of the watch, Brigitte, secure in her physical charms and convinced that she still had a hold over Arnold, made up her mind to pursue him.

In the new year of 1985 Monte Shadow drove her to St. Moritz for a short vacation and to attend a jet-set party. He remembers, "Brigitte was excited that Prince Albert of Monaco was going to be at the party. But she was still desperate because Arnold had got rid of her. I had to stop the car two or three times on the way to St. Moritz because she was so desperate to reach Arnold. She was very nervous. He was trying to avoid her and, at first, wouldn't accept her calls. But she ran after him and, after three days in St. Moritz, managed to talk to him.

"Brigitte was crazy about Arnold. She is wild, loves sex, and adores someone who is physically stronger than she is. She told me she was always dreaming about incredibly healthy, strong, good-looking muscle men. So Arnold was ideal.

"Brigitte really wanted Arnold desperately. She is very

impressionable, like a chameleon. If you put her with a
nun, she would become like a nun. She had been with
Arnold; now she wanted to be like him. She did everything
to look strong because she wanted to be a female Stallone or
Schwarzenegger." Shadows adds, "She was incredibly ambitious."

Indeed she was. Some time in the spring of 1985 Brigitte arrived in America, ostensibly to begin promoting *Red
Sonja* but also determined to win Arnold back. Whether or
not she succeeded at that point is debatable. One thing is
certain. She definitely did meet Sylvester Stallone. Both he
and Brigitte have always claimed that they met because she
sent Stallone a fan letter and a striking photograph of
herself. Yet there is a second version of their meeting, one
that puts forward the theory that it was not Cupid, but
Arnold Schwarzenegger, who engineered Brigitte's first
meeting with Stallone.

For, some time after his return from Austria, Arnold
confided to an intimate friend that he had arranged for one
of his associates to set Brigitte up with Stallone because he
wanted to get rid of her. Arnold himself has confessed, in
an interview published in the German edition of *Playboy*,
that Brigitte had wanted to marry him and that when he
reminded her of his commitment to Maria she announced,
"I am unbeatable," and that he then suggested she look for
fresh fields to conquer. He adds that, as chance would have
it, Brigitte knew his attorney, Jake Bloom (probably having
met him in Rome during the *Red Sonja* shoot), and that
Jake invited her to dinner. And, according to Arnold, it was
at that dinner that Brigitte met Stallone (also a Jake Bloom
client). Stallone, says Arnold, took one look at Brigitte and
fell madly in love with her. "I was happy about that," said
Arnold, "because I didn't want her after me."

Completely unaware that from the first Arnold had
been pulling the strings by setting his new romance in
motion, Stallone was enchanted by Brigitte. Due to start
filming *Rocky IV* in Canada, he quickly rewrote the script,

creating a part specifically for Brigitte, that of the Russian interpreter wife of Ivan Drago, played by Dolph Lundgren. According to an eyewitness on the set, "Brigitte couldn't take a word of criticism from Sly. . . . She acted as if she was a star." She did, however, take gifts: a white Canadian fox coat and a diamond-studded Cartier "Panther" watch bearing the legend "I'll love you till the end of time."

Stallone, far more than Arnold, has always been a romantic, ruled by his heart rather than his head. And despite his macho image, when it comes to romance he appears to have marshmallow, not steel, coursing through his veins. A loner who avoids crowds and too much contact with other people, he seems to prefer his own company to that of others, while Arnold, put simply, loves being the center of attention, the life and soul of the crowd, feeding on it for strength and relishing its occasional malice—just as long as he can control it. A man who comes across as vulnerable and introspective, sometimes insecure, moody, temperamental, and receptive to female flattery, Stallone was the perfect rebound romance for Brigitte. And it soon became clear that, if Arnold didn't want her, Stallone definitely did.

During the filming of *Rocky IV* Stallone's heart was bruised in a fight scene with Dolph Lundgren. He was rushed to intensive care, with Brigitte in hot pursuit. Three years later, talking on the set of *Rambo III* in Yuma, Arizona, Stallone remembered, "She was with me twenty-four hours a day. She even slept under my bed. The nurses begged her to leave the room. But she refused. . . .

"I was extremely vulnerable after my divorce from Sasha. And I was looking for somebody to hold on to. Brigitte seemed to be the perfect woman. She sent me roses, showered me with love and was the warmest woman in the world. She seemed demure and devoted to me. She was one of the kindest, most outgoing women I had ever met. I fell madly in love with her." By playing Florence Nightingale to a glamour-laden superstar, Brigitte had at last found the perfect synthesis of her teenage ambitions. She also must

have been aware that Stallone was Arnold's archrival and
that her affair with him might provoke Arnold so much
that she would be able to win him back. In the meantime,
she wasn't lax in consolidating her power over Stallone,
even banning his mother, Jacqueline, from her son's hospital room.

By May 1985 Brigitte's hold on Stallone's heart had
tightened. Arnold, meanwhile, had turned his attention to
real estate. On March 20th he had paid nearly $1 million
for property in Denver near the site of a proposed $129
million convention center. His latest book, *Encyclopedia of
Modern Bodybuilding*, which as a manuscript totaled one
thousand pages, was due for July publication. In March
Esquire had published a major interview with Arnold that
demonstrated that his fabled sense of humor had remained
unchanged. "As he leaves," journalist Lynn Darling wrote,
"a shy young security guard approaches Schwarzenegger
and offers to escort him back to his limousine. Schwarzenegger is flattered by the awe in the man's eyes and begins
to ask him questions. The guard tells Schwarzenegger that
he is going to night school to study business and that he
hopes eventually to start his own small shop. 'You should
sell dildoes,' Schwarzenegger tells him. 'I beg your pardon,
sir?' stammers the bewildered guard. 'Sure,' explains
Schwarzenegger. 'People buy them for presents, they like to
be funny at parties. They really sell.' "

Red Sonja was released in July to appalling reviews
(one labeling it "shamelessly silly," another "bubble-
headed"), but given the paucity of his part, that didn't affect
Arnold. Perhaps out of deference to Maria, he did no promotion for the film, leaving all publicity to the limelight-
hungry Brigitte. Instead he focused his attention on his
upcoming part in *Raw Deal*, a promising project due to be
directed by De Laurentiis. All in all, professionally his life
appeared to be on schedule.

Privately, however, it was another thing. Although
there is no documentary evidence, it is highly likely that
Maria had discovered the truth about Arnold's liaison with

Brigitte. When asked in 1986 by journalist Monica Collins if she would like to be a muscle man's consort like Brigitte, the normally diplomatic Maria retorted, "Oh gawd, spare me. Have you met her? Gawd."

"Gawd," apparently having been alerted to the danger threatening Maria's romance with Arnold, moved events along to her satisfaction. In May 1985, just four months after he had officially ended his affair with Brigitte, Arnold, while having a sauna with Jim Lorimer, turned his thoughts to the subject of marriage.

It would be difficult not to question the preponderance of coincidences in the sequence of events: Arnold and Brigitte have an affair; Jim Lorimer, one of Arnold's closest friends and a trusted adviser, is in Vienna with Arnold during that affair; a few months later, Maria presumably having discovered the truth about Arnold's affair, Lorimer advises him to marry her.

According to Lorimer, "Arnold and I were in the Jacuzzi at his house, and I said to him, 'Arnold, you've really had a tremendous experience. It exceeds anything you really thought would happen. One thing you haven't had and must have is the experience of a family and children and grandchildren. That will complete the picture for you. You've got to go through all of life's cycles. You've been with Maria for eight years, as far as your courtship is concerned. It would seem to me to be the time for you to move on to the next stage of your life.' " Eight weeks later Lorimer received a telegram from Arnold and Maria, on holiday in Austria together, announcing, "We did it."

Arnold, once so reckless with Brigitte, stage-managed his engagement to Maria with extreme calculation. On his thirty-eighth birthday, exhibiting his flair for dramatics, he took Maria to Thal. A man who has always hated ordinary things, he didn't want to propose in an ordinary way, so he took Maria out in a rowboat on the Thalersee, where it had all begun for him.

According to Arnold, "It was a great sunny day. There were great green mountains all around. And so we were rowing and I said, 'This is the perfect situation.' No one was there to bother us or interrupt as it happens so often when I go somewhere. I thought it was very romantic. So I proposed to her."

According to Maria, she then said, "Hey, Arnold, what's so special about today? Have I been especially *good* lately? Have I gotten really *beautiful?*" Arnold's reply is not known.

Their engagement was announced in the American press on August 10th. On August 8th Brigitte Nielsen's second major American press interview was published in the *New York Daily News*. In her first, published in *People* magazine, she had declared, "Arnold is not that macho," and, affirming her love for Stallone, added, "I'm young, but I've lived a lot. You can't sit in a chair and wait for things to happen. . . . I'm *very* outgoing. I have a lot of energy. I say to myself, 'Hey, let's go for it!' "

In her *People* interview Brigitte "went for it" by in effect goading Arnold. In her *Daily News* interview, published just two days before his engagement to Maria was officially announced, Brigitte, when asked if she and Stallone might get married, declared for the benefit of all the world and, more particularly, Arnold, "Most definitely. I love Stallone very much." Given the timing of her announcement, it is difficult not to conclude that Brigitte had been forewarned about Arnold's intentions by someone who, knowing her designs on him, had wanted to prepare her for the reality that her hopes of marrying Arnold had come to nothing.

She did not, however, admit defeat. Mike Cantacessi, her personal bodyguard during the twenty months that she lived with Stallone, while not alleging that Arnold continued his affair with Brigitte throughout their respective marriages, nevertheless maintains that she remained obsessed with Arnold. Says Cantacessi, "She had tons of photographs of herself with Arnold, which I saw on two visits I made with her to her parents' house in Denmark. Back in Los Angeles, she kept cruising by Arnold's house in the hope of seeing him. For a while she made friends with

Arnold's friends Anna and Sven-Ole Thorsen and kept going over to their house, trying to find out when Arnold was going to come by. She was always talking about Arnold and his muscles. She told me that Arnold was great in bed."

On the surface it appeared to be a schoolgirl crush, fueled by memories of better days past. Yet others allege that Brigitte's feelings for Arnold were sustained by something more substantial than memories.

In July 1987 Stallone announced his divorce from Brigitte amid rumors that she had had affairs with both Tony Scott, director of her latest film, *Beverly Hills Cop II*, and her female personal assistant, Kelly Sahnger. Although she denied the rumors, saying she was hurt most by the ones about Sahnger, newspapers and magazines all over the world, ranging from *People* to *Vanity Fair*, carried reports of Brigitte's flamboyance, accompanied by revealingly sexy pictures.

However, it wasn't just the press that had a field day with the scandalous divorce. Arnold Schwarzenegger did as well. At a time when Stallone's image was that of the cuckolded husband, Arnold had a chance meeting with Stallone's brother Frank at Patrick's Roadhouse and, in tones of sympathy, said, "I feel so bad for your brother. I always knew what she was. I only wish I had warned him."

Given that Arnold had covertly initiated Stallone's first meeting with Brigitte, his condolences to Frank call to mind *Pumping Iron*, the film that made Arnold famous and that focused on his ability to get the better of his rivals. And those who have studied Arnold's past strategies for undermining his competitors believe that while in the past he had used salt jokes, sugar treatments, and screaming techniques, his weapon against Sylvester Stallone may well have been Brigitte Nielsen. As Sue Moray has commented, "Arnold probably knew she was trouble and wanted to give him [Stallone] some trouble. . . . That's right out of *Pumping Iron*."

Whether or not Stallone knew about the part Arnold

played in his abortive marriage, Arnold's next move definitely did not escape Stallone's attention. During an interview with *Playboy*, journalist Joan Goodman asked Arnold the question, "Are you forgetting your friend and fellow action-movie mogul, Sylvester Stallone? Isn't he the highest paid actor?" Arnold responded:

First of all, I don't know about that. Second, he is not my friend. He just hits me the wrong way. I make every effort that is humanly possible to be friendly to the guy, but he just gives off the wrong vibrations.

Whatever he does, it always comes out wrong. I'll give you an example. We had breakfast together not long ago, because we are making films for the same company. We discussed not getting in each other's way and when the films should be released.

It was a very agreeable conversation on every subject, and then he said, "You've got to become a member of my new club." I said, "What club?" He said, "It's going to be an all male club with no women allowed. Just like in the old days. Only men. And we sit around and smoke stogies and pipes and have a good time." I told him it was the worst thing he could do. That we're living in a very sensitive time period, when women are struggling for equality. I said that I didn't agree with half the stuff they were talking about, but a club like that would offend every smart woman in the country. I said to stay away from it. "If you want just guys, invite them up to your house. That's what I do."

Listen, he hired the best publicity agents in the world and they couldn't straighten out his act. There's nothing that anyone can do out there to save his ass and his image. Just the way he dresses. Seeing him dressed in his white suit, trying to look slick and hip, that already annoys people. And the

gold ring and the gold chains that say, "Look how
rich I am," all that annoys people. It's a shame no
one taught him to be cool. He should have L. L.
Bean shoes and corduroy pants with a plaid shirt.
That's cool; that's how a director should look,
rather than have that fucking fur coat when he
directs.

At the time Arnold was interviewed by *Playboy* one
might have expected Stallone to be bitter toward Arnold,
rather than the reverse. After all, it was Stallone who had
loved and lost; he and Brigitte had been divorced in the
summer of 1987, around the time of the *Playboy* interview.
And whether or not Arnold had initiated the romance
between Brigitte and Stallone, he had definitely been there
first, with Stallone following in his amorous footsteps.
Why, then, did Arnold escalate his public campaign of
bitterness against Stallone? It is highly unusual for a major
star to directly attack another major star in print, yet
Arnold had done just that, deliberately provoking Stallone
in three published articles. Looking at Arnold's on-record
comments, they seem to be imbued with more than his
usual competitiveness. And it is easy to conclude that Arnold's vitriolic comments might well have been fueled by
his lingering love for Brigitte as well as his long-standing
jealousy and hatred of the man to whom she had been
married—his cinematic rival who persisted in outearning
him at the box office.

Perhaps, too, Arnold's unprecedented attack on Stallone had been prompted by another phenomenon, trans-
porting Arnold to other times, other places, other competitions in which he had taunted, humiliated, and riled his
more vulnerable rivals. For a brief, damaging moment, he
must have forgotten that the man he was attacking was not
a minor bodybuilder, ripe for extinction, but Sylvester Stallone, one of the most powerful men in Hollywood. And for
a searing moment Arnold may have been listening to Gustav's voice reverberating in the depth of his psyche, causing

him to strike out and assert to the readers of *Playboy* and the world in general, "I am the best."

When asked why he thought Arnold had attacked him in *Playboy*, Stallone's public response was "That's something I'll just have to ponder in private. Whatever difficulties two people have shouldn't be aired publicly, it should be taken care of privately."

Sometime after the *Playboy* interview appeared, Arnold, during a televised interview with Chantal on "Good Morning America," made an apology to Stallone. According to Chantal, "I asked him about the comments in *Playboy*. I think these were off-the-cuff remarks he had made about Stallone that were off the record. He was lovely about it. As always, he was the perfect gentleman."

Later Arnold claimed that the *Playboy* interview had totally misrepresented his feelings about Stallone, saying, "I respect the man as an actor, a director and a human being. Aside from his contributions to the industry, he also does great work for the community and charity and the last thing I want to do is offend him." A spokesman for *Playboy* said that the magazine stood by the story, adding, "It's clear that he said what he said. He may have had second thoughts, but his feelings at that moment are quite clear." *Playboy* insiders later revealed that Arnold's off-the-record comments about Stallone were even stronger than those printed in the magazine.

The apology, at any rate, had now been made. However, Rick Wayne adds an interesting postscript to the entire episode: "Joe Weider taught Arnold to say sorry. He taught him that, after all, it doesn't take much to say sorry. Once the whole world has seen you demonstrate that the other guy is a dog, you turn around and say, 'I am sorry.' What you have said is now out there, on record, but after apologizing, you look pretty good and really human."

Despite assertions to the contrary, both sides continued to feud. On September 17, 1988, "Page Six" of the *New York Post* contained the following item: "The feud between

Hollywood's most muscular men, Arnold Schwarzenegger and Sylvester Stallone, gets nastier with every workout. Sly, with assorted bodyguards, walked into a night spot in LA recently, spotted Arnie's picture on the wall, and told the owner that if it wasn't removed, he'd leave and never come back. The owner took the photo down and handed it to Sly's guys, who promptly destroyed it."

Stallone's reasons for continuing the feud are apparent. Arnold's, however, remain a mystery. His 1988 hit film *Twins* contains a sight gag during which Arnold, passing a *Rambo III* poster, smiles mockingly at it. And although the credits of *Twins* contain the words "Thanks to Sylvester Stallone," thanks or no thanks, that scene merely serves as a reminder of Arnold's continued obsession with his nemesis.

Just one month after her divorce from Stallone was announced, *People* reported that Brigitte and Kelly Sahnger showed up at Arnold's fortieth-birthday breakfast at Patrick's Roadhouse. "Nielsen gave the pec-tacular Schwarzenegger a birthday hug and then twirled around in a circle to show the boys the iridescent bikini she was wearing beneath her micro-mini tank dress."

Six months after her divorce, exuding bravado, Brigitte declared, "I have no regrets. My business is better than ever."

Soon her romantic life also would take a turn for the better, leading to a well-publicized affair with New York Jets star Mark Gastineau. After surviving a cancer scare, Brigitte became pregnant by Gastineau and gave birth to a baby boy on December 15th (two days after Arnold and Maria's baby was born). And, although her film career seems to be in a dormant stage, she and Mark apparently are living happily ever after in Arizona. This, in spite of those who whisper that Brigitte's choice of yet another macho man as mate was merely an attempt to provoke Arnold's interest and seduce him into loving her again.

By the spring of 1988 Arnold was taking great pains to

assure all and sundry that his love for Brigitte had died a stony death. In a conversation with his old trainer, Helmut Cerncic, who was visiting him in Los Angeles from his home in Australia, the mention of Brigitte's name unleashed a flood of invective from Arnold. However, things may not have been entirely what they seemed. During the first week in April 1989 Brigitte's personal press agent, Joel Brokaw, revealed that Arnold and Brigitte had just talked to each other on the telephone.

Although Arnold's true feelings about Brigitte are unknown, it appears that as far as Brigitte is concerned, "I'll love you till the end of time," the words engraved on the Cartier watch given to her by Stallone during those first carefree days of their romance, may well describe her deep and abiding feelings for Arnold.

18
The Wedding and Waldheim

FOLLOWING THE ANNOUNCEMENT OF HIS engagement to Maria on August 10, 1985, events moved swiftly, and with the wedding date set for April 26, 1986, it seemed clear that Arnold was back on the straight and narrow.

Shortly after their return from Austria on September 2nd Maria scored the biggest coup of her television career: replacing the former Miss America, Phyllis George, in the prestigious anchor job on the "CBS Morning News" program.

Despite the power of her new position, Maria still had doubts about whether she owed her success to her family connections or even to her famous fiancé.

Much to the dismay of Maria's agent, Art Kaminsky, her fiancé *had* played a part in the negotiations for her new job at CBS. According to Ed Joyce, who had hired her after making the deal with Kaminsky, when Kaminsky called to check some details with Maria, Arnold grabbed the phone from her and screamed, "Those terms are not good enough for Maria. The deal is off!" before slamming the receiver down.

Kaminsky phoned back, but Arnold apparently refused to allow Maria to come to the phone. The situation was finally rectified by Bobby and Sargent Shriver, who explained to Arnold, in no uncertain terms, that in their family a deal is a deal. Arnold bowed out, the deal was made, and Maria was bound for New York and CBS.

From the start she was completely committed to her

job, living alone in a New York hotel and getting up at 3:00
A.M. every day for the fifteen-block taxi ride from her hotel
to the CBS studios on West 57th Street. At 4:30 she read the
wire report, then went into makeup at 6:15 before going on
the air at 7:00 A.M.

Each day at 9:15, as soon as the show went off the air,
Eunice phoned Maria with a critique of her performance.
Peter McCabe, senior CBS producer, was not enamored of
Eunice's comments, observing, "At times it seemed to me
we were getting an input we didn't need."

Each Friday Maria flew back to Los Angeles to be with
Arnold. Or, if he was making a film, she flew to the on-
location site. But during the week her life off camera was
dull. Refusing to accept weekday dinner invitations, her
primary recreation was riding in Central Park. She ignored the New York night life, avoiding hot clubs like the
Palladium, preferring to have afternoon tea with friends.

In the office, according to Peter McCabe in *Bad News
at Black Rock*, "Maria liked to have fun, and she was fun to
be around, but she could also be remarkably strait-laced at
times. Some of the bookers delighted in telling her stories
about men, or sex, or the peccadilloes of celebrities she
knew. When she professed disbelief, they would tell her she
was naive. Maybe she was, but she mixed well with the
staff, and she was a breath of fresh air. She was competent
and willing to pitch in on stories, and some of her sugges-
tions were good.

"Maria was first-rate with celebrities, but sometimes
she didn't grasp an issue or would see it only from the
peculiar perspective of a privileged Catholic woman, born
to one of America's leading families."

Although she was more successful than Phyllis George
had been, privately Maria seemed racked with conflict:
"People say, 'Oh, she's rich, she's pretty and she's marrying
Arnold.' Well, every day I have to get through the day
wondering if I'm going to eat five muffins and not gain ten
pounds. I've got a relationship that's three thousand miles
away and that's tough. I'm here all alone. I'm thinking,
should I go this weekend and see my parents or should I see

Arnold? It's very difficult. Have I paid enough attention to my friends, my brothers? It's a matter of juggling many things."

In theory, now that they were finally engaged, their relationship should have deepened, yet Arnold and Maria were seeing less of each other than ever. Ostensibly the separation was the result of Maria's career and Arnold's inability to leave Los Angeles. But it was a separation that seemed to suit Arnold, for it proved not to be temporary.

Ever unconventional, Arnold, aided by CBS and Maria's ambitions, had managed to imbue his upcoming married life with that unconventionality. He and Maria would begin as a bicoastal couple and would do nothing to alter the structure they had created. Maria's "CBS Morning News" job lasted just a year, and although she was then offered a Los Angeles job as interviewer on another CBS show, an offer that would enable her to spend more time with Arnold, she rejected it.

In November 1985, just five months before his wedding day, Arnold paid an estimated $5 million for a Spanish-style mansion in Pacific Palisades, where his close neighbors were "Dynasty" star John Forsythe and, ironically, for a time Sylvester Stallone and Brigitte Nielsen. The house was set on two acres of gardens laid out across a series of terraces that led down to a romantic stream. With seven bedrooms and four bathrooms, it included all the obvious accoutrements of Hollywood stardom: a swimming pool, a tennis court, and, naturally, a gym. Arnold planned, he said, for his children to grow up in his new and opulent house.

On November 1st Arnold began filming *Raw Deal* in Chicago. In the film he plays an FBI agent who, as a result of excessive violence, has been fired from the bureau. Hoping for reinstatement, he accepts a plea from an old colleague who asks him to infiltrate and then destroy a top mob family.

The film attempts to humanize Arnold's character,

giving him an alcoholic wife and a subsequent romance
with a gangster's moll, as played by Kathryn Harrold. He
and Dino De Laurentiis argued over the affair throughout
the filming. "Ah! You bang-a de girl!" Dino insisted. "You
bang-a, and you make off! Fuck-a de wife!" But Arnold,
with his intuition regarding the prevalent mood of the
nation, was adamant: "That is you, Dino. Not me. I want
to be bigger in films than I am in life, not smaller, apart
from the overall trend towards conservatism."

That trend, of which he was so aware, pleased Arnold
greatly. In fact, just a month after his engagement to Maria
he had lent his support to a new and, at that point, un-
blemished representative of the conservative ethic, former
U.N. secretary Kurt Waldheim. In September 1985, his
alleged war record not yet the subject of public outrage,
Waldheim had declared his intention to run for office in
the upcoming Austrian presidential election.

Arnold's friend Erika Zimmermann had introduced
him to Viennese architect Gerhard Welley, a representative
of Youth for Waldheim. Subsequently, on September 12,
1985, Arnold voiced his support for Waldheim in a published letter to his Austrian countrymen, explaining that
in his view Waldheim was the man most worthy to hold the
highest office in Austria.

On March 4, 1986, the World Jewish Congress revealed
for the first time that Waldheim had deliberately concealed
the facts about his past. The following day the congress
released documents proving that Kurt Waldheim had been
a member of Hitler's brownshirt storm troopers. On March
20th personnel files from the Austrian Foreign Ministry
were published, showing that Waldheim was a member of
yet a third Nazi organization. On March 22nd a U.S. Army
and U.N. list revealed that Kurt Waldheim had once been
termed a suspected Nazi war criminal wanted for murder.

There was more: on April 1st the World Jewish Congress amplified its charges with documents that showed
Kurt Waldheim was on the operations staff of the military
unit that carried out the "Kozara Massacres"—a Nazi atroc-

ity in wartime Yugoslavia. Finally, on April 24th the United States Justice Department recommended barring Kurt Waldheim from entering the United States. Two days later, in Hyannis, Massachusetts, Arnold Schwarzenegger married Maria Shriver.

The wedding had taken eight months to plan. In February Maria and Eunice flew to Paris and, with the help of Pat Kennedy Lawford, selected a wedding gown for Maria at the House of Dior on the Avenue Montaigne.

The celebrations began long before the April 26th wedding day. On February 22nd a prenuptial party for the happy couple and forty guests was held at Exiles in Manhattan. Eunice and Sargent Shriver, along with John F. Kennedy, Jr., Caroline Kennedy, and Bobby Shriver, sipped vintage Italian wine and supped on cod fritters, antipasto of red pepper, prosciutto, fried vegetables, and pasta filled with ricotta cheese. Next there was trout, followed by chocolate soufflé. The entire meal, including exclusive use of the eighty-seat restaurant, cost a grand total of about $3,000.

Soon afterward in Santa Monica, in April, a bachelor party was thrown for Arnold, the details of which have been shrouded in secrecy, the only information being that it was a raucous affair in which Arnold was chained and handed over to a dominatrix.

The mother of the bride, Eunice Shriver, flew in to Hyannis Port on Tuesday, April 22nd, followed the next day by Maria, who before leaving New York, without mentioning the wedding, announced to the audience of "CBS Morning News" that she would be taking a few days off. The next day Maria went to the Dunfey Hyannis Hotel, worked out, and then had a massage.

On Friday, April 25th, Arnold, who had been filming *Predator* in Puerto Vallarta, flew in to Hyannis Port in a Lear jet chartered for the occasion. The same day, Caroline Kennedy gave a luncheon party at her mother's gray-shingled cottage, situated within the Kennedy compound.

The thirty guests ate chowder from mugs inscribed "Maria and Arnold, April 25, 1986, Chowderheads."

In the evening, at the exclusive Hyannis Port Country Club, which the Shrivers had rented for the evening, Aurelia was hostess at the rehearsal dinner. Billed as "an Austrian clambake," the party featured an Austrian oompah band and waitresses dressed in Austrian national costume, and the club was decorated in a combination of the American and the Austrian national colors. In keeping with the theme, dinner consisted of a mélange of Austrian and American dishes: Wiener schnitzel, lobster, strawberry shortcake, and Sacher torte.

During the dinner Caroline Kennedy, Sydney Lawford McKelvey, and Courtney Kennedy Ruhe sang a song about the newlyweds' transcontinental marriage. Then six of the bridesmaids contributed a skit, "Old MacArnold," sung to the tune of "Old MacDonald Had a Farm." The bridesmaids, led by maid of honor Caroline Kennedy, then presented Maria with their gift—a sterling silver comb, brush, and mirror set with a matching silver tray engraved with the names of all of the bridesmaids. In return Maria gave her bridesmaids black lacquer boxes inlaid with a hand painting of Rose Kennedy's house.

Maria was serene and didn't seem at all nervous about the following day. According to her school friend and bridesmaid Theo Hayes, Maria was in total command of the wedding arrangements, down to the smallest detail.

The guest list had been a matter of great speculation among the members of the international press clustered at Hyannis to cover the wedding. Provincetown-Boston Airline, the commuter line that would fly many family members and guests in for the wedding, was induced by the Shriver/Kennedy clan to lock up its computers a day before the wedding to prevent the guest list from being unwittingly divulged to the press by a passenger agent.

Eager crowds had been gathering outside the white clapboard Church of St. Francis Xavier since 6:00 A.M. on the day of the wedding. Reporters, banned from the wedding ceremony, stood on a viewing stand across the street from the church, craning their necks and jostling for position to take pictures, while droves of police officers on special duty maintained law and order. Mindful of the fiasco caused by press planes flying over Madonna's wedding to Sean Penn, which Maria had covered the previous August, the Kennedys, summoning up every iota of their political clout, arranged to have air traffic barred over the Kennedy compound from ten in the morning until six at night. The ban covered a two-mile radius to an altitude of two thousand feet above sea level. Thus privacy was ensured.

By 10:15 the limos and rented buses began to arrive, bringing guests and members of the wedding party to the church. And despite the fact that both the press and the crowds assembled outside the church eagerly awaited a celebrity turnout rivaling Oscar night in Hollywood, they were disappointed. For not only the guest list, but also the bridal party, would reflect the groom's loyalty to his past and the bride's loyalty to her family. Most of the more visible Hollywood luminaries had been excluded.

Princess Caroline of Monaco, Clint Eastwood, Sylvester Stallone, and Brigitte Nielsen had been rumored to be among those who would attend, but didn't. However, Susan Saint James, Tom Brokaw, Forrest Sawyer, and Abigail Van Buren, who arrived in a white Rolls-Royce Silver Cloud, did. And, always a scene stealer, Grace Jones, Arnold's *Conan the Destroyer* co-star, arrived, to cheers from the waiting crowd, midway during the ceremony, clad in a figure-hugging green Alaïa dress, swathed in black fur, with Andy Warhol by her side.

Maria's bridesmaids were Alexa Halaby, sister of Lisa Halaby, who is now Queen Noor of Jordan; Charlotte Soames Hambro, one of Maria's old friends; Theo Hayes; TV producer Roberta Hollander; cousin Sydney Lawford McKelvey; Timothy Shriver's fiancée, Linda Potter; cousin Courtney Kennedy Ruhe; old friend Renee Meier Schink;

and writer Wanda McDaniel Ruddy, whose three-year-old-son, Maria's godchild, John Ruddy, was ring bearer.

On the groom's side, Franco Columbu was best man. Leading the contingency representing Arnold's bodybuilding past, who had been invited to be ushers, were Albert Busek, the man who had discovered him in Stuttgart; Sven-Ole Thorsen, one of his closest bodybuilding friends; American bodybuilder Bill Drake; his business partner Jim Lorimer; Neal Nordlinger; and Mitsou Kawashima, a promoter and friend of Arnold's from Hawaii. Schwarzenegger and Shriver male family members completed the list of ushers: Karl Schwarzenegger, Arnold's cousin; his nephew and godson, Patrick Knapp; and, of course, Maria's brothers.

Eunice Shriver wore an emerald-green two-piece silk Dior outfit, accessorized with matching green shoes and hat. Aurelia, wearing violet under a mink coat, smiled warmly at all and sundry, her toothy grin uncannily resembling the bride's own.

Arnold, traveling in a limousine, instructed the driver to slow down as he approached the church. Then, rolling down the car window, a cigar in his hand, he flashed a huge grin at the crowd. Once inside the church, he personally greeted as many of the five hundred guests as possible, commenting, "I didn't think there would be so much noise in here," and then added, "We're all a little nervous here." On hand, as he entered the church, were three video cameras primed to film the wedding so that, in Arnold's words, "When I [get] home I can really be part of my wedding."

Maria arrived in a $60,000 limousine, a few minutes late for the ceremony, accompanied by her bridesmaids, all fetchingly dressed in outfits based on sketches executed by the bride herself: long skirts and fitted jackets made from silk moiré, reflecting a rainbow of blue, pink, and violet colors.

Maria's wedding dress, the crowd agreed, was spectacular. The Dior gown, designed by Marc Bohan, who was also invited to the wedding, was fashioned out of white

muslin silk with a tight-fitting bodice of French lace. The
high Victorian collar was edged in pearls, and thirty-three
lace-covered buttons closed the dress at the back. Her train
was eleven feet long, and her bouquet was composed of
lilies of the valley, sweet pea, French ariana roses, Casa-
blanca and Eucharist lilies, orchids, white peonies, freesia,
cherry blossoms, and Queen Anne's lace, tied with French
satin ribbons. The crowds outside the church, shouting,
"Maria, Maria," agreed that she looked beautiful, a fairy-
tale bride fittingly attired to marry her Prince Charming.

She walked down the aisle to the strains of the Wagner
Bridal March from *Lohengrin*. The service, lasting over an
hour, was conducted by the Reverend John Baptist Rior-
dan, assisted by the Reverend Edward Duffy, pastor at St.
Francis. Teddy Kennedy, Eunice Shriver, Sargent Shriver,
and Jim Lorimer all read passages from the Bible, and
Oprah Winfrey, who had known Maria since the days
when they were both employed by the local Baltimore
television station, read Elizabeth Barrett Browning's poem
"How Do I Love Thee?"—which Maria herself had chosen.

In a bow to European tradition both the bride and the
groom had wedding rings. But in a departure from tradition, requested by Maria, she and Arnold were pronounced
"husband and wife," as she had wanted to avoid the sexist
connotation of "man and wife." Then, leaving the church
to the strains of "Maria" from *The Sound of Music*, the
happy couple were met outside by cheers, but refused to kiss
for the benefit of the press photographers. Then Maria and
Arnold disappeared into their waiting limousine, bound
for the Kennedy compound.

The reception, held in two tents on the grounds of the
Kennedy compound, was opulent. The guests were banned
from taking photographs. However, Wag Bennett—Wag
from the early days of London, Wag who knew many of
Arnold's secrets—unafraid, had smuggled his Canon Sure
Shot under his top hat and snapped away. Arnold, eventually alerted, gave his old friend the go-ahead. Consequently

Wag took 350 pictures of the reception, many of which subsequently appeared in the British muscle magazine published by his wife, Dianne, all demonstrating the glory of the event.

The first reception tent was set up for cocktails and the reception line, where guests like Bernd Zimmermann, Art Zeller, and Wag and Dianne Bennett mingled with Jackie Onassis, remote and dignified in navy blue, and other celebrities. The second tent, set up for lunch and dancing, was decorated with fourteen flowering fruit trees, including pear, cherry, apple, plum, and flowering crab apple. To offset the chilly forty-degree weather outside, both tents were warmed with heaters.

Guests ate lunch at tables covered in rose-colored linen, with centerpieces consisting of baskets of lilies, roses, anemones, sweet pea, and Queen Anne's lace, all individually arranged by the Robert Isabell Company in New York.

Lunch, catered by Creative Gourmet of Boston, included such delights as cold lobster, chicken breasts in a champagne sauce served with shrimp and asparagus over pasta shells and julienned vegetables, followed by dessert: long-stemmed California strawberries, Viennese pastries, and the Austrian specialty *Mozart Kugeln*—chocolates filled with marzipan.

The wedding cake, made by Stephen Hesnan, the Shriver family chef, weighing 425 pounds and measuring seven feet high, was composed of eight tiers of carrot and pound cake and was a replica of Eunice and Sargent's own wedding cake. Iced with buttercream frosting, the cake was adorned with pink ribbons, flowers, lace, and white sugar bells and topped with figures of the bride and groom.

Maria and Arnold danced the first waltz together, to the music of Peter Duchin's seven-piece band. By now the bride had changed out of her satin shoes into sneakers. A short while before the wedding she had broken her toe in a freak accident. But with the train of her wedding dress wound around her wrist as she danced, her face radiant with joy, Maria looked more beautiful than ever. This was her day, one she had been planning since she was five years old. She was married now, and Arnold was hers.

During the reception Arnold and Maria slipped away to see Rose Kennedy, who was too ill to attend either the wedding or the reception. As the day went on, Arnold danced with his mother-in-law, then Jackie Kennedy Onassis, pausing only to present his in-laws with a silk-screen Andy Warhol portrait of Maria. "I'm not really taking her away," he told them, "because I am giving this to you so you will always have her." Addressing all the guests, he said, "I love her and I will always take care of her. Nobody should worry."

And given the joy of the occasion, the love and care reflected by the event, it is highly unlikely that anybody did. As Arnold and Maria boarded a private jet bound for Antigua and the honeymoon suite of the luxurious St. James Club Hotel, the good wishes of friends, family, and all the guests at their fabulous wedding went with them. The Kennedys and the Shrivers were delighted that Maria and Arnold were now married. Ethel Kennedy was ecstatic, saying, "It was the most beautiful wedding ceremony I've ever been to in my life." Arnold's old friends were thrilled that he had remembered them, flattered to be part of such a prestigious event. And the international press was pleased, knowing that its coverage of the fairy-tale union between the Kennedy heiress and the Hollywood movie star would delight readers.

Arnold, like his father at the time of his marriage, was thirty-eight. His bachelor days were over. Of his new Kennedy/Shriver in-laws, he commented, "I've always been accepted by them with great admiration and with respect." Indeed he had, especially during his wedding reception, when his new father-in-law, Sargent Shriver, was confronted by an unpleasant event that, he would late concede, took him by surprise.

For there was one flaw in the otherwise perfect Shriver/Schwarzenegger nuptials—one false note that threatened to cloud the brightness of the day. Amid all the good wishes and hopes for future happiness, the love and the kindness, a dark shadow was cast by a gift from someone whom many people had identified as evil.

The gift was two life-size, papier-mâché dolls fabricated by artist Christa Muller, replicas of Arnold, dressed in lederhosen, carrying Maria, dressed in a dirndl. They were sent from Arnold's Austrian homeland by Kurt Waldheim.

The dolls, prominently displayed at the wedding reception, assumed a slightly sinister air, as if they might suddenly open up to reveal the grinning specter of Kurt Waldheim lurking inside their shells. After all, only the day before the press had carried yet another story about Waldheim's duplicity, his concealment of his Nazi past, and evidence of Nazi atrocities with which he may have been connected.

Arnold, naturally, was not responsible for being the recipient of a gift from a leading Austrian politician—indeed one who might well, in the near future, be elected president of Arnold's native Austria. As Arnold pointed out later, he had, after all, out of courtesy, invited Waldheim to his wedding—along with Pope John Paul II and President Reagan. Waldheim had now reciprocated with a gift.

Up until the moment that Waldheim's gift was brought into the reception, the day had been close to perfect: the bride was beautiful, the groom handsome, the guests glittering, the reception superb. All in all, the gift might have passed relatively unnoticed had it not been for Arnold himself.

In a gesture that perhaps was a defiant declaration of independence—and that, according to one guest, caused Jackie Kennedy Onassis to pale—Arnold spoke the following words, later recorded by wedding guest Andy Warhol in his diaries: "My friends don't want me to mention Kurt's name because of all the recent Nazi stuff and the U.N. controversy, but I love him and Maria does too and so thank you, Kurt." CBS's Terry Smith, also a wedding guest, confirms that Warhol's recorded comments encapsulate the gist of Arnold's remarks. Later, in what was described as "an awkward moment," Arnold praised Kurt Waldheim, adding that he was a victim of bad press.

According to another guest, Arnold's friend Richard Burkholder, "He [Arnold] wished Kurt Waldheim was at the wedding. He also assured everyone that Waldheim hadn't done what he had been accused of."

As it turned out, Arnold was partially right, as Waldheim has indeed been cleared of some of the allegations made in 1986. But given that at the time of the wedding the allegations had only just been made, world opinion was against Waldheim, and an assortment of Democrats and journalists was present, Arnold's defense of Waldheim was startling and did not go unnoticed—resulting in coverage in diverse publications, from *People* magazine to the *New York Daily News* to the bodybuilding press. Rick Wayne says he reported in *Flex*, one of Weider's magazines, Arnold's statement that Waldheim had had bad press and wryly observed, "Yes, so did Hitler, so did Idi Amin."

Angered by Rick's observation, Arnold confronted Rick in Columbus, Ohio, just before the Mr. Olympia contest was to begin. According to Rick, Arnold querulously complained, "Rick, you are my friend; how could you have written what you did?" Rick reminded him that he had merely quoted *People* magazine's report on Arnold's wedding day remarks, but Arnold was not pacified, saying, "I can't go to *People* and tell them to retract. They will only tell me, 'Look at the spread we gave you for your wedding.' But I can call on you as my friend. If I boob, I expect you, as my friend, to protect me."

If, indeed, he did believe that he had boobed in defending Kurt Waldheim, Arnold took no steps to remedy the situation. The usually self-protective Arnold seemed to have placed Waldheim's interests ahead of his own. Far from retracting his remarks championing Waldheim, Arnold went on to lend his name to posters that trumpeted his support of Waldheim in the Austrian presidential campaign. The posters were displayed all over Austria but, luckily for Arnold, escaped the attention of the American press.

He has never retracted his defense of Waldheim. Nor has he since withdrawn his support from him. In May 1986, just a few weeks after Arnold's marriage to Maria, Kurt Waldheim was elected president of Austria, winning with 54 percent of the vote. Nobel Peace laureate Elie Wiesel said at the time, "Waldheim's election by the Austrian people is a stain on Austria and all of mankind."

Yet despite the mounting evidence as to Waldheim's alleged past, in August 1986 Arnold visited the Austrian president in his summer home on Lake Attersee, outside of Salzburg. The visit, reported extensively in both the Austrian and the German press, was notable, for Waldheim, then banned from entering the United States (a ban that has never been lifted), rarely received important visitors, having been ostracized by the rest of the world.

Waldheim publicized Arnold's visit with relish, seizing the moment and posing for pictures with him. Arnold, it appears, was not averse to such treatment, later describing the meeting to the press as "a private and friendly get-together." Sissy Waldheim, the president's wife and Austria's first lady, served Arnold a breakfast of muesli, coffee, scrambled eggs, and ham. During the three-hour meeting, the president, wearing blue jeans and a sport shirt, took his visitor for a walk along the lakeshore. According to the press reports, the two men talked further, with Waldheim thanking Arnold for the help he had given him during his election campaign.

In the fall of 1988, when asked by journalist Sharon Churcher about his allegiance to Waldheim, Arnold refused to characterize his meeting with Waldheim as bad judgment.

Arnold is not and has never been responsible for his father's political affiliations. However, one can't help wondering why Arnold, rather than repudiating Waldheim for his duplicity in concealing his Nazi past, rose up so publicly in defense of him. And there are many, allegedly including Maria Shriver, who wish that Arnold had followed a different path.

19
May 1986 to
February 1990

ARNOLD AND MARIA LEFT THEIR WEDDING reception at 5:30 P.M. on April 26th. The following day at 9:30 A.M. Arnold was doing his workout at the St. James Club Hotel in Antigua, where he and Maria were honeymooning. After the workout the newlyweds had brunch, with the new Mrs. Schwarzenegger reportedly looking sexy in a black leotard with a hot-pink bow in her hair.

Their honeymoon in the $800-a-night Roof Garden Suite of the hotel was idyllic. But soon it was time to return to reality and, as was their wont, for the bride and groom to go their separate ways. By May 12th Maria was back at her CBS beat, attending the premiere of *Top Gun* at Manhattan's Astor Plaza, while Arnold was three thousand miles away in California.

The transcontinental nature of their highly publicized marriage caused many a raised eyebrow but seemed to suit Arnold fine, for less than a month after the honeymoon he said, "I'm a very independent person. I can be alone and I enjoy it when we're together. Sometimes Maria and I don't spend enough time together and, at other times, too much. But we make it work. I don't see a problem there at all."

In July 1988, Arnold was still working on projecting a positive image when, in response to a question from *Cosmopolitan* about how their marriage stayed together when they worked so far apart, Arnold claimed, "Maria and I love one another *so much*. Because we both have a tremendous *need* for being together—I *love* being together with Maria, she *loves* being together with me. Whether we're

251

traveling or horseback riding or going to art galleries or hanging out with her family or my mother, we love to be together. We enjoy each other's company so much that we schedule our times together as carefully as we schedule our business—it's all written in our daily calendars, just as work is."

With his sense for what the public wants, Arnold did his best to project his new marriage in the most erotic light possible. During that same period, *People* magazine quoted him as saying, "We fly back and forth as much as possible, and we run up thousands of dollars in phone bills. . . . We have over-the-phone sex." And, lest the arrangement reflect negatively on the couple's normalcy, he also made a point of stressing Maria's own sexuality during an appearance on "CBS Morning News," informing interviewer Forrest Sawyer, "She is a sexy devil. I tell you, what a sexy devil."

Soon thereafter he alluded to his marriage in still more favorable terms, asserting, "I don't feel marriage has changed me. . . . People said I would be held back, not be able to go skiing when I wanted to. I am an independent man, but none of that has happened. But the people around me say that I have become kinder since I got married. That I am more low-key, more considerate and more the homebody."

Arnold and Maria represented the ideal modern couple whose healthy, powerful, successful, and beautiful images were emblazoned across the covers of America's most popular magazines. It was clear to the public that Arnold and Maria's union was here to stay, sweeping them both up in a whirl of activities, travel, social events, and never-ending success.

Raw Deal was released on June 6, 1986, to good business. One reviewer wrote, "Schwarzenegger is a considerably appealing presence in pictures like this. May he make many more." In August Arnold went to Graz with Maria to visit his mother. When Maria returned to America, he and Aurelia went on to Vienna, where they stayed at the Hilton, and on August 22nd they attended the *Raw Deal* premiere together at Vienna's Kolosseum cinema. Next, as if determined to retain his premarital right of stag trips, Arnold traveled to Zurich, where he went hiking with Bernd Zimmermann.

September found Arnold at the 1986 Olympia. After winning an honorary award, he gleefully embarrassed the Weider brothers by reminding them that the now disgraced Ferdinand and Imelda Marcos of the Philippines had been former IFBB patrons. As Joe and Ben squirmed, wishing to forget that they had ever been associated with the Marcoses, Arnold rubbed further salt into their wounds by cracking that, unlike Mrs. Marcos, he didn't own enough pairs of shoes. Naturally the audience loved him, erupting in wild applause at his wit.

On November 6th, Maria's first married birthday, her husband surprised her by hiring the Vienna Boys' Choir to sing at her party in their Los Angeles home. After their performance the boys supped on shrimp, hamburgers, cake, and exotic fruit; then each boy received the gift of a T-shirt with Arnold's picture printed on the front.

Christmas 1986, and New Year's Eve, too, followed the routine Arnold had established during his bachelor days: Christmas with his mother in Seefeld, followed by yet more skiing with Zimmermann, then back to America to spend New Year's Eve with Maria.

His first few months as a married man had demonstrated that Arnold hadn't radically altered his lifestyle. Later, asked what usually caused Arnold and Maria to get upset with each other, he confided to Oprah Winfrey on her talk show, "I think what I'm doing right now, which is leaving town and being away on a promotional tour. She would like me to stay home, because she has such a need for me." At this point Arnold coughed sarcastically. Then he added, "And so I think that we sometimes argue over those things—do I really have to be on the road that many times? Do I really have to ski thirty days every winter? Twenty days out of those is by myself with friends and so on. So I think things like that really bother her, and it would bother me too, of course. That's understandable." Understandable or not, his lifestyle remained unchanged.

In early 1987, Arnold began filming *The Running Man*, an unusual science fiction saga. Also in 1987, on June 2nd, he was to win the honor of having his star on Hollywood Boulevard. With Maria and Aurelia by his side, he seemed moved, citing the sense of wonder he felt that he, a farm boy from Austria, now had his very own star—number 1,847—on Hollywood Boulevard.

Soon after, he met with yet more success, when his latest film, *Predator*, opened on June 12th and grossed an incredible $34.9 million in its first three weeks, winning him the 1987 Star of the Year Award presented by the National Association of Theater Owners.

Predator, the movie he had been making in Puerto Vallarta just before his wedding the previous year, once again featured him in a heroic role, that of an elite agent sent on a mission to South America to kill an invisible predator from outer space who has thermal vision and is able to skin a man alive. *Predator* director John McTiernan was highly impressed with Arnold's skills as an actor. "The range of things he can do is expanding daily," McTiernan said. "I had been warned that I'd have to do 112 takes for him to act it right, but that's just not so. We've never gone more than nine, and four of those were for camera problems and two because Arnold and another actor would break out laughing. The guy could be another John Wayne."

Perhaps. However, Arnold appeared to be drifting slowly away from the macho ideal and, with his characteristic vision, to be searching for a more multidimensional image. At this point in his career there was only a hint of future developments, in the form of his almost wistful comment, "It's hard to do heroic films and bring out vulnerability."

In his private life he tried hard not to let himself be

overwhelmed by stardom, refusing to hire bodyguards or chauffeurs. Instead, roaring around Hollywood in his own red Porsche or on his Harley Davidson, he affirmed, "You see stars who have people drive for them, answer calls for them, make dates for them, pick out their clothes for them, pick up their shoes. They have people practically walk and run for them. And then they begin to wonder why they feel ineffective and disconnected. I like to build my own fire. I like to do things for myself. I can enjoy the fun of being a star and walk away from the bull."

In November 1987 *The Running Man* was released and, according to executive producer Keith Barish, elicited by far the most female enthusiasm of all his pictures. To Arnold's vast amusement a group of women, asked to describe what they liked most about Arnold, replied, "He has a cute ass."

Co-starring Richard Dawson as the host of a futuristic game show, *The Running Man* told of America's first fascist government in which a gladiator-type television program called "The Running Man" forces prisoners to try to escape a variety of killers. The film's considerable tension is relieved by a script that allows Arnold more comedic cracks than usual; for example, when Jim Brown descends on a flamethrower, and a girl exclaims, "Jesus Christ," Arnold quips, "Guess again!" He seemed to relish his moments of light relief and claimed that he would soon make a comedy. Anyone who had followed his career up to now knew without a doubt that Arnold, as always, would achieve his goal.

Nineteen eighty-eight began the way Arnold liked it, skiing in Austria. Before starting his next picture, *Red Heat*, Arnold lost ten pounds at the request of director Walter Hill. He played the part of a Russian policeman, Ivan Danko, sent to America to avenge the death of one of his fellow officers and bring back his killer. Looking at him in his Russian policeman's uniform, so similar to Gustav's uniform, which Arnold had tried on when he was a child, Hill observed, "Arnold's secret is his face. It's the

face of a medieval warrior—a face with great natural dig-
nity and an almost regal quality."

His choice of script—one that painted the Russians in
human terms—was, in the light of *glasnost*, an inspired
choice. Arnold, the brilliant intuitor, had predicted the
mood of the nation.

Unlike his tactics with bodybuilding competitors, his
tactics with his movie colleagues, with the blatant exception of Sylvester Stallone, were to assist, praise, and capti-
vate. His co-star in *Red Heat* was Jim Belushi. Belushi, as
Arnold had intended, was impressed by him and said,
"He's a very intelligent actor. I called him the Professor.
Off screen, he did all the talking. He taught me about
finance, real estate, publicity. . . . When Arnold saw me
before we started shooting the movie, he was shocked. He
thought I was ideal for the role because I was a fat Chicago
slob. When he saw the shape I was in, he started calling me
into his dressing room and opening up a big refrigerator
full of Haagen-Dazs and eating it in front of me, and then
offering me some."

The film, shot partly in Budapest and Chicago, began
in a Russian sauna with Arnold confronting a drug dealer.
The sauna scene was filmed in Schladming, not far from
Graz. Arnold's enjoyment at filming close to home came to
an abrupt halt when tragedy struck the set. On February
6th Arnold's stuntman, Benny Dobbins, fifty-four, died of
a sudden heart attack. According to an eyewitness, Arnold,
who had just given Benny a present commemorating their
work together, liked the stuntman and was upset and genuinely moved by his death.

He had been due to attend the annual Vienna Opera
Ball with his mother and Maria, who was flying in especially for the event, but canceled out of deference to Benny.
On February 9th, 10th, and 11th he and the crew traveled
to Moscow, where they became the first American film
company ever permitted to film in Red Square. Given
Arnold's incredible luck and sense of timing, the *Red Heat*
crew was actually filming in Red Square on the day that

Gorbachev announced the Soviet pullout from Afghanistan, serving to emphasize Arnold's accuracy in gauging the current political climate.

The political climate aside, when *Red Heat* opened on June 17th in fifteen hundred movie theaters nationwide, the film did not do as well as had been expected. However, it was still notable as being the first film for which Arnold was paid the phenomenal sum of $10 million. To top that, the *New York Times* reviewer paid him the compliment of writing, "Though Mr. Belushi is the comedian of the film, the most consistently comic performance is given by Mr. Schwarzenegger."

In March, in keeping with his increasing prominence in Hollywood, Arnold was roasted by the Friars Club. The roast, the longest in Friars history, lasted an amazing five hours and was attended by Jesse "The Body" Ventura, Franco Columbu, Carl Weathers, Danny DeVito, Bruce Willis, James Earl Jones, Milton Berle, Sid Caesar, and Henny Youngman.

The gags were fast and furious, with George Carlin commenting, on meeting Arnold for the first time, "He's so lifelike!" Arnold countered with, "You thought you'd embarrass me with the filth. Well, I heard worse language in Hyannis Port when they found out I was a Republican. . . . I'm such an easy target. They'll go after the name, the muscles, the accent, the Kennedy stuff. It's one of the rare nights when people can insult me and know that I won't kick their butts."

Arnold's roast, with its preponderance of comedians, signaled the latest phase in his career: an Ivan Reitman comedy entitled *Twins*. Following a meeting with Reitman three years before in which Arnold had expressed a desire to play a comic part, Reitman commissioned writers to come up with a concept that eventually evolved into *Twins*.

Filming was under way in the spring of 1988 with Arnold playing Julius Benedict, scientifically created from the sperm of six geniuses and imbued with mankind's most perfect traits. Arnold was delighted that he was doing a comedy, and he and co-star Danny DeVito, who plays his twin, Vincent, developed instant chemistry.

When *Twins* opened on December 5, 1988, director Ivan Reitman approached Maria Shriver and said, "People will finally understand why you married Arnold." He was proved right. The film did, indeed, demonstrate another side of Arnold, a far sweeter and more vulnerable character than that projected by his previous films. He had always been a natural comedian—albeit one whose jokes, streaked with sadism, often misfired—but in *Twins* he was able to indulge himself to the fullest, yet without being cruel. His humor in *Twins*, endearing rather than malicious, rendered him all the more lovable. And his audience did love him.

One of the guests at the *Twins* premiere who also loved Arnold was George Bush. And, as he said, he "was sure grateful to his [DeVito's] twin during the last campaign."

Arnold had loved Nixon, adored Ronald Reagan and, now a major force in Hollywood, had thrown all of his considerable support behind George Bush's campaign to become president.

In addition to contributing financially to the Bush campaign, Arnold attended the Republican Party's national convention in New Orleans, claiming, "I've been a big supporter of Reagan, and I wanted to hear his last speech and visit with Nancy Reagan."

His support for Bush consisted of making speeches on Bush's behalf in various parts of the country, including New Jersey and Ohio. There, due to his bodybuilding contests, which had been held in Columbus for over a decade, Arnold's popularity was at its height, causing Republican insiders to comment that it was Arnold who had won the state of Ohio for Bush!

In early 1990 President Bush rewarded Arnold's support by naming him chairman of the President's Council on Physical Fitness and Sports. Arnold's campaigning had also earned him the nickname of "Conan the Republican" and served to fuel the rumor that he was set on a career in politics. Members of his Arnia still believe that politics is his destiny. In October 1989 the *New York Daily News* published an item citing the rumor that Arnold is "seriously considering" a run for governor of California, and in January 1990 the *Chicago Sun-Times* reported his hope to run for lieutenant governor of California.

In the meantime, his life goes on, a constant round of workouts, filmmaking, publicity, and traveling. The financial rewards increase daily, as do his investments in real estate, where a great part of his fortune is now deployed. In October 1989 *Forbes* estimated that Arnold's gross income for 1989 would be $35 million, up from $6 million in 1988, making him the sixth-highest-paid show business figure— just behind the fifth-ranked Sylvester Stallone, whose 1989 gross income was estimated at $38 million.

In 1987 Maria moved from CBS to co-host NBC's "Sunday Today," and for a short period she spent much more time with Arnold, traveling to Washington for just one night a week. That changed, however, when Maria was offered one of NBC's top jobs, commanding a salary said to be $475,000 a year. Her duties included not only co-anchoring "Sunday Today" but also anchoring "NBC Nightly News" on Saturdays and co-hosting the prime-time news magazine program "Yesterday, Today & Tomorrow."

Maria's ambition and professionalism have never been in question. Owing to her ability and capacity for hard work, her appearances on "Yesterday, Today & Tomorrow" have garnered generally good reviews. Yet, although a *TV Guide* cover story dubbed her "Maria Striver," her co-workers have described her as immature and, according to the *TV Guide* story, exhibiting "the curious mixture of worldly experience and naïveté common to children of privilege."

Eventually, however, marriage interfered with Maria's career plans. Arnold himself has publicly insisted, "Maria wants five kids, because she comes from a family of five, and I want two kids because I come from a family of two kids," and had announced that his house in Pacific Palisades had been purchased with the future Schwarzenegger children in mind. However, three years into the marriage, offspring were not forthcoming. Bodybuilding insiders speculated that steroids, long known to cause sterility after excessive usage, may have affected Arnold negatively. However, when Sue Moray brought up the issue with him in 1985 and asked Arnold if he was able to father children or if steroids had created problems, he told her there were none and assured her, "I've been tested and I'm fine."

Maria's pregnancy was announced in May 1989. She continued working and hosted an NBC special on addiction. Promoting it on "Late Night with David Letterman," she went into detail about her bouts of morning sickness, dissolving into giggles as she graphically described her episodes of vomiting.

Claiming to be ecstatic about his wife's pregnancy, Arnold told Chantal of "Good Morning America" that he couldn't wait for the birth of his "Schwarzenshriver," and enthused to the *National Enquirer* that he was impatient for fatherhood and wants to be a full-time dad.

Katherine Eunice Schwarzenegger, Arnold and Maria's first child, was born on December 13th at St. John's Hospital in Los Angeles. Heiress to the Schwarzenshriver kingdom, Katherine's future appears to be golden. How her birth will alter her proud father's way of life remains to be seen.

During the pregnancy, Arnold saw Maria only an estimated once every two weeks, while spending four months at Churubusco Studios in Mexico filming *Total Recall*, an interplanetary thriller scheduled to be released during the summer of 1990. Arnold's star power had revived the film, a project that producers had been trying to get off the ground for ten years, and he had approval of the script, the cast, and much of the marketing of *Total Recall*.

The film was tailored to project Arnold as king of the action movies and twentieth-century superstar.

Offscreen, however, glimpses of the Arnold of Graz and Munich were still apparent. During an evening out on the town in Mexico City, with crew members in tow, Arnold managed to convince a nondrinking female friend to down a few tequilas, whereupon she threw up. Arnold, according to Jack Mathews of the *Los Angeles Times*, "recalled the story, between spasms of laughter," leading another crew member to comment, "Arnold has that streak in him, he loves to goad people into doing things that embarrass them."

While he waited for the baby to be born, Arnold's routine remained what it has always been. Needing only a maximum of six hours of sleep, he gets up at six o'clock in the morning, starting his daily one-hour World Gym workout at 7:00 A.M. His arrival at the gym usually causes a ripple, especially among women, who tend to sidle up to him, smiling or asking for his autograph. If Maria is not with him, he sometimes exercises the droit du seigneur that is inherent in being a conqueror, relishing the spoils of a victory, and hugs them a trifle tightly.

Fun and games aside, he enjoys his morning workouts. "I relax and gossip with the other guys between setups. It's like a bunch of guys playing cards or sitting at a bar. . . . I don't need a night out with the boys."

After his workout he and a bunch of assorted bodybuilders go to breakfast, with Arnold picking up the tab for whoever joins him. Often he goes to Patrick's Roadhouse, where, at around 9:30 A.M., he can be found at one of the restaurant's four booths. He is greeted warmly by owner Bill Fischler, who invariably serves him a special recipe, reputedly created by Aurelia, consisting of three scrambled eggs, onions, and tomatoes. With it he usually eats a grilled English muffin and drinks lots of coffee.

Sometimes, instead of going to Patrick's, he'll eat at the Rose Café, opposite his Venice office, in an area still populated by hippies—to observers, a strange place for an arch Republican to have his headquarters. At the Rose, which is also close to World Gym, he sticks mainly to oatmeal and eggs. Even when he and Maria are at home, they rarely eat there. If they do invite people over, dinner is catered unless Arnold barbecues steak—in which case he will also do the dishes afterward.

Usually, though, Arnold prefers fish and chicken, and although he enjoys cheese, he avoids it and other dairy products. His sole indulgence is cigars. He smokes two black Cuban Davidoff cigars per day, each one costing $25. During the controversial *Playboy* interview, he informed interviewer Joan Goodman that the interview would not last longer than his cigar, telling her, half jokingly, that when the cigar ended, the interview would be terminated.

Before the pregnancy, for recreation he and Maria played tennis, at which Maria consistently beat him. They also rode horses, Maria in the English style, Arnold preferring western. They often used to ski together in Aspen, where Arnold is a close friend of tycoon Dick Butera, and they stay in the Jerome Hotel. When in Aspen, Arnold likes to breakfast each day at the Wienerstube, enjoying its authentic Austrian-style muesli.

Arnold's homeland is still close to his heart. Although his mother visits him in California at least twice a year, he spends as much time as possible in Austria. In 1988 he went back to Austria four times, first for filming *Red Heat*, then with Maria, another time with Maria and his in-laws Sargent and Eunice Shriver, and the fourth time alone.

One afternoon during his third visit, after Alfred Gerstl had made the appropriate arrangements, Arnold, Aurelia, Eunice, Sargent, and Maria all piled into a Mercedes limousine and made the short ride from Graz to Thal. There the limousine stopped outside 145 Thal-Linak, the house in which Arnold had grown up. Inside, Helga Anderwalt, her three daughters, Susannah, Elizabeth, and Ruth, and her son, David, were waiting for their illustrious visitors. Taking them from room to room, Arnold described the cold, the hardship, the bare wooden floors, the hungry nights, and the dream-filled days of his boyhood.

David Anderwalt is around the same age as Arnold was when he started out on his odyssey, first picked up a barbell, and dreamed his first dream. Today David sleeps in Arnold's old room, looks out on the view of the old ruined castle that Arnold once looked out on, goes to the same school that Arnold once attended, and learns many of the same lessons that Arnold once learned. Arnold asked him what he wanted to be when he grew up, and David replied that he didn't know. Aurelia then chimed in with the story of how Arnold, as a ten-year-old boy, proclaimed when asked about his ambitions, "I don't want to be anything. All I want is to go out in the world with a hat, a stick, and a monkey." The Anderwalts, knowing he had done much more than that, stared at Arnold in wonder.

Arnold made two visits to Thal in 1988, the villagers lost in admiration and delight at the honor. He was their only famous son, and they gathered around him in awe and love. Swiss playwright Friedrich Dürrenmatt wrote a play—filmed starring Ingrid Bergman and Anthony Quinn and entitled *The Visit*—about a peasant girl who, as a pregnant teenager, is thrown out of her village in disgrace. Fifty years after she left, now rich and famous, she returns to the village and persuades the villagers to stalk and kill the man who had made her pregnant and then disowned her. Listening to the Thal villagers, some of whom had once despised him, talking about their Arnold, one gains the distinct impression that during one of his visits he, like Dürrenmatt's heroine, could persuade them to do anything for him.

Not that Arnold has hatred or revenge on his mind. Far from it. How could he, victorious as he has always been, triumphant as he always is? Yet his visits back to Thal must bring him immense joy and an intense awareness of how far he has come, how much he has achieved, how far he has soared as a result of torturing himself, training obsessively all through his youth, formulating his gargantuan future, while all his contemporaries back on earth went about their everyday life, going to the movies, dating girls, and remaining balanced and average.

In a rare moment he allowed his vast delight at his own progress and evolvement to emerge. In Schladming, during filming of the early *Red Heat* scenes, his old friend Franz Hormann came to visit him. Arnold, in a burst of nostalgia and warmth, took him aside and confided, "All those years ago, you were all playing and having fun and I wasn't. I just trained. But now it's my turn. Now I can do everything that you were doing and I never had time for. Now I can have fun."

His confession was not, by any stretch of the imagination, tinged with malice. If anything, his attitude resembled that of a great novelist, luxuriating in the knowledge that the character he has created, the life that he has unfolded, is timeless and will live forever in legend. For Arnold has always been his own creation, which he has fashioned out of an unloved little boy, a misfit floundering amid poverty and neglect. He has created a masterpiece, which the whole world now recognizes and admires. Yet perhaps it is only by going back, by returning to where it all started, that he can really appreciate the magnitude of his achievement and relish all that he has become. It is only by comparison that he can truly savor the sweetness of his victory.

Epilogue

ARNOLD SCHWARZENEGGER HAS BECOME A
Hollywood legend, a latter-day Gatsby, a self-created man
whose unwavering belief in himself has led him to scale
undreamed-of heights in quest of his chosen destiny. His
charm, intelligence, and talent have brought him all that
his heart must desire: wealth, power, adulation, money,
success. But is he happy? Or is he fearful of the next morning, of the essay, of the terrifying possibility of another
mark from his father's red pencil? Now that he has conquered his chosen universe, does he still say to himself, in
the final stage of victory over his past, "Yes, but wait until
next year?" And if he does, what will next year bring for
Arnold Schwarzenegger, for Mr. Supercharm, who holds
the world enthralled in his expansive and muscular hands?
What, in fact, does Arnold still want? And who, ultimately,
has he become?

In 1986, in a rare and revealing moment of introspec-
tion, he said, "People wonder how I've changed, but I
haven't. I have never sold out. I am always the same, no
matter where I am or who I'm with. I felt great ten years
ago, and I feel great now. I was totally fulfilled ten years
ago in every way—with work, with money, with relationships. And I am now. I have to put the brakes on sometimes. Sometimes I'm too driven, and I lose patience with
people around me. I expect everyone out there to be
hungry. I expect too much from people, but there is really
nothing about myself I would change. I have had no big
disappointments in my life. I would not want to live

265

anyone else's life. I don't get depressed. I'm not a person who sits down and analyzes things too much. That's one of the worst things people can do."

Perhaps. However, phenomenon that he is, it is inevitable that those who know him have come to some conclusions about his failures, his weaknesses, the chinks in his armor, and what really does make Arnold run. On that subject Sue Moray tells an illuminating story. Once, in the days of their romance, she and Arnold, bound for Aspen, found themselves stranded in Denver. All flights having been canceled due to snow, they decided to rent a car and, at the car rental office, made the acquaintance of a certain gentleman from Arkansas. These being the days before his vast accumulation of wealth, Arnold, aiming to save money, invited the gentleman to share a car and travel with him and Sue to Aspen.

"Arnold was always complaining because people came up and bugged him for autographs," says Sue. "But when he realized that this man from Arkansas had no idea who he was, Arnold couldn't leave it alone. He spent the entire trip explaining who he was and who he knew." He even showed the man a copy of *Time* magazine, in which Arnold was featured as one of the outstanding people of the year, and told him, "Here I am. If ever you come to L.A. and want to go to the *Playboy* mansion, I can get you in." Says Sue, "He was really working at it. He needs the attention."

He has said, "Everybody likes to be wanted and needed and appreciated and loved and all those things. Some people only have it in a limited way by just being loved by their family or by their children or by their brother or wife. Some people like more than that. I'm one of them." He once found that he could bench-press sixty pounds more in front of an audience than he could alone in a gym. It seems clear that there are no chinks in Arnold's armor—except perhaps a fear of anonymity.

Maria Shriver once said, "You look at people who have great faith in God, like my grandmother, and they have that—inner peace. They know they haven't hurt anyone on the way up, they haven't lied or done anything that they feel horrid about. So no matter what, they're very centered people." Whether Maria's sentiments can be applied to Arnold is, perhaps, debatable. Whatever the case, it seems clear that one day social historians may well regard Arnold's life, achievements, and the hero worship they arouse as being indicative of the world we live in and, in particular, of the success-hungry eighties. For, like Donald Trump, he is representative of a new brand of hero, a twentieth-century idol who has created a religion of self and is celebrated for what he owns, for his ruthlessness, ambition, and financial success, rather than for what he has done for humanity.

On many levels Arnold has indeed done the impossible and, through an act of will, has reversed the classic definition of tragedy and transformed it into a triumph. The great Shakespearean tragic heroes have been likened to perfect statues that possessed a fatal flaw that ultimately destroyed them. Arnold's life, however, is a living reversal of that definition. He began life with nothing but flaws—abused, unloved, a charmless misfit with destructive tendencies and grandiose fantasies—but overcame all those flaws, transcending them by creating what today literally is a perfect statue.

Arnold does, ostensibly, have it all: the world and everything in it. Yet something still is missing. For the unloved child, the child who cried unheeded through those Thal nights, remains unsatisfied, his love still unrequited. He may indeed now be one of the world's favorite sons—but he will never be his father's. And no matter how much mass love he wins, how much acclaim, admiration, and adoration, none of it can transport him back to those childhood days or can compensate for what he longed for but never received.

However, Arnold being Arnold, he tries. On March 11, 1989, at Veterans Memorial Auditorium, he held the first Arnold Schwarzenegger Classic, offering some of the biggest prizes bodybuilding has ever known. He was back where he belonged, back among his family, back where he is the best, back where he is the only one, the king. In Hollywood he might never be number one, but here, among those who adored him, drenched in the shower of their love, his supremacy was unchallenged.

Bodybuilding was the one arena in which he could come close to satiation, to receiving the love that he had always craved. He had retired nearly a decade before, yet still dominated the sport. He had vanquished and humiliated many of his peers, yet still they admired him. And no matter how they felt about him, no matter how deep their bitterness or how rampant their jealousy, yet still they cheered him, stamping their feet, shouting until they were hoarse.

The auditorium rang with his name: "Arnold! Arnold! Arnold!" The adulation was overwhelming, deafening, all-embracing. As their love welled up and cascaded over him, he stood there smiling. And, for a moment, was fulfilled. Forever victorious. Forever the conqueror. Forever supreme. Forever Arnold.

Author's Note and Acknowledgments

I FIRST ENCOUNTERED ARNOLD SCHWARZENEGGER in 1980, when he escorted Maria Shriver to Jerry Rubin's "The Event." He appeared to be strong, silent, gargantuan, and closer to my idea of a Frankenstein's monster than to a potential superstar. I was not impressed. In January 1985 I sat a few rows away from him on the *Concorde*, flying from London to New York. Completely alone and without the trappings of his fairly newly acquired stardom, he seemed vulnerable and far more handsome than when I had first seen him. I found him attractive. In 1986 my husband, Steve, and I attended the *Top Gun* premiere just a few days after Maria and Arnold's wedding. We were standing at the top of the escalator as Maria Shriver was coming up toward us. She struck me as being beautiful and strangely isolated.

Nearly two years later, in the course of a journalistic project, I met and spent many hours with one of Arnold's ex-girlfriends, who gave me a unique perspective on him, one that convinced me that the story of his epic life had never before been fully told and definitely merited a book.

My first step was to contact bodybuilding journalist Rick Wayne, author of a major study on bodybuilding, *Muscle Wars*, for I had heard that he intended to write Arnold's biography himself. Wanting to find out the status of the book before beginning my own, I spent a few days with Rick and his girlfriend, Mae Mollica, in St. Lucia, where Rick is the publisher of the *St. Lucia Star*. He told me that he had indeed planned to write Arnold's biography

269

but that Arnold had been adamantly opposed to the idea and had dissuaded him from doing so.

Taking Rick's experience into account, as well as the remarks of journalist Joan Goodman—who in *Playboy* characterized Arnold as "one of the more finely tuned control freaks I have met in a career of celebrity journalism"—I decided not to contact Arnold until my research for the book was well under way.

I made no secret of the project, however, contacting Arnold's friends and family at an early stage. When any of them asked me if Arnold had authorized the book, I told them he had not and that I hadn't yet contacted him but planned to when I was ready. As a result, Arnold was aware of the book from the start. His close associates Art Zeller, Frank Zane, and Joe Weider confided to me during taped interviews that they had asked Arnold's permission to talk to me and that he had agreed to let them. Weider, however, had a court reporter present during our interview, and beforehand he insisted that I see him alone (without Steve, who was with me) and went on to interrogate me about what I intended to write in my book. I explained that the content of my book depended on the outcome of my research. Weider left me with the distinct impression that his questions had been dictated by Arnold. After allowing Steve back into the room, he then proceeded to give me a half-hour interview during which he was polite but didn't go into great detail. A few days afterward, I interviewed a leading bodybuilder who confided to me that Arnold had asked him to "get her over to your house and tape-record her without her knowing it."

Confident that I was armed with enough facts to interview him in depth, I wrote to Arnold in the summer of 1989 to request an interview. His secretary, Lynn Marks, wrote back with a request for more details about my project. This response was couched in terms designed to give the impression that Arnold knew nothing about the book. Judging from what the people I interviewed had said, however, that was not true. I replied to the letter, giving the requested details. However, Arnold would grant me an interview only under circumstances that would give him control of the book and that no responsible journalist would agree to.

After that, the next Arnold intimate whom I contacted and who asked Arnold's permission to talk to me, Charles Gaines, told me that Arnold's secretary had told him that Arnold "very strongly discouraged him" from speaking to me. I also wrote to Maria Shriver requesting an interview, received a request for more details from a representative of hers, and then responded with the relevant details, but I never received a reply to my second letter. Aurelia Schwarzenegger, Dianne Bennett, Franco Columbu, and Brigitte Nielsen ignored my written requests for interviews. Franco had previously agreed to talk to me in Los Angeles but then stood me up for lunch.

Albert Busek said he didn't have time to talk to me. Mr. C of the salt joke refused to talk, though he didn't deny the story. As I am fluent in German, it was easy for me to arrange and conduct the German and Austrian interviews. Everyone in Thal was very forthcoming, with the exception of Frau Schrott, who was a close friend of Gustav and Aurelia's and owned a guesthouse where they spent many an evening. Among the celebrities, bodybuilders, and friends of Arnold's who refused my request for an interview for this book are Loni Anderson, the late Lucille Ball, George Butler, Bob Birdsong, Dino De Laurentiis, Lou Ferrigno, Joe Gold, Arthur Jones, Grace Jones, Mike Katz, Peter Laden, George Pipisak, Sergio Oliva, Joe Sanceri, Sylvester Stallone, and Bernd Zimmermann.

In Europe I talked to Arnold's aunt Hertha, his uncle Alois, and his cousin Gerold and was scheduled to talk to his aunt Cilly. We set up an appointment, but then I was told that Arnold would prefer that I talk to his public relations representative. Kurt Marnul, to whom I first talked in the fall of 1988 in Graz and later over the telephone on repeated occasions, told me that, although Arnold had been in Graz on two previous occasions and hadn't contacted him, he received a telephone call from Alfred Gerstl late one night, inviting him over to his house, as Arnold wished to see him. Delighted, Marnul rushed over, spent a nice evening with Arnold and Gerstl, then was asked in detail about me and the questions I had asked. Marnul assured Arnold that he had nothing to be afraid of.

Sometime in the spring of 1989 Arnold met Sue Moray at World Gym, where they both train, and asked her if she had talked to me. Sue said she had. Arnold asked her what she had told me. Sue replied, "The truth." Arnold reproachfully said, "I don't know how you could have talked to her without asking me. If someone had asked me to talk about you for a book, I wouldn't have done so without asking you."

Many of the key people in Arnold's life agreed to talk to me, largely on the record in taped interviews. The book is based on over five hundred interviews. Surprisingly, some of the material least favorable to Arnold came from men who claim to idolize Arnold, such as Helmut Riedmeier, who told me that he has a *Terminator II* concept that he wants to give to Arnold, and Kurt Marnul. Some of my major sources were interviewed over ten times. In one-and-a-half years of work Steve and I made two research and interview trips to Graz, Thal, Vienna, and Munich; three trips to London; three trips to Los Angeles; and also conducted research and interviews in Paris, Monte Carlo, Kitzbühel, Essen, Aspen, Palm Springs, Weiz, Krefeld, Axams, Nottingham, Portsmouth, Newcastle, and St. Lucia.

High points of the project include lunch with Frank Zane in Palm Springs; Sacher torte in Landsberg with Erika Knapp Lohrer, the fiancée of Arnold's brother, Meinhard; dinner in Graz with Wilma and Kurt Marnul; listening to David Anderwalt and the children of the Hans Gross School—Arnold's old school in Thal—singing to us in English; lunch with Frederich Gsols, Gustav's sergeant, by the Thalersee; lunch with Hans Janaschek, former assistant to Kurt Waldheim, at the U.N. Plaza in New York;

talking to Sue Moray on the porch of her house in Venice, while her baby daughter, Skylar, played in the background; seeing Wag Bennett's Arnold photo gallery in his house in East London; spending the weekend with Rick Wayne and Mae Mollica in St. Lucia; lunching with Serge Nubret in Paris; having drinks with Ken Waller at Chinois on Main in Santa Monica; lunch with Helmut Riedmeier at the Hard Rock Cafe in London; having tea with Mr. R in Chelsea; and chatting to Herr and Frau Hautz in Kitzbühel.

Some of my sources were off the record, and I appreciate their honesty in talking to me. Although it would be impossible to thank everyone I interviewed or who helped in various capacities, I would like to thank Mindy Alberman in Dino De Laurentiis's office; Gordon Allen; Robert Altman; Stefan Amsuss; the Anderwalt family; Lowell Banks; Hans Bender; Wag Bennett; Byron Berline; Marie Bernard; Karl Blomer; Kathy Brady; Richard Burkholder; Sara Campbell; Mike Cantacessi; Peter Carrette; Jim Caruso; Helmut Cerncic; Chantal; Sharon Churcher; John Citrone; Boyer Coe; Ron D'Ippolito; Benno Dahmen; Wayne de Milia; Chris Dickerson; Jim Dolinksy; Stephania Duncan; David DuPre; Richard Ellis; Richard Fleischer; the Fröbel School, Graz; Charles Gaines (who, although bowing to Arnold's request that he not talk to me, did verify facts); Alfred Gerstl; Hans Gobetz; Bill Grant; Roy Greenslade; Manfred Grossler; Frederich Gsols; Edward Hankey; the Hans Gross School, Thal; Barbara Harvey; Ian Harmer; Maria and Johann Hautz; Oscar Heidenstam; Professor Robert Herzstein; Herr Hess; Walter Hill's office; Dave Hogan; the Hollywood Foreign Press; Franz Hormann; Adam Horowitz; Kevin Horton; Dan Howard; Hans Janaschek; Erich Janner; Christian Jauschowetz; Karl Kainrath; Willi Kalcher; Freddy Kattner; Herr Klink; Herr Koller; Norbert Kossler; Frau Krainer; Imre Kuzterich of Bunte; D. Levin; Erika Lohrer; Jim Lorimer; Ton Maessen; Kurt and Wilma Marnul; Ruth Matthews; Ronald Matz; Herr Mayer; Wil McArdle; Peter McGough; Ray Mentzer; Mae Mollica; Sue Moray; Eric Morris; Gene Mozee; Jack Neary; Hal Needham; Serge Nubret; Danny Padilla; John Paignton; Bill Pearl; the Pontchartrain Hotel, New Orleans; Raaba Gemeinde; Helmut Riedmeier; Frank Richards; Donna Rosenthal; Don Ross; Jimmy Savile; Francesco Scavullo; Michael Schwartz; Alois Schwarzenegger; Gerold Schwarzenegger; Hertha Schwarzenegger; Barbara Seaman; Monte Shadow; Lud and Pat Shusterich; Morty Sills; Frau Sinkovitz; Terry Smith; Anton Spuler; Margarate Stanzer; Gloria Stewart; Armand Tanny; Noreen Taylor; Manfred Thellig; Russell Turiak; Dick Tyler; Ron Vandenburg; Helga Verschink; Mary Vespa; Nicole Watts, Commercial Bank of Saudi Arabia; Rick Wayne; Joe Weider; Mark Weitzman of the Wiesenthal Institute of New York; Wiesenthal Institute in Los Angeles; Bob Woolgar; Frank Zane; the Zarem office; Art Zeller; Monika Zimmermann.

Libraries and information services consulted include:
Academy of Motion Pictures Library
Associated Newspapers
Austrian Institute, London, Library
Berlin Document Center's Archival Records
Die Kronen Zeitung, Vienna
Dynamic Information Services
Express Newspapers
Kleine Zeitung, Graz
Lincoln Center Library for the Performing Arts
Mirror Group Newspapers
Münchner Abend Zeitung
Munich Public Library
New York News Service
New York Public Library
Santa Monica Public Library
Star
Sud Deutsche Zeitung
Sunday Times Library at News International
Time Inc.
Today
Vienna Kurier
Wiener Library, London

Special thanks go to my publisher, Harvey Plotnick, for his faith in me and in the book; to my wonderful editor, Bernard Shir-Cliff, for his perception and guidance; to Michael Antonello, Kathy Willhoite, Georgene Sainati, Julia Walski, Christine Albritton, Donna Adkins, John DeRoo, Cyndy Raucci, Christine Benton, and all the others at my publishing house for devoting their considerable talents to the book; and, of course, to my agent, Elizabeth Kaplan at Sterling Lord Literistic for her patience, understanding, creativity, and commitment.

Source Notes

Prologue

Wedding details from Deirdre Donahue and Susan Reed, "A Hyannis Hitching," *People*, May 12, 1986; Jeannie Williams and Greg Katz, "Maria and Arnold Tie the Knot in Style," *USA Today*, April 28, 1986; Beverly Ford, "It's the Wedding of the Year," *Boston Herald*, April 20, 1986; Michael Kilian, "Are You Invited to 'The' Wedding?," *Waterbury Sunday Republican*, April 20, 1986; Norma Nathan, "Conan Weds a Kennedy," *Star*, April 1986; Rosemary Breslin, "Kennedys Gain a Son," *New York Sunday News*, April 27, 1986; Elizabeth Kastor, "And 450 Close Personal Friends," *Washington Post*, April 26, 1986.

Chapter 1: A Pride of Lions

Pages 5, 6, 7. Description of Gustav from author interviews with his sister-in-law, Hertha Schwarzenegger; his brother, Alois; and his co-worker at the Thal Gendarmerie, Frederich Gsols. "Gentleman of the family," cheering Franz up, Cecilia, Karl, and Cary Grant, all from Hertha, repeated and confirmed by Alois. Gsols was the source on the musical instruments. Description of Aurelia from author interview with Erika Lohrer.

Page 5. Emperor Franz Josef anecdote from confidential source who knew Gustav.

Page 6. Details on Gustav's participation in the Gendarmerie Musik from author interview with Willi Kalcher of the Musik.

Page 6. Statistics on number of Austrians who joined the Nazi party from author interview with Professor Robert Herzstein, University of South Carolina, who discovered the Waldheim documents and is author of the books *Waldheim: The Missing Years* and *Roosevelt and Hitler: Prelude to War*; and Richard Grunberger, author of *Social History of the Third Reich* and editor of *The Association of Jewish Refugees Information*, London. The Nazi party illegal 1933–1938 from author interview with employee of the Austrian Institute, London.

Page 6. Gustav's Nazi party membership is on record at the Berlin Document Center's Archival Records. His membership number is registered as being 8439?80 (one number is obscured in copy).

Page 6. Nazi party membership not being compulsory for Austrian policemen from author interview with Robert Herzstein.

Page 7. Schwarzenegger family background from author interviews with Hertha Schwarzenegger, Alois Schwarzenegger, and Gerold Schwarzenegger, who is Alois's son and Arnold's first cousin.

Page 7. Description of Aurelia (her looks, etc.) from author interview with Erika Lohrer.

Page 7. Aurelia working at a war office from author interview with Hertha Schwarzenegger.

Page 7. Aurelia's marriage to Herr Barmuller from Herr Mayer at the Mürzsteg Gemeinde.

Page 7. Gustav in the German military police in Belgium from Frederich Gsols and confidential source.

Page 7. Aurelia's claim that she didn't know the details of Gustav's war work from author interview with confidential source.

Page 7. Gustav and Aurelia's wedding date from Herr Mayer, Mürzsteg Gemeinde.

Page 8. Hitler's entry into Graz from Frederich Gsols and Kurt Marnul.

Page 8. Aurelia's reaction to Hitler from author interview with Sue Moray.

Page 8. Schwarzenegger house and lifestyle information from author interviews with Freddy Kattner and the Anderwalt family, which now lives in the house and whom Arnold, Aurelia, Maria, and the Shrivers visited in the summer of 1988. Also details from Arnold Schwarzenegger and Douglas Kent Hall, *Arnold: The Education of a Bodybuilder* (New York: Pocket Books, 1977), 20.

Page 8. Aurelia's weak heart from author interview with Frau Krainer, who owned the local guesthouse.

Page 9. Aurelia and pants information from Joan Goodman, "Playboy Interview: Arnold Schwarzenegger," *Playboy*, January 1988.

Page 9. Aurelia and hair, nails, shoes, buckles, and shirts from Jami Bernard, "Muscled Mirth," *New York Post*, June 11, 1987; and Nancy Collins, "Pumping Arnold," *Rolling Stone*, January 17, 1985.

Page 9. Gustav's salary from Nancy Collins, "Pumping Arnold."

Page 9. Gustav's drinking from author interviews with Frederich Gsols, Karl Kainrath, and confidential source.

Page 10. Thalersee Restaurant details from author interview with Herr Klink, whose family owns the restaurant.

Page 10. Arnold's birth time from author interview with Erich Janner of the Germany Bodybuilding Federation.

Page 10. Meinhard's birth date from author interview with Erika Lohrer.

Page 10. Favoritism toward Meinhard from author interviews with Erika Lohrer, Kurt Marnul, Joe Weider, and Frederich Gsols; Arnold Schwarzenegger and Douglas Kent Hall, *Arnold: The Education of a Bodybuilder*, 24; Joan Goodman, "Playboy Interview"; and confidential source from Thal.

Page 10. Arnold sent to stay with Alois alone from author interview with Alois.

Page 10. Gustav saying Arnold wasn't his from author interview with two confidential sources.

Page 10. Gustav's jealousy from author interviews with Frederich Gsols and confidential source.

Page 11. Arnold's nightmares and not being comforted from Jean Vallely, "The Promoter," *GQ*, July 1986.

Page 11. Aurelia and baby teeth and hair from author interview with Erika Lohrer.

Page 11. Aurelia wanting both boys to be same height and giving less food from author interview with confidential source.

Page 11. Meinhard favoritism from author interview with Erika Lohrer.

Page 11. Arnold's sickness from "Celebs," *Chicago Sun-Times*, February 10, 1988; and Arnold Schwarzenegger and Douglas Kent Hall, *Arnold: The Education of a Bodybuilder*, 109.

Page 11. Arnold going to Hans Gross from author interview with Margarate Stanzer, headmistress and daughter of now-deceased headmaster.

Pages 11, 12. Arnold's appearance, glasses, "Cinderella" from author interview with confidential source from Thal.

Page 12. Details on Arnold's fear of his father from author interview with confidential source from Thal.

Page 12. Arnold and Meinhard's early-morning weekday duties from Dotson Rader, "I Wanted to Be a Champion," *Parade*, May 31, 1987.

Page 12. Gustav demanding that the boys eat with books under their elbows from Joyce Wadler, "Arnold Schwarzenegger: Body Language," *New York Post*, January 15, 1977.

Page 12. Arnold's monkey ambition from author interview with Frau Helga Anderwalt, who was told it by Aurelia in 1988.

Page 13. Sunday outings and Gustav's required essays from Joan Goodman, "Playboy Interview"; and Marguerite Michaels, "A Son's Quest to Be the Best," *Parade*, January 9, 1983.

Page 13. Arnold's postvictory attitude of planning for next year from author interview with confidential source.

Pages 13–14. Gustav encouraging a rivalry between Arnold and Meinhard, "Let's see," and "Tell me" quotes from Marian Christy, "Winning According to Schwarzenegger," *Boston Globe*, May 9, 1982.

Page 14. "You really beat your brother" from Marguerite Michaels, "A Son's Quest to Be the Best."

Page 14. Arnold and games from author interview with Freddy Kattner.

Page 14. No birthday parties due to poverty from author interview with Arnold's boyhood friend, Franz Hormann.

Page 15. No TV or refrigerator from Nancy Collins, "Pumping Arnold."

Page 15. Arnold's Thal school days from author interviews with schoolmates Helga Verschink, Monika Zimmermann, and Franz Hormann; Margarate Stanzer; and confidential source who went to school with Arnold and Meinhard.

Page 16. Arnold dressing up in his father's uniform from Dotson Rader, "I Wanted to Be a Champion."

Page 16. The stinging nettles from author interview with confidential source from Thal.

Page 16. Fröbel School from author interview with current administrator.

Page 16. Meinhard and Marschall School problems from author interview with confidential source.

Page 16. Meinhard and reform school from author interviews with confidential source from Thal to whom Gustav told this, and a second confidential source.

Pages 16–17. The book-filled schoolbag and the milkman stories from author interview with confidential source from Thal.

Page 17. The Schinerl story from author interview with confidential source close to Gustav Schwarzenegger.

Page 17. Why the Schwarzeneggers were hated from author interview with confidential source from Thal.

Page 17. Playing soccer for the Graz Athletic Club from Richard W. Johnston, "The Men and the Myth," *Sports Illustrated*, October 14, 1974.

Pages 17–18. Arnold and team sports from Arnold Schwarzenegger and Douglas Kent Hall, *Arnold: The Education of a Bodybuilder*, 14.

Page 18. Arnold and the arts information from Marguerite Michaels, "A Son's Quest to Be the Best."

Page 18. Arnold and Sieguard, Reg Park, Steve Reeves from Arnold Schwarzenegger and Douglas Kent Hall, *Arnold: The Education of a Bodybuilder*; author interview with Rick Wayne; Tom Sciacca, "Arnold Trades in His Sword for a Ray Gun—and Becomes a Menie!," *Starblazer*, December 1984; Rosemary Breslin, "Pumping Arnold," *New York Sunday News*, September 15, 1985; and author interview with confidential source.

Chapter 2: Escape from Thal

Pages 22–23. Details on Marnul and Athletic Union Graz from author interviews with Kurt Marnul and Helmut Cerncic.

Pages 23–25. Bodybuilding history information from Margaret Roach, "Bodybuilders Labor to Develop an Image," *New York Times*, March 20, 1977; Stephen Karten interview with Oscar Heidenstam of NABBA; and Jim Stingley, "Bodybuilding: State of the Art, 1975," *Los Angeles Times*, November 16, 1975.

Page 24. Description of Muscle Beach and Vic Tanny's shows from author interview with Armand Tanny.

Page 25. Alistair Murray quote and powerlifting quote from Richard W. Johnston, "The Men and the Myth," *Sports Illustrated*, October 14, 1974.

Page 25. Details on Athletic Union Graz from author interviews with Kurt Marnul and Helmut Cerncic.

Page 26. Arnold suggesting he had made many friends in the Graz bodybuilding scene from Arnold Schwarzenegger and Douglas Kent Hall, *Arnold: The Education of a Bodybuilder* (New York: Pocket Books, 1977), 14, 15, 17.

Page 26. Helmut Cerncic quotes from author interview with Cerncic.

Page 27. Arnold taking steroids at thirteen from author interviews with Kurt Marnul and Rick Wayne and confidential source who trained with him and saw him take them.

Pages 27–28. Steroids and sexuality from author interview with bodybuilder Dave DuPre, who trained with Arnold.

Page 28. Ronald Matz details from Stephen Karten interview with Matz.

Pages 28–29. Arnold's Union training habits from author interviews with Kurt Marnul, Karl Kainrath, and Hans Gobetz, who all trained with him there, and Helmut Cerncic.

Pages 28–29. Karl Kainrath quote from author interview with Kainrath.

Page 29. Helmut Cerncic quote from author interview with Cerncic.

Page 29. Gustav's teachings from Joan Goodman, "Playboy Interview: Arnold Schwarzenegger," *Playboy*, January 1988.

Page 29. School, parents, girls, friends not mattering to Arnold from Arnold Schwarzenegger and Douglas Kent Hall, *Arnold: The Education of a Bodybuilder*, 28.

Page 30. Gerstl information from author's German researcher's interview with Gerstl.

Page 30. Information on both parents disapproving of Arnold's pursuing bodybuilding from Arnold Schwarzenegger and Douglas Kent Hall, *Arnold: The Education of a Bodybuilder*, 31, 56.

Page 30. Arnold on religion from Arnold Schwarzenegger and Douglas Kent Hall, *Arnold: The Education of a Bodybuilder*, 32.

Page 30. Arnold going to church "when I think about it" from James Delson, "Penthouse Interview: Arnold Schwarzenegger," *Penthouse*, December 1981.

Pages 30–31. Gustav's departure from Thal for Raaba from the Raaba Gemeinde and author interviews with confidential source in Thal, and ex-policeman Herr Koller, who worked with him.

Page 31. Meinhard leaving school and taking a job without telling Gustav from author interview with Frederich Gsols.

Page 31. Gustav telling Arnold that he would never succeed and needed a psychiatrist from Marian Christy, "Winning According to Schwarzenegger," *Boston Globe*, May 9, 1982; and Teresa Carpenter, "The Self-Made Man," *Premiere*, January 1989.

Pages 31–32. Quotes from Dr. Maurice White and Laurie Taylor from John McVicar, "Body-Builders: Men or Beasts?," *Sunday Telegraph Magazine* (London), January 17, 1988.

Page 32. Riklin quote from Leonard Todd, "Muscle Madness: The Incredible Boom in Male Body-Building," *Cosmopolitan*, August 1977.

Page 32. Frank Zane and Boyer Coe quotes from author interviews with Zane and Coe. Ronald Matz quote from Stephen Karten interview with Matz.

Page 33. Arnold's work and salary from author interview with confidential source from Graz.

Page 33. Steirer Hof contest from researcher's interview with Alfred Gerstl.

Page 33. Curling championship details from Albert Busek, "Der Junge Gigant," German-language publication, 1964.

Page 34. Correspondence with Benno Dahmen from author interview with Dahmen.

Page 34. Details of Arnold's army service from Arnold Schwarzenegger and Douglas Kent Hall, *Arnold: The Education of a Bodybuilder*, 35, 36; Nancy Collins, "Pumping Arnold," *Rolling Stone*, January 17, 1985; and Roman Schliesser, "Adabei," *Die Kronen Zeitung*, February 12, 1985.

Page 34. Tank rolling into river from Roman Schliesser, "Adabei."

Page 35. Arnold eating meat every day from Nancy Collins, "Pumping Arnold."

Page 35. Benno Dahmen financing Stuttgart trip from author interview with Dahmen.

Pages 35–36. Details of Stuttgart contest from author interviews with Karl Blömer and Erich Janner as well as "Arnold Schwarzenegger: Top Secret Dossier," *Sport and Fitness* (the Netherlands), 1988.

Page 36. Franco Columbu details from Jane Ardmore, "Arnold Schwarzenegger, the Gentle Giant," *The Sunday Times (Northeast Woman)*, June 8, 1986; Richard Corliss (cinema page), "Arnold Wry (Red Heat)," *Time*, June 20, 1988; Richard W. Johnston, "The Men and the Myth," *Sports Illustrated*, October 14, 1974; and Ruth Ryon, "Body Builder Turns Home Builder," *Los Angeles Times*, September 21, 1986.

Pages 36–37. Details about Rolf Putziger from author interviews with Benno Dahmen and Helmut Riedmeier. Putziger died in 1977.

Page 37. Arnold's army punishment and later encouragement from Arnold Schwarzenegger and Douglas Kent Hall, *Arnold: The Education of a Bodybuilder*, 37.

Pages 37–38. Salt story from author interviews with Hans Gobetz, Kurt Marnul, and Karl Kainrath, who were around at the time, and from author interviews with Bill Pearl, Frank Zane, and Gene Mozee, to whom Arnold told the story. Mr. C was approached by the author and did not deny the story, but blanched and refused to comment.

Chapter 3: Munich

Page 39. Information on Aurelia's attitude toward Arnold's victories from Arnold Schwarzenegger and Douglas Kent Hall, *Arnold: The Education of a Bodybuilder* (New York: Pocket Books, 1977), 31.

Page 39. Arnold's father providing wine and Arnold viewing women as sexual tools from Arnold Schwarzenegger and Douglas Kent Hall, *Arnold: The Education of a Bodybuilder*, 32; and author interview with Karl Kainrath.

Page 40. Gustav and Aurelia's vision of Arnold's future from Arnold Schwarzenegger and Douglas Kent Hall, *Arnold: The Education of a Bodybuilder*, 31, 33.

Page 40. Thal details (pencil factory, etc.) from author interview with Frederich Gsols.

Pages 40–41. Arnold's dislike of routine, convention from Arnold Schwarzenegger and Douglas Kent Hall, *Arnold: The Education of a Bodybuilder*, 34.

Page 41. "I look down at people" quote from Michael Tolkin, "More Than Just a Beautiful Body," *New York Sunday News*, September 5, 1976.

Page 41. "Ever since I was a child" quote from Diane K. Shah, " 'Pumping Iron' Pumps Up Arnold," *National Observer*, February 19, 1977.

Pages 41–42. "Strength does not come from winning," "As a kid I always idolized," "We all have great inner power," and "Good things don't happen by coincidence" quotes from Marian Christy, "Winning According to Schwarzenegger," *Boston Globe*, May 9 1982.

Page 42. "What I am most happy about" quote from Jean Vallely, "The Promoter," *GQ*, July 1986.

Page 42. Date of Arnold's commencement at Putziger's from "Arnold Schwarzenegger: Top Secret Dossier," *Sport and Fitness* (the Netherlands), 1988.

Pages 42–43. Meinhard arguing with Gustav over politics, "troubled boy," "artist," and drifting from job to job from author interview with Erika Lohrer.

Page 43. Meinhard borrowing money and not returning it from author interviews with confidential source in Thal to whom Gustav told it and Austrian bodybuilder who knew Meinhard.

Page 43. 1965 dollar value of Austrian schillings from Nicole Watts, Commercial Bank of Saudi Arabia.

Pages 43–44. Meinhard meeting Erika Lohrer from author interview with Lohrer.

Page 44. Erika not knowing about Arnold from author interview with Lohrer.

Page 44. Arnold's answer to questions about his brother from author interview with Benno Dahmen.

Page 44. Gustav's complaints about Arnold's letters from Bart Mills, "Muscling His Way Up in Hollywood," *Newsday*, September 29, 1985.

Page 45. Details on Putziger's gym from author interviews with Helmut Riedmeier and Kurt Marnul as well as two confidential sources, German bodybuilders who trained there.

Page 45. Arnold drinking lots of beer in Munich from Dennis Hunt, ". . . While Schwarzenegger Pumps Life into His Mate," *Us*, November 11, 1980.

Page 45. Arnold displaying his muscles in beer halls from author interview with Helmut Riedmeier.

Page 45. Arnold's joke with the dog from author interview with Karl Kainrath, who was there.

Pages 45-46. Arnold not paying for dinner from author interview with Rick Wayne.

Page 46. "I am Styrian" quote from author interview with Kurt Marnul.

Page 46. Arnold's waitress pickup and steroid use from author interview with Helmut Riedmeier.

Page 46. Arnold's dangerous driving from author interviews with Erich Janner, Rick Wayne, and Gene Mozee and from Arnold Schwarzenegger and Douglas Kent Hall, *Arnold: The Education of a Bodybuilder*, 64.

Pages 46-47. Arnold's Munich fights from author interview with John Citrone; author interviews with Erika Lohrer and Kurt Marnul; and Arnold Schwarzenegger and Douglas Kent Hall, *Arnold: The Education of a Bodybuilder*, 64.

Pages 46-47. Oktoberfest anecdote from author interview with Erich Janner.

Page 47. Gustav's trip to Munich from author interview with Karl Kainrath.

Page 47. "Arnold always made a fool of people" quote from author interview with Helmut Riedmeier.

Page 48. Ice cream joke from author interview with Hans Gobetz.

Page 48. Sugar treatment from author interview with Kurt Marnul.

Page 48. "Vitamin apple" from author interview with Kurt Marnul.

Page 49. Mountaineer joke from author interview with Erich Janner.

Pages 49-50. Screaming competitor joke told by Arnold himself in the film *Pumping Iron*.

Page 50. Teaching Americans and others rude German words from author interview with Kurt Marnul.

Page 50. Arnold taking Marnul from brothel to brothel from author interview with Kurt Marnul.

Pages 50-51. Homosexuals offering bodybuilders money to pose (in Munich gym) from author interview with Helmut Riedmeier and confidential source who trained at the gym.

Page 51. "Schneck" story from Arnold Schwarzenegger and Douglas Kent Hall, *Arnold: The Education of a Bodybuilder*, 40-43.

Chapter 4: London

Page 53. Gym members paying for Arnold's trip to London from Helmut Riedmeier, who was one of them, and Arnold Schwarzenegger and Douglas Kent Hall, *Arnold: The Education of a Bodybuilder* (New York: Pocket Books, 1977), 45.

Page 53. Arnold reprimanding his friend for speaking German from Stephen Karten interview with Oscar Heidenstam.

Pages 53-54. That Arnold has spoken German in front of Sue Moray and Maria Shriver from author interview with Moray and Kurt Marnul.

Page 54. Arnold backstage at the Universe from author interview with Rick Wayne.

Pages 54-55. 1966 Universe details from author interview with Jimmy Savile and Stephen Karten interview with John Citrone.

Pages 55-56. Rick Wayne quotes and description of Arnold after the contest from author interview with Wayne.

Pages 56-57. Wag Bennett details from Stephen Karten interview with Bennett; Arnold Schwarzenegger and Douglas Kent Hall, *Arnold: The Education of a Bodybuilder,* 57, 58, 59; "Arnold Really Is Just a Big Softie," *London Daily Mail,* January 22, 1986; and author interview with British bodybuilding journalist Peter McGough.

Page 56. Dianne Bennett's mother being a Tiller Girl from Stephen Karten interview with her husband, Dianne's father, Bob Woolgar.

Pages 57-58. Wag Bennett quotes from Stephen Karten interview with Bennett.

Page 58. Arnold's brief fling with Dianne Bennett from author interviews with Rick Wayne, Peter McGough, and Mr. R.

Pages 58-59. Information on Wag teaching Arnold to pose and the theme from *Exodus* from Arnold Schwarzenegger and Douglas Kent Hall, *Arnold: The Education of a Bodybuilder,* 58.

Page 59. Arnold's first meeting with Reg Park from Arnold Schwarzenegger and Douglas Kent Hall, *Arnold: The Education of a Bodybuilder,* 61, 63, 64; author interviews with Rick Wayne; and Stephen Karten interview with Wag Bennett.

Page 59. Reg Park quotes and promise to bring Arnold to South Africa from author's South African researcher's interview with Park.

Page 60. "I personally don't know" quote from Jim Stingley, "Bodybuilding: State of the Art, 1975," *Los Angeles Times,* November 16, 1975.

Page 60. "It didn't belong in the movie" quote from Michael Tolkin, "More Than Just a Beautiful Body," *Sunday News,* September 5, 1976.

Pages 60-61. "The biggest cliché" quote from Jennifer Seder, "Schwarzenegger: He's Quit Going Shirtless in Hollywood," shortened version of article in *Los Angeles Times,* July 6, 1979.

Page 61. Ronald Matz statement from Stephen Karten interview with Matz.

Page 61. John Citrone comments from Stephen Karten interview with Citrone.

Pages 61-62. Details on Spanish millionaire from Stephen Karten interview with Oscar Heidenstam and author interview with Rick Wayne. The millionaire's close friend Serge Nubret confirmed details.

Page 62. The pictures of Arnold from author interviews with Rick Wayne and a confidential source.

Page 62. The weekend with the Spanish millionaire from author interview with a confidential source.

Pages 62-65. The material on Mr. R from author and Stephen Karten interviews with Helmut Riedmeier, Rick Wagner, and Mr. R himself. Also, in his book *Muscle Wars* (New York: St. Martin's Press, 1985), 92, Rick refers to being in Munich with Arnold and discussing a British industrialist and his affairs.

Pages 64-65. Quotes and information from author and Stephen Karten interview with Mr. R.

Chapter 5: Escape to America

Pages 67-68. Details of Portsmouth visit, Arnold's interest in history, and the girl whom Arnold went out with there from Stephen Karten interview with Gordon Allen.

Page 68. Reg Park's invitation to Arnold from author's South African researcher's interview with Park.

Pages 68-69. Arnold on apartheid from author interview with Rick Wayne.

Page 69. Arnold's "Nazi salute" anecdote from Rick Wayne, *Muscle Wars* (New York: St. Martin's Press, 1985), 91.

Page 69. Union contest and Arnold and Karl Kainrath's confrontation from author interview with Helmut Cerncic.

Pages 69-70. Helmut Cerncic quotes from author interview with Cerncic.

Pages 70-71. Joe Weider details from Rick Wayne, *Muscle Wars*, 111-14.

Pages 71-72. Arnold's interview from Uwe Dick, "Wie Habe Ich Meinen 54er Oberarm Erreicht?," *Münchner Merkur*, October 6, 1967.

Pages 72-74. Christopher Ward interview from "It's Not Easy, Being Arnold Schwarzenegger," *London Daily Mirror*, March 8, 1968.

Page 74. Arnold's reaction to the Ward interview from author interview with Rick Wayne.

Page 75. Details of Newcastle trip from Stephen Karten interview with John Citrone.

Page 75. Patrick Knapp's birth details from author interview with his mother, Erika Lohrer.

Pages 75-76. Jimmy Savile quote from author interview with Savile.

Pages 76-79. Details involving Ludwig and Pat Shusterich (Munich meeting, departure from London) from author interviews with both.

Chapter 6: Florida and California: 1968

Page 81. "I'll eat them up" quote from author interview with Lud Shusterich.

Page 81. "I could not speak the language" quote from Wanda McDaniel and Cheryl Lavin, "Pumping Arnold and the Fast Track," *Los Angeles Herald Examiner*, July 29, 1984.

Page 81. "I had no money" from Nancy Collins, "Pumping Arnold," *Rolling Stone,* January 17, 1985.

Page 81. Details on 1968 IFBB Universe from author interviews with Frank Zane and Rick Wayne; Michael Kilian, "Are You Invited to 'The' Wedding?," *Waterbury Sunday Republican,* April 20, 1986; and Arnold Schwarzenegger and Douglas Kent Hall, *Arnold: The Education of a Bodybuilder* (New York: Pocket Books, 1977), 92, 93.

Page 81. Arnold crying himself to sleep after Miami defeat from author interview with Rick Wayne and Arnold Schwarzenegger and Douglas Kent Hall, *Arnold: The Education of a Bodybuilder,* 93.

Page 82. Arnold's attitude toward losing from Arnold Schwarzenegger and Douglas Kent Hall, *Arnold: The Education of a Bodybuilder,* 93.

Page 82. Joe Weider quote from Jerry Kindela, "In the Eye of the Beholder: How Joe Weider Saw the Future in Arnold," *Flex,* January 1990.

Pages 82–83. Weider's attitude toward Arnold's defeat from author interview with Rick Wayne.

Page 83. "Weider and his brother Ben" quote from Gene Stone, "The Money in Muscle," *California Business,* October 1988.

Page 83. Details on Arnold's contract with Weider from author interview with Lud Shusterich.

Page 84. Weider teaching Arnold about art and real estate from author interview with Joe Weider.

Page 84. Weider's pragmatism from Arnold Schwarzenegger and Douglas Kent Hall, *Arnold: The Education of a Bodybuilder,* 95.

Page 84. Armand Tanny quote from author interview with Tanny.

Page 84. Dan Howard quote from Stephen Karten interview with Howard.

Pages 84–85. "Joe visibly shrinks" from author interview with confidential source.

Page 85. The man Arnold "most admires" quote is from Joe Weider in Rick Wayne, *Muscle Wars* (New York: St. Martin's Press, 1985), 193.

Page 85. Joe Weider on Arnold from author interview with Weider.

Pages 85–86. *Sports Illustrated* quote from Richard W. Johnston, "The Men and the Myth," *Sports Illustrated,* October 14, 1974.

Page 86. Joe Weider's dual role in Arnold's life from author interview with Weider.

Page 87. Montreal stay with Jim Caruso from author interview with Caruso.

Page 87. Art Zeller meeting Arnold in California from author interview with Zeller.

Page 87. Details on posing lessons from author interview with Dick Tyler.

Page 87. Arnold saying that he admired Hitler in cut portion of *Pumping Iron* from Stephen Karten interview with George Butler.

Page 88. *Pumping Iron* not being scripted from author interview with Charles Gaines.

Pages 88–89. Manfred Thellig quotes from Stephen Karten interview with Thellig.

Page 89. In author interview one of Arnold's girlfriends, Sue Moray, said she was half Jewish.

Page 89. Arnold's Jewish friends and aides include Alfred and Karl Gerstl, Art Zeller, Joe Gold, Joe Weider, and his publicist, Charlotte Parker.

Page 89. Wiesenthal Center support, friendship with Wiesenthal, and attendance at his birthday party in Los Angeles from Stephen Karten interview with spokesperson at center.

Page 89. Witnesses who have seen Arnold do the "Sieg Heil" include Gene Mozee, Rick Wayne, Dan Howard, Wil McArdle, and two confidential sources.

Page 89. Arnold owning and listening to records of Hitler's speeches from author interviews with Sue Moray and a confidential source.

Page 89. Arnold's denial that he is interested in the Nazi era from Sharon Churcher, "Schwarzenegger's Kurt Replies," *Penthouse*, January 1989.

Page 89. "It was expected of him" quote from Stephen Karten interview with Dan Howard.

Page 90. Dick Tyler quote from author interview with Tyler.

Page 90. Gironda's comment to Arnold from John Balik, "Arnold: Celebrating 20 Years in America," *Ironman*, December 1989.

Page 90. Vince Gironda training Arnold for nine months from author interview with Gironda.

Pages 91–92. Bill Grant quotes from author interview with Grant.

Page 92. "Arnold was dedicated beyond belief" quote from author interview with confidential source.

Page 92. Comment about Nixon from Joan Goodman, "Playboy Interview: Arnold Schwarzenegger," *Playboy*, January 1988.

Page 92. Arnold's speeding tickets from author interviews with Dick Tyler, Frank Zane, and Lud Shusterich.

Page 92. Car race with Art Zeller from author interviews with Zeller and Dick Tyler.

Page 92. Comment to Benno Dahmen from author interview with Dahmen.

Page 93. Frank Zane friendship, Tijuana trip, and Zane quotes from author interview with Zane.

Pages 93–94. Bill Grant quote from author interview with Grant.

Page 94. Little Swede and antique shop incident from author interview with Wil McArdle.

Page 94. Ron D'Ippolito anecdote from author interview with D'Ippolito.

Page 94. Arnold shocked at bodybuilders lying on the beach from Larry Kart, "Schwarzenegger's Barbarian Has a Heart of Gold," *Chicago Tribune*, May 9, 1982.

Pages 94–95. Arnold's pickup techniques from author interviews with Armand Tanny, Wil McArdle, and Jim Caruso.

Chapter 7: Love and Victory: 1969–1970

Page 97. Barbara's meeting with Arnold from Arnold Schwarzenegger and Douglas Kent Hall, *Arnold: The Education of a Bodybuilder* (New York: Pocket Books, 1977), 112.

Page 97. Arnold educating himself to be an American from writer unknown, "Ten Routes to the American Dream," *Time*, 1986.

Page 97. Description of Barbara Outland from author interview with Erika Lohrer.

Page 98. Barbara Outland's education from Arnold Schwarzenegger and Douglas Kent Hall, *Arnold: The Education of a Bodybuilder*, 110.

Page 98. Barbara Outland's family background from author interview with Sue Moray.

Page 98. Barbara Outland's profession as English teacher from Richard W. Johnston, "The Men and the Myth," *Sports Illustrated*, October 14, 1974.

Page 98. Description of Barbara and Arnold's relationship from author interviews with Gene Mozee, Art Zeller, and Frank Zane.

Page 98. Dan Howard quote from Stephen Karten interview with Howard.

Page 98. Boyer Coe quote from author interview with Coe.

Page 99. Rick Wayne quotes from author interview with Wayne.

Page 99. Dick Tyler quote from author interview with Tyler.

Page 99. Arnold on Sergio Oliva from Rick Wayne, *Muscle Wars* (New York: St. Martin's Press, 1985), 132–33.

Page 100. Arnold saying at the 1969 NABBA that he wanted to beat everyone from author interview with Serge Nubret.

Page 100. *Hercules* made for Italian TV on a $300,000 budget from Brian Lowry, "Arnold Schwarzenegger: The Complete Barbarian," *Starlog*, May 1984.

Page 100. Arnold's phone calls from friends about *Hercules* from Teresa Carpenter, "The Self-Made Man," *Premiere*, January 1989.

Page 100. Description of *Hercules* from Filmpartners, Inc., press release, March 3, 1983.

Page 101. Quote on acting from "The Body Meets the Face," an exchange between Arnold Schwarzenegger and Natalie Wood, *The Hollywood Reporter's 48th Annual*.

Page 101. Details on Arnold's training from Rick Wayne, *Muscle Wars*, 107.

Page 101. Arnold memorizing other bodybuilders' routines from Stephen Karten interview with Dan Howard.

Pages 101–102. Arnold's comments about blacks and Jews from author interview with Dave DuPre.

Page 102. Hatcheck girl incident from author interview with Rick Wayne, who was with Arnold at the time.

Page 102. Arnold's mail order business from author interview with Gene Mozee.

Page 102. Arnold not opening envelopes unless they contained checks from author interviews with Armand Tanny and Rick Wayne.

Pages 102–103. Details on Pumping Bricks business from December 2, 1988, "20/20," 1988; Susan Peters, "Schwarzenegger, Inc.," *California Business*, June 1986; and Ruth Ryon, "Body Builder Turns Home Builder," *Los Angeles Times*, September 21, 1986.
Pages 103–104. Palmdale investment from "20/20," December 2, 1988; and documents from Los Angeles county clerk's office.
Page 104. Letter to Park and Gordon Allen quote on NABBA Universe from Stephen Karten interview with Allen.
Page 104. Participation being a surprise to Arnold from Arnold Schwarzenegger and Douglas Kent Hall, *Arnold: The Education of a Bodybuilder*, 103.
Pages 104–105. Rick Wayne quote from Rick Wayne, *Muscle Wars*, 119.
Page 105. Information on John-John Park and Arnold from author's South African researcher's interview with Reg Park.
Pages 105–106. Arnold's relationship with Jim Lorimer, Columbus contest, and Arnold quote from author interview with Lorimer.
Pages 106–107. Information on Oliva from author interview with Rick Wayne.
Page 108. Wil McArdle quote from author interview with McArdle.
Page 108. Oil story from author interviews with Dan Howard, who saw Arnold play his trick twice, Boyer Coe, Rick Wayne, Ray Mentzer, and confidential source, a German bodybuilder. Also referred to in Rick Wayne, *Muscle Wars*, 165.
Pages 108–110. Details on Erika Lohrer and Meinhard's relationship, Patrick, Gustav, and Aurelia, and Meinhard's death from author interview with Lohrer.
Page 110. Arnold not attending funeral from author interviews with Erika Lohrer and Maria Hautz.
Page 110. Arnold on Meinhard from Nancy Collins, "Pumping Arnold," *Rolling Stone*, January 17, 1985.
Pages 110–111. Arnold helping Erika Lohrer and Patrick and Erika's 1988 visit from author interview with Lohrer.
Pages 111–112. All Meinhard details and Meinhard in prison from author interviews with Maria Hautz, to whom he told it, Anton Spuler, who worked with Gustav, and confidential source in Thal to whom Gustav told it.

Chapter 8: Success, Death, and *Stay Hungry*

Page 115. Barbara and Arnold's Kufstein visit from author interview with Erika Lohrer.
Page 115. Barbara's thoughts and feelings from Arnold Schwarzenegger and Douglas Kent Hall, *Arnold: The Education of a Bodybuilder* (New York: Pocket Books, 1977), 112; and author interviews with Frank Zane, Art Zeller, and Gene Mozee.
Page 115. Arnold's New Year's resolutions from author interview with Frank Zane.
Page 116. Arnold not being faithful to Barbara from author interview with Pat Shusterich.

Page 116. Arnold not wanting to get married till past thirty from "How 'Barbarian' Arnold Won Kennedy Approval of His Love for Maria Shriver," *Star*, June 1, 1982.

Page 116. Barbara providing secretarial services from author interviews with Lud Shusterich and Dick Tyler.

Page 116. Arnold's education from Stephen Karten interview with confidential source and D. Levin at UCLA extension.

Page 116. Barbara helping Arnold in research from author interview with Gene Mozee.

Page 116. George Butler information from " 'Pumping Iron' Builds Muscles and Shapes a New Body Trend," *Chicago Tribune*, April 24, 1977.

Page 116. George Butler quote from Teresa Carpenter, "The Self-Made Man," *Premiere*, January 1989.

Page 117. Frank Zane toasting Gustav from author interview with Zane.

Page 117. Arnold not wanting to pay prostitute in Essen from author interview with Serge Nubret.

Page 117. Arnold on Sergio Oliva from Rick Wayne, *Muscle Wars* (New York: St. Martin's Press, 1985), 132.

Page 117. Rick Wayne's definition of Oliva's weakness from author interview with Wayne.

Page 117. Peter McGough quote from author interview with McGough.

Page 118. "I was far more interested" quote from Rick Wayne, *Muscle Wars*, 134.

Page 118. Obituary of Gustav Schwarzenegger from *Graz Kleine Zeitung*, December 14, 1972.

Page 118. Gendarmerie Musik playing Chopin from author interview with Willi Kalcher, one of the players.

Page 118. Arnold not going to his father's funeral because he was training from author interview with Art Zeller.

Page 118. Arnold on French bodybuilder from Nancy Collins, "Pumping Arnold," *Rolling Stone*, January 17, 1985.

Page 118. Arnold's saying that a leg injury had prevented him from going to Gustav's funeral from Joan Goodman, "Playboy Interview: Arnold Schwarzenegger," *Playboy*, January 1988.

Page 118. Arnold saying he was not notified in time to go to Gustav's funeral from Rob Lowing, "Brain & Brawn," *Sun Herald*, January 22, 1989.

Page 119. Barbara's comment to Ken Waller from author interview with Waller.

Page 119. Arnold saying he would pay anything for his father to be alive from Marguerite Michaels, "A Son's Quest to Be the Best," *Parade*, January 9, 1983.

Page 119. Gustav not seeing the full circle from Joan Goodman, "Playboy Interview: Arnold Schwarzenegger."

Page 119. Wayne de Milia quote from author interview with de Milia.

Page 119. Arnold's trip to Hawaii from author interview with Art Zeller.

Page 120. Robert Altman quotes from Stephen Karten interview with Altman.

Page 120. Art Zeller anecdote about Arnold driving him to the airport from author interview with Zeller.

Pages 120–121. Arnold at 1974 Olympia from author interviews with Frank Zane and Rick Wayne.

Page 121. Arnold quote on bodybuilding from Joan Goodman, "Playboy Interview: Arnold Schwarzenegger."

Page 122. Lucille Ball hiring Arnold from Nina Darnton, "He-Man Humor," *New York Post*, November 11, 1987; and Tom Sciacca, "Arnold Trades in His Sword for a Ray Gun and Becomes a Menie!," *Starblazer*, December 1984.

Page 122. Charles Gaines quote from Teresa Carpenter, "The Self-Made Man," *Premiere*, January 1989.

Page 123. Eric Morris quotes from Stephen Karten interview with Morris.

Page 123. Arnold's breakup with Barbara from Arnold Schwarzenegger and Douglas Kent Hall, *Arnold: The Education of a Bodybuilder*, 112.

Page 123. "Arnold is the most goal-oriented person" quote from Richard W. Johnston, "The Men and the Myth," *Sports Illustrated*, October 14, 1974.

Page 123. "A woman is like a car" from author interview with Rick Wayne.

Page 124. Byron Berline quote from Stephen Karten interview with Berline.

Page 125. Arnold quote on Sally Field from Tom Burke, "Sexy, Fun-Loving Schwarzenegger!," *Cosmopolitan*, July 1988.

Page 125. Quote on Arnold on set of *Stay Hungry* from author interview with confidential source.

Chapter 9: Filming *Pumping Iron* and Retirement

Page 127. Arnold's refusal to change his name from author interview with confidential source.

Page 127. Arnold's observation on the unforgettability of his name from Rosemary Breslin, "Pumping Arnold," *New York Sunday News*, September 15, 1985.

Page 127. Arnold's comment on getting laid from Cliff Jahr, "A Sex Symbol for the Seventies?," *New Times*, November 1976.

Page 127. Rafelson's conversation with Eric Morris and Arnold's acting courses from Stephen Karten interview with Morris.

Page 128. Arnold seeing Elvis from author interview with Art Zeller.

Page 128. Serge Nubret information from author interview with Nubret.

Page 128. "I wanted every single person" quote from Arnold Schwarzenegger and Douglas Kent Hall, *Arnold: The Education of a Bodybuilder* (New York: Pocket Books, 1977), 108.

Page 130. Arnold guest posing in San Francisco from Jim Stingley, "Bodybuilding: State of the Art, 1975," *Los Angeles Times*, November 16, 1975.

Page 131. Arnold's friendship with the Koornhofs from Rick Wayne, *Muscle Wars* (New York: St. Martin's Press, 1985), 141.

Pages 131–132. Information on Serge Nubret's trip and Robinson's being thrown out from Rick Wayne, *Muscle Wars*, 141–42, 145.

Page 132. Arnold's visit to Graz and Vienna from " 'Mister Olympia' in Graz," German language publication, date unknown.

Page 132. Arnold's gifts and income details from Cliff Jahr, "A Sex Symbol for the Seventies?"

Page 133. Whitney Museum exhibition from Stephen Karten interview with museum spokesperson.

Page 133. Exhibition description and "I'm in heaven" quote from Cliff Jahr, "A Sex Symbol for the Seventies?"

Page 133. George Butler quote about Arnold's naïveté and Algonquin Hotel information from Teresa Carpenter, "The Self-Made Man," *Premiere*, January 1989.

Page 133. Arnold's shirt size from Jennifer Seder, "Schwarzenegger: He's Quit Going Shirtless in Hollywood," shortened version of article in *Los Angeles Times*, July 6, 1979.

Page 133. Arnold's jeans and shoe size from Judy Klemesrud, "What Body-Building King Finds Uplifting," *New York Times*, May 8, 1976.

Page 133. Arnold's jeans costing $150 from Jennifer Seder, "Schwarzenegger: He's Quit Going Shirtless in Hollywood."

Page 133. Arnold's jeans being from Nudies from Stephen Karten interview with store spokesperson.

Page 133. Morty Sills being Arnold's tailor from Stephen Karten interview with Sills.

Pages 133–134. Arnold's taste in preppy and country-and-western clothes from Jonathan Roberts, "Arnold Schwarzenegger," *Interview*, October 1985.

Page 134. Arnold's taste for country music from author interview with Rick Wayne.

Page 134. Frank Zane Hare Krishna Mexico anecdote from author interview with Zane.

Page 134. Critic's comments from Diane K. Shah, " 'Pumping Iron' Pumps Up Arnold," *National Observer*, February 19, 1977.

Page 134. Scavullo details from Stephen Karten interview with Scavullo.

Pages 134–135. Montreal escapade from author interviews with Kurt Marnul and Karl Kainrath.

Page 135. Austrian trip from author interview with Franz Hormann.

Page 135. Quote on Miss America from Cliff Jahr, "A Sex Symbol for the Seventies?"

Pages 135–136. *Sunday Times* article is Michael Roberts, "The King of Muscle Beach Heads for Hollywood . . . and a Star Is Brawn?," *London Sunday Times*, October 3, 1976.

Chapter 10: Stallone, *Pumping Iron*, and Sue Moray

Page 137. Details on Golden Globe Awards from author interview with Hollywood Foreign Press spokesperson.

Pages 137-138. Details on Frank Stallone and Jacqueline Stallone from 1986 and 1987 author interviews with Jacqueline Stallone.

Page 138. Stallone seeing Ali fight, getting idea for Rocky, then fighting to play part from Nancy Collins, "Sylvester Stallone," *Rolling Stone*, December 19, 1985.

Pages 139-144. *Pumping Iron* premiere from Tom Shales, "Bringing Biceps Chic to the Uptown Crowd," *Washington Post*, January 19, 1977.

Page 144. Date of "Dallas" premiere from Stephen Karten interview with Lorimar Productions spokesperson.

Page 144. Larry Hagman quote from Larry Hagman, "J.R. on the Couch," *TV Guide*, February 11, 1989.

Pages 144-145. Cohn quote from Nik Cohn, "Pumping Chic: The Launching of a New Folk Hero," *New York*, January 24, 1977.

Page 145. *Soho Weekly* quote from *Pumping Iron* press release, Cinegate Film Distribution, 1977.

Page 145. *Time* quote from Richard Schickel, "A Delicate Beefcake Ballet," *Time*, January 24, 1977.

Page 145. Gary Arnold quote from Gary Arnold, " 'Pumping Iron': A Witty Psych-Out by Mr. Olympia," *Washington Post*, February 19, 1977.

Page 145. Bobby Zarem as PR man confirmed by Zarem employee to Stephen Karten.

Pages 145-146. Alexander Walker quote from Alexander Walker, "Beautiful," *London Daily Mail*, May 19, 1977.

Page 146. Ratazzi party from Diane K. Shah, " 'Pumping Iron' Pumps Up Arnold," *National Observer*, February 19, 1977.

Page 146. Aurelia quote from Joyce Wadler, "Arnold Presses Bulges into a Tux as Celebs Give Lift to Premiere," *New York Post*, January 18, 1977.

Page 146. Arnold at Park Lane Hotel and carrying only $100 bills from Joyce Wadler, "Arnold Schwarzenegger: Body Language," *New York Post*, January 15, 1977.

Page 146. Offers of free cars, Austrian Airlines offer, and Arnold at "21" from Diane K. Shah, " 'Pumping Iron' Pumps Up Arnold."

Pages 146-147. Barbara Walters story from Jean Vallely, "The Promoter," *GQ*, July 1986.

Page 147. Liz Smith quote from Tom Shales, "Bringing Biceps Chic to the Uptown Crowd."

Page 147. Gaines on Arnold from Lynn Darling, "How Much Bigger Can Arnold Schwarzenegger Get?," *Esquire*, March 1985.

Page 147. Shirt incident from Marcia Stamell, "Arnold Wants an Oscar," *Bergen Record*, November 3, 1977.

Page 147. Arnold conflict about getting film print to Vienna and meal with Bernd and Erika Zimmermann from German language publication, May 7, 1977.

Page 148. Cannes Film Festival quote from Alexander Walker, "Muscling in on the Movies," *London Evening Standard*, May 19, 1977.
Pages 148–150. Sue Moray and Arnold from author interview with Moray.

Chapter 11: Maria

Page 153. Bobby Zarem arranging RFK Tennis Tournament invitation from Teresa Carpenter, "The Self-Made Man," *Premiere*, January 1989.
Page 153. Invitation to Hyannis Port from "Valentines" column, "Conan the Affectionate," *Vanity Fair*, February 1985.
Page 153. "I felt like I was going into the unknown" quote from James Delson, "Penthouse Interview: Arnold Schwarzenegger," *Penthouse*, December 1981.
Page 154. Arnold being at ease in Hyannis Port from Marie Brenner, "Growing Up Kennedy," *Vanity Fair*, February 1986.
Page 154. Rose Kennedy story from James Delson, "Penthouse Interview: Arnold Schwarzenegger."
Page 154. Joe Kennedy quote from Peter Collier and David Horowitz, *The Kennedys: An American Drama* (New York: Summit Books, 1984), 58.
Page 154. Arnold's admiration of Joe Kennedy from confidential source.
Pages 154–155. Joe Kennedy details from Peter Collier and David Horowitz, *The Kennedys*, 85, 87, 150.
Page 155. Bobby Shriver quote from Marie Brenner, "Growing Up Kennedy."
Pages 155–156. Sargent and Eunice Shriver details from Peter Collier and David Horowitz, *The Kennedys*, 40, 84, 159, 214, 415.
Page 156. Maria on her mother from Susan Price, "Maria Shriver—No Kennedy Clone."
Page 156. Maria's mother reminding her of Lucille Ball from Marie Brenner, "Growing Up Kennedy."
Page 157. Sargent Shriver's uneasiness with the Kennedy ethic and "Kennedys don't cry" quote from Peter Collier and David Horowitz, *The Kennedys*, 383.
Page 157. Maria praying daily and keeping rosary beads on desk from Monica Collins, "A Problem Like Maria's," *USA Weekend*, April 18–20, 1986.
Page 157. Shrivers being daily communicants from Marie Brenner, "Growing Up Kennedy."
Page 157. The Shrivers being workaholics from Monica Collins, "A Problem Like Maria's."
Page 157. Quote on Maria being the only girl in the family from Jill Brooke, "What's in a Name?," *Elle*, April 1986.
Pages 157–158. Eunice's estimated inheritance from Tamara Manjikan, "The Kennedy Connection," *California Business*, June 1986.
Page 158. Maria's education and life in Paris from Marie Brenner, "Growing Up Kennedy."

Page 158. Kibbutz quote from Susan Watters, "Maria Shriver: Screening Out the Illusion," *W*, June 17–24, 1983.

Page 158. Eunice's comments on being pretty from Monica Collins, "A Problem Like Maria's."

Page 158. Maria and journalism during Shriver campaign from Marie Brenner, "Growing Up Kennedy."

Page 158. Rose Kennedy's TV program from Peter Collier and David Horowitz, *The Kennedys*, 188.

Page 159. Maria being watched like a hawk from Susan Price, "Maria Shriver—No Kennedy Clone."

Page 159. Maria's thesis from Peter Collier and David Horowitz, *The Kennedys*, 409.

Page 159. Graduation date from Stephen Karten interview with University of Georgetown registrar.

Page 159. Arnold losing tennis matches to Shriver from Martin Burden, "Amazing Arnold: Gentle Giant Muscles in on Kennedy Clan," *New York Post*, October 21, 1985.

Page 159. Arnold's boat ride with Eunice and Bobby quote from Tamara Manjikan, "The Kennedy Connection."

Page 159. Maria on Arnold from Marie Brenner, "Growing Up Kennedy."

Pages 159–160. George Butler quote from Teresa Carpenter, "The Self-Made Man."

Page 160. "She was filled with all kinds of dreams" quote from Marie Brenner, "Growing Up Kennedy."

Page 160. "I knew instantly" quote from Tom Burke, "Sexy, Fun-Loving Schwarzenegger!," *Cosmopolitan*, July 1988.

Page 160. Rick Wayne quote from author interview with Wayne.

Pages 160–161. Maria being impressed by Arnold from Susan Price, "Maria Shriver—No Kennedy Clone."

Chapter 12: Maria and Sue

Quotes and information in this chapter on Arnold's relationship with Sue Moray from author interviews with Moray.

Page 165. Maria and Arnold spending New Year's Eve together from author interview with Frank Zane.

Page 166. Eunice asking Teddy if Jack was a womanizer from Peter Collier and David Horowitz, *The Kennedys: An American Drama* (New York: Summit Books, 1984), 413.

Page 167. Maria and Arnold's trip to Hawaii from German language publication, August 27, 1978; and author interview with Sue Moray.

Page 168. Maria's move to Baltimore from Stephen Karten interview with Ruth Matthews at the Philadelphia TV station she left.

Pages 168–169. Maria and Arnold's trip to New Orleans and the Mile High Pie incident from author interview with Boyer Coe.

Page 169. Maria on Arnold's sense of humor from Alan Richman, "Commando in Love," *People*, October 14, 1985.

Page 169. Wag Bennett quote from Stephen Karten interview with Bennett.

Page 170. Arnold's work in the Special Olympics from Stephen Karten interview with Sara Campbell of the Special Olympics.

Page 170. Arnold's weightlifting quote and quote from Sandra Hembd from Wendy Olson, "Schwarzenegger Gives Them a Lift," *Los Angeles Times,* June 2, 1987.

Page 171. "I found an enormous need for prisoners to have something positive" quote from "Conan the Destroyer," Universal Studios press release, May 14, 1984.

Page 171. "Weight training helps make prisoners less violent" quote from "Schwarzenegger: Bodybuilding Is for Every Body," *Los Angeles Herald Examiner,* December 3, 1979.

Page 171. Arnold's $275,000 salary from German language publication, August 27, 1978.

Pages 171–172. "was not interesting" quote from "People" page, *Time,* December 4, 1978.

Page 172. Hal Needham quotes from author interview with Needham.

Page 172. Arnold's comments about Kirk Douglas and Ann-Margret from "People" page, *Time,* December 4, 1978.

Page 172. Film critic's quip from Teresa Carpenter, "The Self-Made Man," *Premiere,* January 1989; and Marian Christy, "Winning According to Schwarzenegger," *Boston Globe,* May 9, 1982.

Page 172. Arnold's confession of being hurt from Marian Christy, "Winning According to Schwarzenegger."

Page 172. Eunice wanting to take Maria plus details of her Vienna trip with Arnold from Roman Schliesser, "Adabei," *Die Kronen Zeitung,* December 29, 1978.

Page 173. Arnold in Cannes promoting *The Villain* and then visiting his mother from Roman Schliesser, "Adabei," *Die Kronen Zeitung,* May 22, 1979.

Page 173. Details on Arnold's degree from Stephen Karten interview with Lowell Banks, registrar's office at the University of Wisconsin in Superior.

Page 173. Arnold turning down commercial from Jennifer Seder, "Schwarzenegger: He's Quit Going Shirtless in Hollywood," *Los Angeles Times,* July 6, 1979.

Page 173. Details on "The Streets of San Francisco" appearance from Stephen Karten interview with Dan Howard.

Page 174. Frank Zane encounter with Arnold from author interview with Zane.

Chapter 13: Australia and the Comeback

Page 175. Arnold meeting with De Laurentiis from Nancy Collins, "Pumping Arnold," *Rolling Stone,* January 17, 1985.

Page 175. Dino De Laurentiis not wanting Arnold and calling Arnold a Nazi from Pat H. Broeske, "Barbarian Arnold Schwarzenegger," *Drama-Logue,* June 17–23, 1982.

Pages 175-176. Milius telling De Laurentiis he'd have to build a replica of Arnold from Nancy Collins, "Pumping Arnold," and Brian Lowry, "Arnold Schwarzenegger: The Complete Barbarian," *Starlog*, May 1984.

Page 176. Arnold's comment on his instincts from Kenneth Turan, "The Barbarian in Babylon," *New West*, August 27, 1979.

Page 176. "He sets a very positive example" quote from Tom Burke, "Sexy, Fun-Loving Schwarzenegger!," *Cosmopolitan*, July 1988.

Page 176. Maria's "All those commas" quote from Marie Brenner, "Growing Up Kennedy," *Vanity Fair*, February 1986.

Page 177. Arnold's comment on women supporting their men from Marie Brenner, "Growing Up Kennedy."

Page 177. "Arnold has specific opinions" quote from Jill Brooke, "What's in a Name?," *Elle*, April 1986.

Page 178. Arnold on Maria's politics from Nancy Collins, "Pumping Arnold."

Page 178. Arnold's comment on politics from Eva Windmoller and Thomas Höpker, "Mit Zehn Jahren bei Seiner Erstkommunion in Thal Nahe Graz, Beschloss der Krankliche Arnold Weltmeister zu Werden. Er Wusste nur Noch Nicht, Worin," *Stern*, 1977.

Pages 178-179. Rick Wayne's Miss Olympia interview with Arnold from author interview with Wayne.

Page 179. Frank Zane asking Arnold for advice from author interview with Zane.

Pages 179-180. Mike Mentzer details from Joe Weider, *The IFBB Album of Bodybuilding Allstars* (New York: Hawthorn/Dutton, 1979).

Page 180. Mike Mentzer criticizing Arnold's training methods from author interview with Rick Wayne.

Pages 180-181. Arnold's interview with Roman Schliesser, "Adabei," *Die Kronen Zeitung*, September 28, 1980.

Page 181. Maria suggesting that Arnold not make a comeback but instead learn a language from Rick Wayne, *Muscle Wars* (New York: St. Martin's Press, 1985), 163.

Page 181. Arnold on music and Serge Nubret quote from author interview with Nubret.

Page 181. Boyer Coe quote from author interview with Coe.

Page 182. Frank Zane quote from author interview with Zane.

Pages 182-183. Boyer Coe, Mike Mentzer, and Arnold confrontation from author interview with Coe.

Page 183. Mentzer shaking in anger and the tactic Arnold said he used with Zane from James Delson, "Penthouse Interview: Arnold Schwarzenegger," *Penthouse*, December 1981.

Page 183. *Comeback* information from the film *The Comeback*, 1981.

Page 184. Dan Howard quote from Stephen Karten interview with Howard.

Page 184. Erasure of the film's sound track, audience reaction to 1980 Olympia results, and Arnold's words to Maria from author interview with Helmut Cerncic, who worked for Paul Graham and witnessed them.

Page 185. Franco toweling off Arnold from author interview with Rick Wayne.

Page 185. Dan Howard quote from Stephen Karten interview with Howard.

Page 185. Jack Neary and Arnold quotes from author interview with Neary.

Pages 185–186. Fallout in Columbus from author interview with Boyer Coe.

Page 186. Frank Zane story from author interview with Zane.

Pages 186–187. Arnold's gloating over 1980 title from George Butler and Charles Gaines, *Pumping Iron*, revised edition (New York: Simon & Schuster, 1981), 248.

Page 187. Arnold quote from author interview with Rick Wayne.

Chapter 14: Jayne Mansfield and *Conan the Barbarian*

Page 189. Arnold's love scene with Loni Anderson from "TV Sizzler Is Too Hot to Handle," *News of the World*, October 26, 1980.

Pages 190–191. Quote on what Arnold learned from Jayne Mansfield from Joan Goodman, "Playboy Interview: Arnold Schwarzenegger," *Playboy*, January 1988.

Page 191. Arnold's comments to Rick Wayne from author interview with Wayne.

Pages 191–192. Information on Robert E. Howard's life and quotes from Conan books from Kenneth Turan, "Conan the Fad," *International Herald Tribune*, May 20, 1982.

Page 192. Film budget, Arnold quote, and Mussolini statue from Brian Lowry, "Arnold Schwarzenegger: The Complete Barbarian," *Starlog*, May 1984.

Pages 192–193. Details on John Milius's career, "zen fascist" quote, motorcycle gang, and mock Nazi salute from Kirk Honeycutt, "Milius the Barbarian," *American Film*, May 1982.

Page 193. Arnold quote on Milius from "Civilized Barbarian," *Us*, July 20, 1982.

Page 193. Details on *Conan* locations from Kirk Honeycutt, "Mr. Universe Conquers a New World," *American Film*, May 1982.

Page 193. Milius quote on pain being temporary from Kirk Honeycutt, "Milius the Barbarian."

Page 193. Promise about pain and dirt from "Civilized Barbarian."

Page 193. Arnold quote on vultures and swords from Kirk Honeycutt, "Milius the Barbarian."

Pages 193–194. Arnold quote on physical dangers from Marian Christy, "Winning According to Schwarzenegger," *Boston Globe*, May 9, 1982.

Page 194. Arnold quote on jumping into boxes from Kirk Honeycutt, "Mr. Universe Conquers a New World."

Page 194. Milius quote on Arnold's acting from Lynn Darling, "How Much Bigger Can Arnold Schwarzenegger Get?," *Esquire*, March 1985.

Page 194. Milius memorizing Arnold's facial expressions from Kirk Honeycutt, "Mr. Universe Conquers a New World."

Pages 194-195. Arnold quote on love scenes, Sandahl quote, and nicknames for Arnold and Sandahl from Larry Kart, "Schwarzenegger's Barbarian Has a Heart of Gold," *Chicago Tribune*, May 9, 1982.

Page 195. *Conan* review from Peter Rainer, "Conan: Muscling in on Sword and Sorcery," *Los Angeles Herald Examiner*, May 14, 1982.

Pages 195-196. Arnold quote on being a salesman from Rita Kempley, "Schwarzenegger Looking for Respect Without Having to Flex Bulging Muscles," *New Haven Register* (reprint from *Washington Post*), November 10, 1985.

Page 196. Maria's encounter with agent from Susan Price, "Maria Shriver—No Kennedy Clone," *McCall's*, October 1988.

Pages 196-197. Arnold quote on Maria being well-rounded and gorgeous from Victor Davis, "The Teatime Titan Takes Up His Warrior's Sword," *London Daily Express*, August 24, 1982.

Chapter 15: *Conan the Destroyer*

Page 199. Aurelia in hospital from "Schwarzenegger: Muskeln aus Eisen, Herz aus Butter," *Vienna Kurier*, January 25, 1982.

Page 199. Aurelia's visits and relationship with Arnold from Joan Goodman, "Playboy Interview: Arnold Schwarzenegger," *Playboy*, January 1988; and Fred Schruers, "Just Another Mama's Boy?—Pumping Dollars," *New York Sunday News Magazine*, May 9, 1982.

Page 199. Arnold quote on his European mentality from Jonathan Roberts, "Arnold Schwarzenegger," *Interview*, October 1985.

Pages 199-200. Gerstl arranging his dual citizenship from author's researcher's interview with Alfred Gerstl.

Page 200. Arnold's TV ads for Gerstl from author interview with Kurt Marnul.

Page 200. Details on Arnold becoming U.S. citizen and quote on becoming an American from Carol McGraw, "Schwarzenegger Flexes Muscles as U.S. Citizen," *Los Angeles Times*, September 18, 1983.

Page 201. "That's why I came to this country" quote from Rex Morgan, "Schwarzenegger," *Cable Guide*, September 1985.

Page 201. "My dream" quote from Studs Terkel (excerpt from *American Dreams: Lost and Found*), "World's No. 1 Torso," *New York Post*, November 19, 1980.

Page 201. "I will always be a Styrian" quote from author interview with Wilma Marnul.

Page 201. Charles Gaines quote from Lynn Darling, "How Much Bigger Can Arnold Schwarzenegger Get?," *Esquire*, March 1985.

Page 201. Republican convention breakfast from unpublished interview for *Time*, October 1985.

Page 201. "I admire him very much" quote from Nancy Collins, "Pumping Arnold," *Rolling Stone*, January 17, 1985.

Page 202. Lynn Darling quote from Lynn Darling, "How Much Bigger Can Arnold Schwarzenegger Get?"

Page 202. "I can't imagine the scrutiny" quote from Peter Keough, "Arnold Schwarzenegger Stays Hungry," *Chicago Sun-Times*, November 15, 1987.

Page 202. Fleischer quotes from author interview with Fleischer.

Pages 202–203. Alicia Figueroa incident from United Press International report, November 1, 1983; and Ken Flynn, United Press International news analysis, November 10, 1983.

Page 203. Regency Hotel incident from "Page Six" column, "Camera-Shy Arnold Blitzes Photog," *New York Post*, May 16, 1987.

Pages 203–204. Phil Gramm incident from "Arnold Talks Politics," *USA Today*, August 17, 1988.

Page 204. Adam Horowitz story from Stephen Karten interview with Horowitz; and Bill Bell, *New York Daily News*, August 18, 1988.

Page 204. Arnold and the press from author interviews with Peter McGough and two confidential sources.

Page 205. "I realized as time went on" quote from Jack Mathews, "The Man Inside the Muscle," *Los Angeles Times*, September 3, 1989.

Page 205. Maria's CBS work appointment and details from Peter McCabe, *Bad News at Black Rock: The Sell-Out of CBS News* (New York: Morrow, 1987), 169–71, 182, 184.

Pages 205–206. Maria refusing to ask Linda Evans about her sex life and quote about being the person you see on air from Susan Watters, "Maria Shriver: Screening Out the Illusion," *W*, June 17–24, 1983.

Page 206. Sarah Douglas quote from Liz Hodgson, London *Sunday Mirror*, July 22, 1984.

Page 206. Arnold and Maria's car accident from United Press International report, "Bodybuilder Loses Control of Car," December 29, 1983.

Page 206. Arnold's New Year's resolution from Don Chase, "Conan the Comedian," *New York Sunday News*, January 29, 1984.

Chapter 16: Gitte

Page 207. Date *The Terminator* shooting began from Stephen Karten interview with Orion Pictures spokesperson.

Page 207. Arnold trying out for hero's part and throwing himself into terminator role from Deborah Caulfield, "Bodybuilder Turns Unhuman," *Los Angeles Times*, October 16, 1984.

Page 207. Arnold loving futuristic weapons from Tom Sciacca, "Arnold Trades in His Sword for a Ray Gun and Becomes a Menie!," *Starblazer*, December 1984.

Page 208. Dino De Laurentiis discovering Brigitte from author interview with Mindy Alberman, his assistant.

Page 208. Occupations of Brigitte's parents, their house, and her problems mixing from Patrick Hill, *London Daily Mail*, July 23, 1987.

Pages 208–209. Brigitte singing in school, smoking grass in the bathroom, her jobs, and her weight from Corrina Honan, *London Daily Mail*, July 23, 1987.

Page 209. Brigitte's nicknames, her ambitions, and her father's advice from Jane Ardmore, "The Woman Who Dumped Stallone," *Woman's World*, October 1988.

Pages 209–210. Brigitte's discovery by Marianne Diers and quotes from Trice Tomsen and Riccardo Gay from Patrick Hill, *London Daily Mail*.

Page 210. Monte Shadow details and quotes from author interview with Shadow.

Page 210. Brigitte living with Lucca Rossi from Jane Ardmore, "The Woman Who Dumped Stallone."

Pages 210–211. Details of Kasper Winding's marriage to Brigitte from Garth Pearce, *London Daily Express*, June 18, 1986.

Page 211. Details about Brigitte wanting to name her son Sylvester from Nancy Collins, "Pumping Arnold," *Rolling Stone*, January 17, 1985.

Page 211. Details on De Laurentiis's search for Red Sonja and quote from Davis from Victor Davis, "Why Brigitte Is Worth a £15m Gamble," *London Daily Express*, December 27, 1984.

Pages 211–212. Details on *Red Sonja* shoot and Fleischer quote from author interviews with Mindy Alberman and *Red Sonja* director Richard Fleischer.

Page 212. Arnold's attempt to back out of *Red Sonja* from Tom Sciacca, "Arnold Trades in His Sword for a Ray Gun and Becomes a Menie!"

Pages 213–214. Author interview with Brigitte Nielsen was published as Wendy Leigh, "Brigitte Nielsen," *Us*, March 21, 1988.

Page 214. Arnold's statement to Brigitte that they were working together and the relationship should remain professional and "I was going to go for it" quote from author interview with Mike Cantacessi.

Page 214. Brigitte reminding Arnold of Sue Moray from author interview with Moray.

Page 214. Brigitte being warm-hearted, solicitous, eager to learn from author interview with Monte Shadow.

Page 214. The *Vienna Kurier* story from October 11, 1984.

Page 214. Aurelia's visit to *Red Sonja* set from Roman Schliesser, "Adabei," *Die Kronen Zeitung*, November 4, 1984.

Page 214. Aurelia asking who this stupid person was from author interview with confidential source in Graz who knows Aurelia.

Page 215. Maria's spies from author interview with Sue Moray.

Pages 216–217. Arnold and Brigitte's stay in Vienna and that Jim Lorimer was there from Reinhard Bimashofer, "Arnold Kommt zum Skifahren Wieder," *Vienna Kurier*, December 11, 1984.

Pages 216–217. Arnold at Zimmermann's and his behavior toward Brigitte and the reaction of the Viennese press present from author interview with Norbert Kossler, who took the picture of Arnold and Brigitte that appears in this book.

Page 217. Arnold introducing Brigitte to Lou Pitt and his quote on her being heavenly from *Vienna Kurier*, December 27, 1984.

Page 217. Details of who was on holiday with Arnold and Brigitte in Axams from Rainer Gerzabek, "Tiroler Chronik" section, *Vienna Kurier*, January 9, 1985.

Pages 217-218. Arnold and Brigitte at Heidegger's in Axams from author interviews with Austrian photographer Christian Jauschowetz and Gerlinde Voppichler and Robert Schartenrat, employees at the skiwear shop next door to Heidegger's. Also from author interview with Sue Moray, whom Arnold told about his skiing holiday with Brigitte.

Page 218. Arnold and Maria at Schloss Fuschl from author interview with receptionist there.

Page 218. Ski quote from Dan Yakir, "Former Body-Builder Fights Mob in 'Raw Deal,'" *Chicago Sun-Times*, June 1, 1986.

Page 219. Arnold on Brigitte's vulnerability from author interview with Sue Moray.

Chapter 17: Arnold, Brigitte, Maria, and Stallone

Page 221. Joel Silver quote from interview with Denise Worrell for *Time*, October 1985.

Page 222. Arnold's first attack on Stallone and quote from Stallone spokesman from Ian Harmer, "Stallone Slogs It Out for Real with Film Rival," *News of the World*, October 20, 1985.

Page 222. Comments on Stallone from Jean Vallely interview with Arnold, "The Promoter," *GQ*, July 1986.

Pages 222-223. Stallone's call to Arnold from Pat H. Broeske, "Clash of the Titans," *Hollywood Magazine*, February/March 1990.

Page 223. Rick Wayne quote from author interview with Wayne.

Page 223. Arnold giving Brigitte a watch from author interview with confidential source.

Pages 223-224. Monte Shadow quote from author interview with Shadow.

Page 224. Arnold arranging to set up Brigitte with Stallone from author interview with confidential source.

Page 224. Brigitte saying "I am unbeatable," Arnold feeling happy and Brigitte's Jake Bloom connection from Joan Goodman, "Playboy Interview: Arnold Schwarzenegger," German edition of *Playboy*, January 1988.

Page 225. Eyewitness quote on Brigitte's behavior on the set of *Rocky IV* from author interview with confidential source.

Page 225. Watch inscription from author interview with Lisa Gastineau, Mark Gastineau's ex-wife.

Page 225. "She was with me" quote from author interview with Stallone for the *London Sun* in January 1988.

Page 226. Jacqueline Stallone banned from sick room from author interview with Jacqueline Stallone.

Page 226. Denver real estate from United Press International wire report, March 20, 1985.

Page 226. Arnold telling security guard he should sell dildoes from Lynn Darling, "How Much Bigger Can Schwarzenegger Get?," *Esquire*, March 1985.

Page 226. *Red Sonja* "shamelessly silly" from Kathleen Carroll, "The Terminator Meets His Match," *New York Daily News*, July 3, 1985.

Page 226. *Red Sonja* "bubble-headed" from Archer Winsten, "Silly 'Red Sonja' Joins Arnie's Army," *New York Post*, July 3, 1985.

Page 227. Maria's quote on Brigitte from Monica Collins, "A Problem Like Maria's," *USA Weekend*, April 18-20, 1986.

Page 227. Jim Lorimer's exchange with Arnold from author interview with Lorimer.

Pages 227-228. Arnold's proposal to Maria from interview by Denise Worrell for *Time*, October 1985.

Page 228. "Hey, Arnold" quote from "Faces & Places" column, "The Shriver-Schwarzenegger Bash," *Us*, April 7, 1986.

Page 228. Brigitte Nielsen quotes from Richard Sanders, "Brigitte Nielsen Likes Life as Rambo's Lady, But This Dane Is Nobody's Pastry," *People*, July 22, 1985.

Page 228. *Daily News* interview with Brigitte from Phil Roura and Tom Poster, "Sly's Great Dane Getting Physical," *New York Daily News*, August 8, 1985.

Pages 228-229. Mike Cantacessi quote from author interview with Cantacessi.

Page 229. Brigitte hurt by Sahnger rumor from Jane Ardmore, "The Woman Who Dumped Stallone," *Woman's World*, October 1988.

Page 229. Arnold meeting with Frank Stallone, Jr., from author interview with Jacqueline Stallone, June 1987.

Page 229. Sue Moray quote from author interview with Moray.

Pages 230-231. *Playboy* comments on Stallone from Joan Goodman, "Playboy Interview: Arnold Schwarzenegger," *Playboy*, January 1988.

Page 232. Stallone's response to Arnold from author, "Sylvester Stallone," *Us*, June 13, 1988.

Page 232. Chantal quote from Stephen Karten interview with Chantal.

Page 232. "I respect the man" quote and *Playboy* spokesman quote from "Conan Cries Foul to Remarks on Rambo," *New York Daily News*, November 25, 1987.

Page 232. Arnold's off-the-record comments being stronger from Pat H. Broeske, "Clash of the Titans," and confidential source.

Page 232. Rick Wayne quote from author interview with Wayne.

Page 233. Brigitte showing up at Arnold's birthday breakfast from Rebecca Bricker, "Take One" page, *People*, August 17, 1987.

Page 233. "I have no regrets" quote from Wendy Leigh, "Brigitte Nielson," *Us*, March 21, 1988.

Page 234. Arnold railing against Brigitte to Helmut Cerncic from author interview with Cerncic.

Page 234. Joel Brokaw's statement that Brigitte had just talked to Arnold in April 1989 from author conversation with Brokaw.

Chapter 18: The Wedding and Waldheim

Wedding details covering Arnold flying into Hyannis Port, Caroline's party, the prewedding dinner, air traffic being banned over the compound, Arnold's attendants, Eunice's dress, Arnold's quote about noise, Maria's bouquet, Arnold and Maria refusing to kiss, food, decor, flowers, cake, and Warhol's portrait from Deirdre Donahue and Susan Reed, "A Hyannis Hitching," *People*, May 12, 1986; and confidential source.

Page 235. Arnold's intervention in Maria's business from Ed Joyce, *Prime Times, Bad Times* (New York: Doubleday, 1988), 498–99.

Page 236. Maria's getting up at 3:00 A.M. from "Beauty Secrets" column, "Maria Shriver," *Harpers Bazaar*, September 1986; Rosemary Breslin, "Frankly, We'd Like It Red," *New York Sunday News*, October 27, 1985; and Marie Brenner, "Growing Up Kennedy," *Vanity Fair*, February 1986.

Page 236. Maria's preparation for work, Eunice's telephoning, and Maria flying to Arnold on Fridays from Marie Brenner, "Growing Up Kennedy."

Page 236. Maria refusing dinner invitations and riding in Central Park from "Beauty Secrets" column, "Maria Shriver."

Page 236. Maria avoiding the Palladium and preferring tea from Rosemary Breslin, "Frankly, We'd Like It Red."

Page 236. Maria at CBS from Peter McCabe, *Bad News at Black Rock: The Sell-Out of CBS News* (New York: Morrow, 1987), 183, 235.

Pages 236–237. Maria's conflicts from Monica Collins, "A Problem Like Maria's," *USA Weekend*, April 18–20, 1986.

Page 237. Maria rejecting CBS job from Peter McCabe, *Bad News at Black Rock*, 280.

Page 237. Description of Arnold's house from Martin Dunn, "Street of Stars," *London Sun*, May 2, 1986.

Page 238. De Laurentiis quote from Eva Windmöller, "Macho Macht Karriere," *Stern*.

Page 238. Erika's introduction of Arnold to Welley and Arnold's letter of support to Waldheim from Reinhard Bimashofer, "Leute Von Heute, "Muller-Puppen als Gag Bei Schwarzeneggers Hochzeit mit Maria," *Vienna Kurier*, May 3, 1986.

Pages 238–239. Waldheim's past from "Waldheim's Nazi Past: The Dossier." From the Commission on the Holocaust and Crimes of the Nazis, published by the World Jewish Congress, 1988.

Page 239. Party at Exiles from John Roca, "The Engaging Kennedys," *New York Daily News*, February 24, 1986.

Page 239. Arnold's bachelor party a raucous affair from Teresa Carpenter, "The Self-Made Man," *Premiere*, January 1989.

Page 239. Maria flying to Cape Cod from Sara C. Medina, "Keeping It All Very Private," *Time*, May 5, 1986.

Page 240. Austrian band, decor of club, and waitresses from author interview with confidential source.

Page 240. Provincetown-Boston Airline locking computers from Sara C. Medina, "Keeping It All Very Private."

Page 241. Reporters on stands from Seth S. King, "The Shriver Wedding: Security for Celebrities," *New York Times*, April 26, 1986.

Page 241. Air traffic ban from Sara C. Medina, "Keeping It All Very Private."

Page 241. Guest list rumors from Roman Schliesser, "Adabei," *Die Kronen Zeitung*, April 28, 1986.

Page 241. Brigitte, Stallone, Princess Caroline, and Clint Eastwood invited to wedding from Beverly Ford, "It's the Wedding of the Year," *Boston Herald*, April 20, 1986.

Page 241. Saint James, Brokaw, Sawyer, Van Buren, Jones, and Warhol attending the wedding from Rosemary Breslin, "Kennedys Gain a Son," *New York Sunday News*, April 27, 1986; Jeannie Williams and Greg Katz, "Maria and Arnold Tie the Knot in Style," *USA Today*, April 28, 1986; Norma Nathan, "Conan Weds a Kennedy," *Star*, April 1986; and Stephen Karten interview with Wag Bennett.

Pages 241-242. Maria's bridesmaids from "Social Events," "Maria Owings Shriver Wed to Arnold Schwarzenegger," *New York Times*, April 27, 1986.

Page 242. Aurelia's dress from Norma Nathan, "Conan Weds a Kennedy."

Page 242. Arnold rolling the windows down from Sara C. Medina, "Keeping It All Very Private."

Page 242. Arnold quote on all being nervous and Arnold's video from transcript of "The Oprah Winfrey Show," June 3, 1987.

Page 242. Maria's bridesmaids' dresses from "Beauty Secrets" column, "Maria Shriver."

Pages 242-243. Maria's wedding gown from Rosemary Breslin, "Kennedys Gain a Son."

Pages 243, 244, 245. Details on the ceremony and reception from Stephen Karten interview with Wag Bennett; author interviews with Art Zeller and Richard Burkholder; "Social Events," Maria Owings Shriver Wed to Arnold Schwarzenegger"; and Norma Nathan, "Conan Weds a Kennedy."

Pages 243-244. Wag Bennett anecdote from Stephen Karten interview with Bennett.

Page 244. Bernd Zimmermann as guest from Roman Schliesser, "Adabei," *Die Kronen Zeitung*, April 27, 1986.

Page 244. Maria and Arnold's dance from Roman Schliesser, "Adabei," *Die Kronen Zeitung*, April 28, 1986, and Norma Nathan, "Conan Weds a Kennedy."

Pages 244-245. Maria's injury and planning her wedding since she was five from Susan Price, "Maria Shriver—No Kennedy Clone," *McCall's*, October 1988.

Page 245. Arnold and Maria seeing Rose Kennedy from Roman Schliesser, "Adabei," *Die Kronen Zeitung*, April 28, 1986.

Page 245. "I'm not really" and "I love her" quotes from Deirdre Donahue and Susan Reed, "A Hyannis Hitching."

Page 245. Arnold and Maria in Antigua from Carol Lynn Mithers, "Waking Up with Maria Shriver," *Us*, August 12, 1985; and Linda

Stevens, "Honeymoon Is Over for Maria & Arnie," *New York Post*, April 30, 1986.

Page 245. Ethel Kennedy quote from Jeannie Williams and Greg Katz, "Maria and Arnold Tie the Knot in Style."

Page 245. Arnold on his in-laws from "How 'Barbarian' Arnold Won Kennedy Approval of His Love for Maria Shriver," *Star*, June 1, 1982.

Pages 245, 246. Sargent Shriver's surprise at Arnold's defense of Waldheim and Arnold having invited Reagan and the pope to the wedding from Jeannie Williams and Greg Katz, "Maria and Arnold Tie the Knot in Style."

Page 246. Details on the dolls from picture in "Arnold," *Bodypower*, October 1988 (*Bodypower* is Dianne Bennett's magazine); and Reinhard Bimashofer, "Muller-Puppen als Gag Bei Schwarzeneggers Hochzeit mit Maria," *Vienna Kurier*, May 3, 1986.

Page 246. Arnold's response to the Waldheim gift from Pat Hackett, ed., *The Andy Warhol Diaries* (New York: Warner Books, 1989), 728.

Pages 246–247. Terry Smith confirmation from author interview with Smith.

Page 247. Arnold saying that Waldheim was the victim of bad press from Deirdre Donahue and Susan Reed, "A Hyannis Hitching."

Page 247. Richard Burkholder quote from author interview with Burkholder.

Page 247. Rick Wayne on *Flex* article from author interview with Wayne.

Pages 247–248. Arnold's visit to Kurt Waldheim from German language publication, August 30, 1986; and "Arnolds Frühstück mit Waldheim," *Vienna Kurier*, August 30, 1986.

Page 248. Meeting not bad judgment from Sharon Churcher, "Schwarzenegger's Kurt Replies," *Penthouse*, January 1989.

Page 249. Maria wishing Arnold had taken a different path from author interview with confidential source.

Chapter 19: May 1986 to February 1990

Page 251. Details of honeymoon from Linda Stevens, "Honeymoon Is Over for Maria & Arnie," *New York Post*, April 30, 1986.

Page 251. "I'm a very independent person" quote from Dan Yakir, "Former Body-Builder Fights Mob in 'Raw Deal,' " *Chicago Sun-Times*, June 1, 1986.

Pages 251–252. "Maria and I love one another" quote from Tom Burke, "Sexy, Fun-Loving Schwarzenegger!," *Cosmopolitan*, July 1988.

Page 252. Quote about phone sex from Michael Neill, "Chatter," *People*, June 2, 1986.

Page 252. Quote to Forrest Sawyer from transcript of "CBS Morning News," June 13, 1986.

Page 252. Arnold quote on marriage from Tom Green, "Schwarzenegger Is Going Strong," *USA Today*, June 30, 1987.

Page 252. *Raw Deal* review from Jay Maeder, "Bodies to the Left of Him, Bodies to the Right . . .," *New York Daily News*, June 6, 1986.

Page 252. Arnold's trip to Graz from author interview with Christian Jauschowetz, who was with him.

Page 253. *Raw Deal* premiere from Reinhard Bimashofer, "Leute von Heute" column, "Mutti stiehlt Mir die Show!," *Vienna Kurier*, August 24, 1986.

Page 253. Trip to Vienna and hiking with Zimmermann from German language publication, August 23, 1986; and Roman Schliesser, "Adabei," *Die Kronen Zeitung*, August 3, 1986.

Page 253. Olympia details from author interview with Peter McGough.

Page 253. Vienna Boys' Choir at Maria's party from Roman Schliesser, "Adabei," *Die Kronen Zeitung*, December 11, 1986.

Page 253. Christmas and New Year's Eve from Reinhard Bimashofer, "Schwarzenegger War mit Mama in Tirol," *Vienna Kurier*, December 31, 1986.

Pages 253–254. "I think what I'm doing right now" quote from transcript of "The Oprah Winfrey Show," June 3, 1987.

Page 254. Star on Hollywood Boulevard from tape of speech and Stephen Karten interview with Hollywood Chamber of Commerce.

Page 254. Details on *Predator* box office performance from Tom Green, "Schwarzenegger Is Going Strong," *USA Today*, June 30, 1987.

Page 254. National Association of Theater Owners award from Stephen Karten interview with spokesperson; and Peter Keough, "Arnold Schwarzenegger Stays Hungry," *Chicago Sun-Times*, November 15, 1987.

Page 254. John McTiernan quote from Donald Chase, "The Man in the Blood-Spattered Suit," *New York Daily News*, June 6, 1986.

Page 254. Arnold on vulnerability from Jami Bernard, "Muscled Mirth," *New York Post*, June 11, 1987.

Page 255. Arnold on stardom from Jeanne Wolf, "The High Price of Sudden Fame," *Cosmopolitan*, November 1988.

Page 255. Barish anecdote from Tom Burke, "Sexy, Fun-Loving Schwarzenegger!"

Pages 255–256. Walter Hill asking Arnold to lose weight and Hill quote from Lloyd Sachs, "Schwarzenegger: Mind Over Muscle," *Chicago Sun-Times*, June 19, 1988.

Page 256. Belushi quote from Roger Ebert, "Jim Belushi Brings a Taste of Chicago to 'Red Heat' Role," *Chicago Sun-Times*, June 19, 1988.

Page 256. Benny Dobbins's death from Werner Kopacka, "Der 'Vater Der Stuntman' Ist Tot!," Austrian publication, February 7, 1988.

Page 256. Eyewitness on set is photographer Christian Jauschowetz.

Page 256. Arnold canceling opera ball from Roman Schliesser, "Adabei," *Die Kronen Zeitung*, February 7, 1988.

Page 256. Dates of Moscow filming from Stephen Karten interview with Walter Hill's assistant.

Page 257. Arnold's *Red Heat* salary from Jay Maeder, "Reinventing Schwarzenegger," *New York Daily News Magazine*, June 19, 1988.

Page 257. *New York Times* review of *Red Heat* from Vincent Canby, "US-Soviet Buddy Movie with a Chicago Backdrop," June 17, 1988.

Page 257. Friars roast details from "Well Done, Arnie," *USA Today*, March 31, 1988.

Page 257. Details on Arnold's character in *Twins* from Teresa Carpenter, "The Self-Made Man," *Premiere*, January 1989.

Page 258. Reitman quote and George Bush quote from Jeannie Williams, "A Premiere with a 'Twins' Purpose," *USA Today*, December 6, 1988.

Page 258. Arnold's quote on being a Reagan supporter from "Arnold Talks Politics," *USA Today*, August 17, 1988.

Page 259. Arnold possibly running for governor from "Here and There" column, "Arnold to Muscle into Politics?," *New York Daily News*, October 5, 1989.

Page 259. Arnold's hope to run for lieutenant governor from Michael Sneed, "Sneed," *Chicago Sun-Times*, January 23, 1990.

Page 259. *Forbes* estimates from Peter Newcomb, "The Magic Kingdom," *Forbes*, October 2, 1989.

Page 259. Maria's salary and NBC duties and *TV Guide* quote from Joanmarie Kalter, "What Makes Maria Shriver Run So Fast?," *TV Guide*, July 29, 1989.

Pages 259–260. Quote on children from Rita Kempley, "Schwarzenegger Looking for Respect Without Having to Flex Bulging Muscles," *New Haven Register* (reprint from *Washington Post*), November 10, 1985.

Page 260. Arnold having bought house for children from Martin Dunn, "Street of Stars," *London Sun*, May 2, 1986.

Page 260. Sue Moray quote from author interview with Moray.

Page 260. Information on Arnold wanting to be a father from "'Conan' Star Thrilled at Upcoming Role—Real-Life 'Mr. Mom,'" *National Enquirer*, June 6, 1989.

Page 260. Background on *Total Recall* from Jack Mathews, "Part 2: Arnold to the Rescue," *Los Angeles Times*, September 10, 1989.

Page 261. Jack Mathews and crew member quotes from Jack Mathews, "The Man Inside the Muscle," *Los Angeles Times*, September 3, 1989.

Page 261. Arnold waking up at six from Tom Burke, "Sexy, Fun-Loving Schwarzenegger!"

Page 261. Arnold at World Gym from author interview with Ron D'Ippolito, who works there.

Page 261. Arnold's behavior with women at the gym from author interviews with two confidential sources who work out there.

Page 261. Arnold enjoying his workouts from Vernon Scott, "He's Wearing a Shirt—He Must Be Serious!," *New York Daily News*, June 10, 1987.

Page 261. Arnold's breakfasts at Patrick's from Jean Vallely, "The Promoter," *GQ*, July 1986.

Pages 261–262. Arnold's visits to the Rose from Tom Burke, "Sexy, Fun-Loving Schwarzenegger!"

Page 262. Arnold and Maria eating out from Jean Vallely, "The Promoter."

Page 262. Arnold doing the dishes from Martin Burden, "Amazing Arnold: Gentle Giant Muscles in on Kennedy Clan," *New York Post*, October 21, 1985.

Page 262. Arnold's cigars, diet, riding, and tennis from Tom Burke, "Sexy, Fun-Loving Schwarzenegger!"

Page 262. Aspen visits from Beverly Ford, "It's the Wedding of the Year," *Boston Herald*, April 20, 1986; and author interview with photographer Russell Turiak.

Page 262. Wienerstube breakfasts from author interview with management.

Page 262. Arnold's first two visits to Graz from author interviews with the Anderwalts and Kurt Marnul.

Pages 262–263. Arnold's third visit from author interview with Marnul, who saw him there.

Page 264. Franz Hormann story from author interview with Hormann.

Epilogue

Pages 265–266. Arnold quote on not having changed from Jean Vallely, "The Promoter," *GQ*, July 1986.

Page 266. Sue Moray story from author interview with Moray.

Page 266. Arnold quote on needing love from *The Comeback*, 1980.

Page 266. Bench-pressing statement from Lynn Darling, "How Much Bigger Can Arnold Schwarzenegger Get?," *Esquire*, March 1985.

Pages 266–267. Maria quote from Susan Price, "Maria Shriver—No Kennedy Clone," *McCall's*, October 1988.

Index